COLUMBIA COLLEGE

659.143G313L   C1   V0

THE LANGUAGE OF TELEVISION ADVERTISIN

W9-DEA-892

659.143 G31.3L

Geis, Michael L.

The language of television
advertising

MAY 98

JAN 5 1987		
JAN 2 4 1987	JUN 1 4 2004	
APR 1 1987		
MAY 5 1987		
OCT 7 1987		
DEC 1 5 1987		
APR 7 1988		
MAY 2 6 1988		
JUL 5 1988		
JUN 0 4 1990		
APR 1 8 1991		
DEC 1 8 1991		
	OCT 1 8 1993	
NOV 2 4 1993		
APR 2 8 1997		

WITHDRAWN

HIGHSMITH 45-220

The Language of
Television Advertising

LIBRARY
OF
COLUMBIA COLLEGE
CHICAGO, ILLINOIS

PERSPECTIVES IN
NEUROLINGUISTICS, NEUROPSYCHOLOGY, AND
PSYCHOLINGUISTICS: A Series of Monographs and Treatises

Harry A. Whitaker, Series Editor
DEPARTMENT OF HEARING AND SPEECH SCIENCES
UNIVERSITY OF MARYLAND
COLLEGE PARK, MARYLAND 20742

HAIGANOOSH WHITAKER and HARRY A. WHITAKER (Eds.).
Studies in Neurolinguistics, Volumes 1, 2, 3, and 4

NORMAN J. LASS (Ed.). Contemporary Issues in Experimental Phonetics

JASON W. BROWN. Mind, Brain, and Consciousness: The Neuropsychology of Cognition

SIDNEY J. SEGALOWITZ and FREDERIC A. GRUBER (Eds.). Language Development and Neurological Theory

SUSAN CURTISS. Genie: A Psycholinguistic Study of a Modern-Day "Wild Child"

JOHN MACNAMARA (Ed.). Language Learning and Thought

I. M. SCHLESINGER and LILA NAMIR (Eds.). Sign Language of the Deaf: Psychological, Linguistic, and Sociological Perspectives

WILLIAM C. RITCHIE (Ed.). Second Language Acquisition Research: Issues and Implications

PATRICIA SIPLE (Ed.). Understanding Language through Sign Language Research

MARTIN L. ALBERT and LORAINE K. OBLER. The Bilingual Brain: Neuropsychological and Neurolinguistic Aspects of Bilingualism

TALMY GIVÓN. On Understanding Grammar

CHARLES J. FILLMORE, DANIEL KEMPLER, and WILLIAM S-Y. WANG (Eds.). Individual Differences in Language Ability and Language Behavior

JEANNINE HERRON (Ed.). Neuropsychology of Left-Handedness

FRANÇOIS BOLLER and MAUREEN DENNIS (Eds.). Auditory Comprehension: Clinical and Experimental Studies with the Token Test

R. W. RIEBER (Ed.). Language Development and Aphasia in Children: New Essays and a Translation of "Kindersprache und Aphasie" by Emil Fröschels

GRACE H. YENI-KOMSHIAN, JAMES F. KAVANAGH, and CHARLES A. FERGUSON (Eds.). Child Phonology, Volume 1: Production and Volume 2: Perception

A list of titles in this series continues at the end of this volume.

The Language of Television Advertising

Michael L. Geis

Department of Linguistics
Ohio State University
Columbus, Ohio

LIBRARY
OF
COLUMBIA COLLEGE
CHICAGO, ILLINOIS

ACADEMIC PRESS   1982
A Subsidiary of Harcourt Brace Jovanovich, Publishers

New York   London
Paris San Diego San Francisco São Paulo Sydney Tokyo Toronto

659.143 G313L

Geis, Michael L.

The language of television advertising

COPYRIGHT © 1982, BY ACADEMIC PRESS, INC.
ALL RIGHTS RESERVED.
NO PART OF THIS PUBLICATION MAY BE REPRODUCED OR
TRANSMITTED IN ANY FORM OR BY ANY MEANS, ELECTRONIC
OR MECHANICAL, INCLUDING PHOTOCOPY, RECORDING, OR ANY
INFORMATION STORAGE AND RETRIEVAL SYSTEM, WITHOUT
PERMISSION IN WRITING FROM THE PUBLISHER.

ACADEMIC PRESS, INC.
111 Fifth Avenue, New York, New York 10003

United Kingdom Edition published by
ACADEMIC PRESS, INC. (LONDON) LTD.
24/28 Oval Road, London NW1   7DX

Library of Congress Cataloging in Publication Data

Geis, Michael L.
    The language of television advertising.

    (Perspectives in neurolinguistics, neuropsychology,
and psycholinguistics)
    Includes index.
    1. Television advertising. I. Title. II. Series.
HF6146.T42G44 1982   659.14'3   82-8686
ISBN 0-12-278980-6   AACR2

PRINTED IN THE UNITED STATES OF AMERICA

82 83 84 85   9 8 7 6 5 4 3 2 1

To Jonnie and Karlyn

WITHDRAWN
LIBRARY
OF
COLUMBIA COLLEGE
CHICAGO, ILLINOIS

Contents

Preface

Advertising is as ubiquitous as the air we breathe. It arrives with the morning newspaper. We encounter it on our radios and on billboards while driving to work. It comes with the mail each day, in magazines and circulars. It interrupts the television programs we watch. It can be found on virtually every product package. I seriously doubt that any of us is ever out of sight or sound of some sort of advertisement during our waking hours. Anything that we experience with this sort of frequency wants, I think, to be understood.

In this study, I examine the language of American advertising, focusing for the most part on television advertising. I adopt this focus for four reasons. First, television, since it employs both the auditory and visual communications channels and occurs in "real" time, places a much greater perceptual and cognitive burden on consumers than does any other advertising medium. Second, television is the primary vehicle for advertising to children, especially young children. Third, television advertising is less accessible for study than is advertising in other media. It cannot be studied without access to videotapes, and relatively few people have such access. As a result, less is known about television advertising than about advertising in other media. Finally, focusing on television advertising allows us to restrict the focus of the study without significantly restricting its scope, for virtually anything that can be done linguistically in print and radio advertising can be done in television advertising.

I know of only one other comprehensive study of the language of advertising (Leech, 1966), and it was published over a decade ago and concerned British, rather than American, advertising. The focus of the present study is quite different from that of the Leech study. The latter was concerned with documenting the various linguistic devices employed by advertisers. This book concerns not only how advertisers use language but also how consumers can be expected to interpret it. My focus, then, is largely psycholinguistic in character.

This study is divided into two parts. The first six chapters are devoted primarily to television advertising directed at adults. In Chapters 7, 8, and 9, I consider children's television advertising. These latter chapters are considerably revised versions of my written and oral testimony to the Federal Trade Commission during its hearings on proposals to ban television advertising directed to young children (children under age 8) and to restrict the television advertising of heavily sugared foods to older children.

In Chapter 1, the Introduction, I examine the special properties of television advertising and provide preliminary discussions of the question of truth in advertising and the role of language in persuasion. In Chapter 2, I take up indirect communication in advertising. I argue that consumers untutored in logic do not control the distinction between valid and invalid inferences (as is presumed by standard theories of sentence interpretation and literalist theories of truth in advertising), and I go on to provide the outlines of a theory of sentence interpretation not based on this distinction. According to this alternative theory, advertisers should be held responsible not only for what their advertisements assert and entail but also for what they imply. I elaborate on this theory of sentence interpretation in Chapter 3, where I discuss how consumers interpret claims employing such "logically weak" words as the quantifier *many*, modal verbs like *may, can,* and *could,* and the very commonly used verb *help*. I argue that in some cases claims employing these words are not as weak as has been believed.

In Chapter 4, I take up the use of comparatives in advertising, focusing on elliptical comparatives and several problematic "more for less" claims. In Chapter 5, I discuss three phenomena: the use of descriptive terms in brand names, some problems with terms used to refer to the symptoms that over-the-counter drugs are designed to treat, and the use of explicit and implicit similes in advertising. In Chapter 6, I discuss commercials that employ language conversationally, arguing that advertisers are sometimes indifferent to questions of style and register in commercials employing conversation.

In the three chapters devoted to children's television advertising, I take up, first, the issue of the ability of young children to cope with television advertising and then consider advertisements for fruit-flavored products and for cold breakfast cereals. As we shall see, those responsible for monitoring children's television advertising, the National Association of Broadcasters and the three major television networks, evidence a considerable disregard for what advertisers say to children.

I would have liked to focus more attention on the question of the effectiveness of the various linguistic devices employed by advertisers, but solid information on what linguistic techniques are and are not effective is hard to come by. As a result, I have focused on those devices which are of special linguistic interest or are problematic on linguistic grounds. Concern with the latter topic may seem unscholarly to some, for I am led from time to time to question the propriety of certain linguistic properties of advertisements, especially in the area of children's advertising. I make no apology for this, for if language scholars do not draw attention to linguistic abuses in public uses of language we leave the field open to various self-styled language experts whose critiques are usually shallow and misinformed. I believe scholars have an obligation to concern themselves with issues of social importance, for we are citizens of the society we live in, and we have an obligation to contribute to the societies that have trained us.

I am indebted to quite a number of people and institutions—to Julia Welch, who drew my attention to the language of advertising, to Arnold Routson for many illuminating discussions on advertising, to Larry Schourup for his very useful comments on Chapter 6, to Greg Stump for numerous conversations on the topics addressed in Chapters 2 and 3, and for his comments on a very early version of Chapter 9, to S-H. Tsang for his tireless work on transcriptions, to Jean Staten for preparing the index, and, most importantly, to Marlene Deetz Payha for her gracious and expert work on the manuscript. I am indebted to the Department of Linguistics at Ohio State University for making S-H. and Marlene available to me and to the College of Humanities for making a word processor available to Marlene. I am especially indebted to my wife, Jonnie, and my daughter, Karlyn, for sustaining and supporting me in a personal way as well as for putting up with my chaotic working habits. Finally, I owe a great debt to Harry Whitaker, my academic editor, for his interest in my work and for his comments on it.

Although I shall focus here on television advertising, I make occasional reference to advertising in other media including, in particular, national magazines. I use advertising in media other than television only when the advertising in question is tied to a television campaign or illustrates a point that either cannot be made or cannot be made as well using my television data.

Some Special Features of Television Advertising

There can be no doubt that television advertising imposes a much greater perceptual and cognitive burden on consumers than does advertising in other media. Television commercials occur in real time and use both visual and auditory communications channels. As a result of the fact that television commercials are presented in real time, they cannot be reviewed in the way print advertisements can. The fact that television commercials use both the auditory and visual communications channels very much complicates the problem of evaluating the message, for viewers are not normally able to focus their attention simultaneously on both channels.

A commercial that illustrates how the real time character of television can be exploited is the following:

(1)   **Duration Nasal Spray** (NBC, 2/25/78, @ 9:03 p.m.) [5]
       Type: Live action
       Setting: Outdoors
       Characters: None

       TEXT
       Voice over (adult male): *Introduce yourself to a remarkable nasal spray that lasts and lasts up to 12 continuous hours. Duration. Duration Nasal Spray relieves up to 12 continuous hours. Duration relieves nasal stuffiness and sinus congestion. So just one use lets you work all day. Just one use lets you sleep all night. Duration relieves 12 continuous hours, and that's Duration—with the longest lasting nasal decongestant.*

---

second. I used black-and-white TRI-X film (ASA 400) rated at ASA 250. The prints were also made by me. The reader should recognize that what he or she sees here is a reproduction of a photograph of an enlargement of a photograph of a videotape of a cable television broadcast of a television signal broadcast over the air waves. What the reader sees therefore does not do justice to the original broadcast signal. I would like to thank Eric Krause, Mike Pogany, and Pati DeCesaro of the Don McAlister Camera Company, Columbus, Ohio, for their help in the nontrivial task of getting usable negatives and prints.

[5]In general, I provide information about the type of commercial (live action versus animated), its setting, and the characters that appear on screen along with transcripts.

As we watch this commercial, a giant figure 12 dominates the screen (see Photograph 1.1). At one point the legend *UP TO 12 HOUR RELIEF* appears over the figure 12 (see Photograph 1.2). The claim that Duration relieves up to 12 continuous hours and the claim that Duration relieves 12 continuous hours, both of which occur in (1), are very different claims. Such claims are usually based on measurements of the concentration of the drug in the body over time. Within this framework, the claim that Duration relieves certain cold symptoms for up to 12 continuous hours would be justified if there were to be a therapeutic concentration of Duration in some one person's body approximately 12 hours after it had been taken. On the other hand, the claim that Duration relieves certain cold symptoms for 12 continuous hours would be justified only if there were to be a therapeutic concentration of Duration in every person's body 12 hours after it had been taken. Since advertisers can normally be assumed to make the strongest claims they can defend, the fact that the manufacturer of Duration bothers to make the weaker of these two claims suggests that he cannot justify the stronger claim.

The Duration commercial begins by claiming twice that Duration relieves up to 12 continuous hours and concludes with the claim that

Photograph 1.1

Photograph 1.2

Duration relieves 12 continuous hours. In between, we find claims (2) and (3).

(2)   *So just one use lets you work all day.*

(3)   *Just one use lets you sleep all night.*

Normally, we think of days and nights as consisting of 12 hours each, even though it may be true that people normally work and sleep only 8 hours. Note in this connection that (4) and (5) strike one as a bit strange.[6]

(4)   *So just one use lets you work all day, but only if you work 8 hours.

(5)   *Just one use lets you sleep all night, but only if you sleep for 8 hours.

Since (4) and (5) are rather odd at best, I believe we must conclude that (2) and (3) promise 12 hours of relief.

We may summarize what has been said by noting that commercial (1) begins by making the weaker *up to 12 continuous hours* claim twice and concludes by making the much stronger *12 continuous hours* claim three

[6]I mark sentences that are odd in one way or another with an asterisk.

times. In general, people tend to recall later messages better than earlier messages (the "recency effect," Klatzky, 1975) and may also recall stronger claims better than weaker claims. If this is true, then the effect of the oral text of (1) will be to plant the claim that Duration relieves 12 continuous hours in viewers' minds. This may be forestalled in the case of consumers who attend carefully to the visual elements of the commercial (see Photograph 1.2). However, viewers who do not attend carefully to television advertising will clearly be quite vulnerable to the technique of presenting disparate statements in commercials.

The Duration commercial exploits the real time character of television advertising. A commercial for Contac exploits the fact that television uses both oral and visual communications channels by way of blurring the distinction between *lasts n hours* and *lasts up to n hours*.

(6)   Contac[7]
        Type: Live action
        Scene: Movie theater
        Characters: Man, woman, and usher

        TEXT
        Man: [Sneezes]
        Woman: *You didn't take your Contac, did you?*
        Man: *No.*
        Woman: *What did you take?*
        Man: [Whispers]
        Woman: *Well no wonder. That only works for 4 hours.*
        Man: [Sneezes]
        Voice over (adult male): *Interesting fact about what he took. Its decongestant lasts only 4 hours per dose, and it contains aspirin, which can upset your stomach.* **Contac lasts up to 12 hours per dose and does not contain aspirin. Contac. Twelve hours, not four** [emphasis added].
        Usher: *Trouble here?*
        Man: *Ah. Some guy didn't take his Contac.*
        Voice over (adult male): *Give your cold to Contac.*

In this commercial, as in the Duration commercial, the verbal distinction we have been discussing is blurred orally, for the voice over announcer says that *Contac lasts up to 12 hours per dose* but then says *Twelve hours, not four*. There is also a conflict between what is said orally and what is printed on screen. As the voice over announcer recites the light italic

---

[7]This commercial was taped during recreational use of the videotape machine.

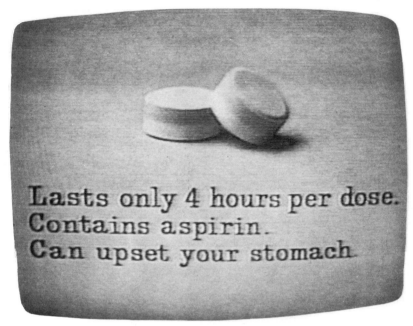

Photograph 1.3

portion of his message we see statement (7) on screen (see Photograph 1.3).

(7)   *Lasts only 4 hours per dose. Contains aspirin. Can upset your stomach.*

As the voice over announcer says the bold italic portion of (6), we see statement (8) (see Photograph 1.4).

(8)   *Lasts 12 hours per dose. Does not contain aspirin.*

I have noted that people cannot focus their attention on simultaneously presented oral and visual messages if they differ from each other and are of any great complexity. However, the oral and visual messages of this commercial are quite similar and are relatively simple, and therefore, I believe that viewers will be able to comprehend both what is said and what is seen. The question arises as to which Contac claim viewers will retain. There appears to have been no experimental studies of the relative saliency of slightly different, simultaneously presented oral and visual linguistic communications. Nevertheless, the manufacturer of Contac has nothing to lose even if the stronger visual message (8) is less salient than the parallel, but weaker, oral message of (6), as I suspect it is.

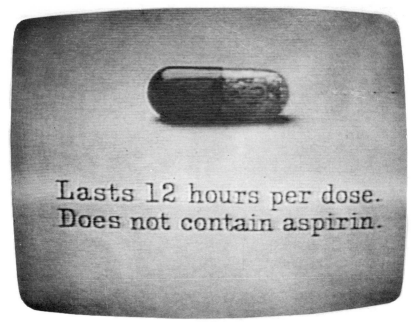

Photograph 1.4

Interestingly, the Duration and Contac commercials differ in this re-spect, for the weaker of the two claims is presented graphically in the Duration commercial.[8]

The fact that television advertising uses both the auditory and visual communications channels is very commonly exploited by advertisers in their presentation of printed disclaimers. Frequently lengthy, small-print disclaimers are presented on screen in competition with the oral message and other visual material. In some cases, the disclaimers are presented too briefly to be read under the best of circumstances. In others, the oral message will distract viewers from the printed disclaimers, for one nor-mally cannot simultaneously read one thing and listen to another and it is easier to listen to someone talk than to read something. A particularly significant example of small-print disclaimers is cited in Chapter 4 in connection with a Chevette commercial.

[8]There is one other feature of (6) worth mention. In the oral text of commercial (6) and in printed message (7), the presence of aspirin is linked to the possibility of an upset stomach. Note that in the bold italic portion of (6) and in (8), it is noted that Contac does not contain aspirin. In this context, the voice over message of (6) and printed message (8) imply that Contac cannot cause upset stomachs. The advertiser is careful not to assert this however.

It is interesting that advertisers are required to present disclaimers in a variety of circumstances, but they are not required to make them intelligible. Just how viewers' interests are served by disclaimers they cannot read is a mystery to me. Generally, the only types of disclaimers that have a serious chance of being understood by viewers are oral disclaimers and very brief printed ones.

As we saw, the fact that television advertising occurs in real time can be exploited by presenting conflicting claims at different points in a commercial. A second way in which the real time character of television advertising can be exploited is by presenting flawed arguments of various sorts. Since viewers cannot review the text of a commercial, unless they see it a number of times, the odds are that they will fail to see through at least some faulty arguments. This probability is enhanced by the fact that viewers are unlikely to attend carefully to television advertising.

Nonsequiturs are not uncommon in television advertising. In some cases they are used as attention getters, as can be seen quite clearly in the following commercial for Freedent gum.[9]

(9)   **Freedent** (NBC, 1/2/81, 10:11 a.m.)
        Type: Live action
        Setting: Art museum
        Characters: Woman

        TEXT
        Woman: *People say I have a million dollar smile. Well, I should. Sometimes I think I invested that much on it.* **That's why I chew Freedent.** *Freedent is the one gum that won't stick to my dental work. And I like that fresh minty taste. Freedent gives me all the chewing pleasure I can ask for in a gum and, where my dental work's concerned, there's nothing tacky about it. Freedent, the pleasure sticks, the gum won't* [emphasis added].

The statement *That's why I chew Freedent* signals the drawing of a conclusion from an argument. However, the actual argument for chewing Freedent is presented after this statement is made, not before it. I believe that the use of a nonsequitur in this statement is designed to attract attention to what the woman is saying.

Perhaps the clearest case of a problematic use of nonsequitur in television advertising occurs in the following commercial for Ty-D-Bol.

[9]I am indebted to Bill Boslego for drawing my attention to this advertising technique.

(10)   **Ty-D-Bol** (WUAB, Cleveland, 2/24/78, @ 12:01 p.m.)
        Type: Live Action
        Setting: Bathroom
        Characters: Man

        TEXT
        Man: *Now there are two great ways to help this part of your bathroom be
        clean and fresh. There's famous blue Ty-D-Bol automatic bowl
        cleaner with lemon-fresh borax. And now there's new green Ty-D-Bol
        with pine-scented borax. Both have the power of borax to clean and
        deodorize.* **So both are even tougher on stains, tougher on odors.** *Get
        Ty-D-Bol with borax. In original lemon-fresh blue or new pine-scented
        green Ty-D-Bol* [emphasis added].

The claim that both green and blue Ty-D-Bol are *even tougher on stains,
tougher on odors* makes no sense whatever in the context of this commercial. The claim that new green Ty-D-Bol is somehow tougher on stains,
tougher on odors cannot possibly be true. Consider (11) and (12).

(11)   New green Ty-D-Bol is even tougher on stains.

(12)   New green Ty-D-Bol is even tougher on stains than it was
        before.

Sentence (11) makes sense in this context only if it has the same meaning
as (12), but (12) is true only if there was an earlier, inferior version of
green Ty-D-Bol. No such version of green Ty-D-Bol appears to have
existed. The claim that blue Ty-D-Bol is even tougher on stains, tougher
on odors than before would be true only if some new ingredient has
been added to an earlier version of blue Ty-D-Bol that makes it more
effective, but this also appears to be false.

  What will be the effect on consumers of commercial (10)? Some consumers may notice that the line *so both are even tougher on stains, even
tougher on odors* is a nonsequitur, but many consumers, especially inattentive ones, may "reconcile" the conflict presented by this claim simply by
assuming (apparently falsely) that something or other was said that
motivates this claim, i.e., by assuming that both blue and green Ty-D-Bol
each contains some novel ingredient not contained in an earlier version
of blue Ty-D-Bol that makes both tougher on stains and odors than blue
Ty-D-Bol used to be.

  If television advertising presents special cognitive and perceptual
problems for viewers, the special character of television also presents
problems for advertisers. Because of the costs of creating television advertising and of buying commercial time, most television advertisements
are just 30 seconds in length. To the advertiser of products of little

intrinsic worth, even a 30-second commercial must be difficult to fill in a substantive way. Consider the problem of presenting 30 seconds worth of substantive information about a soft drink or beer or toilet tissue, etc. On the other hand, in cases of products about which much can be said, e.g., various brands of 35 mm cameras, copying machines, and automobiles, the 30-second commercial presents all too brief an opportunity for product promotion. It is instructive to compare a 30-second television advertisement for, say, a 35 mm camera with one-page advertisements appearing in national magazines like *Time* or *Newsweek,* and to compare the latter with multipage advertisements in photography magazines. It is clear from this sort of comparison that television is not the optimal vehicle for presenting substantive arguments for products.

The fact that viewers are not likely to examine television commercials very carefully makes them more vulnerable to defective arguments for products, but it also makes them less vulnerable to good arguments for products than they would otherwise be.[10] As a result, it should not be surprising if television advertisers were frequently to resort to what we might call "fluffery," the presentation of advertisements that have little substance. To some degree, viewers get the commercials they deserve, that is, commercials to which they respond.

Deception

Of all the issues raised by advertising, none seems to attract more attention than that of what is and is not a deceptive practice. There can be no doubt that language scholars have much to contribute to an understanding of this issue.

The question of whether or not a specific advertising claim is true is normally not something that language scholars would be in a position to answer. However, there are three aspects of this question on which language scholars are in a position to shed light, and these are (a) the determination of exactly what a given claim does claim; (b) the determination of the conditions that must be satisfied if a given claim is to be judged true; and (c) the determination of how those who hear a given claim will interpret it. I believe that language scholars can also make an important contribution to the establishment of a realistic standard of truth in advertising.

Presumably, the determination of what a claim claims and the deter-

---

[10]As we shall see later on in this chapter, the attentiveness of a listener to a message that is persuasive in intent is indispensable to the effectiveness of the message.

mination of how that claim will be understood by those who hear or read it should agree. The only context in which this might not occur is one in which what is asserted is different from what is implied. Consider the following claim on behalf of the nonexistent product Wartsoff.

(13)   Wartsoff contains vivaline and vivaline removes warts instantly.

Sentence (13) would normally be taken to imply that (14) is true.

(14)   Wartsoff removes warts instantly.

However, (13) does not assert the truth of (14) nor is the speaker of (13) logically committed to the truth of (14), for (13) could be true even if Wartsoff does not remove warts at all. Wartsoff might contain so small a dose of vivaline as to be totally ineffective.

Claims like (13) commonly occur in the advertising of over-the-counter (OTC) drugs. Over and over again, we are told that such and such a drug contains the ingredient doctors recommend or prescribe most. The question is whether or not advertisers should be held responsible for the implication that the drug in question is therefore effective. What makes this question especially interesting is that an inference like (14) does not derive solely from what was said, but derives in part from what was said and in part from consumer reasoning. The question is, then, should advertisers (or anyone else, for that matter) be held responsible for inferences that derive from listener reasoning when they have no control over this reasoning.

In Chapter 2, I examine two standards of truth in advertising, a literalist standard, and a pragmatist standard. According to the literalist standard, advertisers should be held responsible only for what they assert and for what the things they say entail.[11] According to the pragmatist standard, advertisers should also be held responsible for nonidiosyncratic inferences drawn by consumers.

The literalist standard of truth in advertising is based on the logical distinction between valid and invalid inferences. In Chapter 2, I shall argue that English speakers untutored in logic do not control this distinction, that is to say that they (including those who are quite intelligent) do not normally distinguish valid inferences from invalid but nevertheless quite compelling inferences of the sort Grice (1975, 1978) called "conversational implicatures." Not only do logically untutored speakers not control this distinction, they are, in fact, quite commonly required to

---

[11]A sentence S entails a proposition P if and only if in every possible circumstance in which S is true, P is also true. That advertisers should be held responsible for entailments should not be controversial.

draw invalid inferences if they are to use the language properly. Thus, for example, someone who says

(15)   I'll give you $5 if you mow the lawn.

would normally expect the listener to draw the inference that

(16)   I won't give you $5 if you don't mow the lawn.

is true even though this inference is not valid.

In Chapter 2, I argue that if our standard of truth in advertising is to be a realistic one, it must be based on actual, rather than ideal, human cognitive and semantic abilities. This in turn forces us to take the view that advertisers should be held responsible for those inferences drawn by consumers that are nonidiosyncratic, that is, for those inferences that follow from principles of language use of the sort Grice has proposed. In Chapter 3, I go on to elaborate the implications of this pragmatist standard of truth in advertising.

A theory of deception in advertising must, of course, be clear about what counts as a deceptive practice. Chisolm and Feehan (1977) identify eight ways in which one person can deceive another. I would like to consider these eight possibilities in connection with contemporary advertising practices. The most straightforward way in which one person can deceive another is by asserting or implying that something false is true. Advertisers are clearly in a position to do this, and a number of examples will be cited in the pages to follow. Corresponding to this sort of deception by commission is a parallel deception by omission, where instead of causing someone to acquire a false belief one simply allows someone to acquire a false belief. A particularly clear case of this occurs in the advertising of fruit-flavored products to young children. As I shall argue in Chapter 8, children are disposed to believe that if a food is fruit flavored then this is because it contains fruit or is made from fruit. To guard against the drawing of this inference by consumers in the case of artificially flavored products, makers of artificially flavored products are required to state this on product packages. However, television commercials are not required to present disclaimers stating that artificially flavored products are artificially flavored. By failing to include such disclaimers, advertisers of artificially flavored products could be said to be allowing children to acquire the false belief that products that do not contain fruit do contain fruit. In television advertising generally, the widespread practice of presenting lengthy disclaimers that cannot be read in the time they are on screen is, in my view, another example of this type of deception.

Chisolm and Feehan note that one person can deceive another by causing (commission) or allowing (omission) someone to continue to believe something false. Advertisers can do this by causing or allowing someone to acquire a false belief in earlier advertising and by causing or allowing someone to continue in this false belief in later advertising. A number of cases of this type have occurred over the years, of course. Much more interesting are cases in which advertising exploits false beliefs that they may not be responsible for starting, as when advertising of OTC drugs actively or passively encourages consumers, who believe that OTC drugs normally treat causes rather than symptoms, to continue with this belief. I discuss possible cases of this in Chapter 5.

The next types of deception identified by Chisolm and Feehan concern cases in which someone deceives another by causing (commission) or allowing (omission) someone to cease to hold a true belief. Consider the following Keebler Cookie commercial:

(17)   **Keebler Double Nutty cookies** (NBC, 9/2/78, 10:58 a.m.)
         Type: Animated
         Setting: Outdoors, near the Keebler tree
         Characters: Keebler elf, animal trainer, and Gracie, the elephant

         TEXT
         Animal trainer: *Look, Keebler, a dancing elephant. She loves peanut
            butter. Dance for some peanut butter, Gracie. Come on, show the elf.*
            [The elephant refuses to dance.]
         Elf: *Try our new Keebler peanut butter sandwich cookies. Double Nutty.
            There's peanut butter inside and out.*
         Animal trainer: *Really?*
         Elf: *Rich creamy peanut butter in the filling and in the cookies, for
            double peanut butter taste.* [The animal trainer and elephant each eat
            a cookie.]
         Animal trainer: *Delicious. Dance for a Double Nutty Cookie, Gracie.*
            [The elephant dances.]
         Voice over (adult male): *New Double Nutty sandwich cookies with
            peanut butter inside and out.*

In commercial (17), the elephant, through her behavior, demonstrates a preference for the Keebler peanut-butter-flavored cookies over peanut butter. I believe it is entirely possible that some children, especially very young ones, might be led by this commercial to abandon the presumably true belief that peanut butter cookies are not normally an acceptable alternative to peanut butter sandwiches.

The last types of deception identified by Chisolm and Feehan concern cases in which someone prevents (commission) someone from abandoning a false belief or allows (omission) someone to fail to abandon a false belief. I see no way an advertiser, through his advertising alone, could deceive consumers in this way.

How Advertisers Talk to Viewers

A fully predictive theory of speech behavior would be a visionary goal of the study of language. However, a determination of the parameters that govern what a speaker might say, how he or she might say it on any given occasion, and how a listener will interpret what is said on that occasion is an attainable goal. Two parameters that govern what a speaker might say are the context which conversants find themselves in and the relative social statuses of the conversants.

There are four aspects of the speech context which are relevant to an understanding of any particular speech behavior: the **physical context,** the **epistemic context,** the **linguistic context,** and the **social context.** The physical context consists of the tangible aspects of context, including where the conversants are, what is present in that context, and what is going on in that context. The epistemic context consists of background knowledge shared by the conversants. The linguistic context consists of what has already been said prior to any speech behavior in question. The social context consists of the social occasion which brings the conversants together. An example will clarify the roles these aspects of context can play.

Suppose a group of people are sitting around a table eating together and that person B can, but A cannot, reach a salt boat (physical context). Suppose further that the conversants are gathered together for a formal dinner party as opposed to a family-style meal (social context) and that the conversants are discussing the most recent presidential election (linguistic context). Finally, suppose that A says to B:

(18)   Would you mind passing the salt?

B will interpret A as having requested that B pass A the salt even though (18) is an interrogative sentence. B will recognize that (18) is inconsistent with the topic of conversation (linguistic context) but will assume that (18) is nevertheless relevant to what is going on, will recognize that people often add salt to their food at the table (epistemic context), will know that listener-oriented yes–no questions are commonly used to make requests (epistemic context), and that he or she, but not A, can reach the salt (physical context). Having made these observations, B must recognize (18) as a request for salt.

The social context has less to do with what people say than how they say it, that is, with style rather than content. At a formal dinner party, A would, for instance, be more likely to say (18) than

(19)   Pass the salt.

or

(20)   I need the salt.

Sentence (18) is more polite than the command (19) or the speaker-oriented assertion (20) and thus is more appropriate at a formal dinner party.

How conversants say what they say not only reflects the social context they are in but also the social relationships that hold among them. Suppose an Army sergeant wants a private to pick up a cigarette butt while both are on duty. In this social context, the sergeant enjoys a sufficient social advantage over the private to issue an order, perhaps,

(21)   Pick up that butt, private.

On the other hand, should the sergeant and private be playing a friendly game of cards while both are off duty, the sergeant might say (21), but would be more likely to make a polite request, perhaps,

(22)   Could you pick up that butt?

In this context the social relationship between the two soldiers would approximate that of friends. Thus, context can serve to determine which of various social relationships conversants might participate in will obtain on a given occasion.

How we talk to each other can be factored into considerations of style (which reflects the social context), and register (which reflects the social relationships), among conversants.[12] The former is usually measured along a formal–informal scale. The latter involves specialized language used when conversants enjoy a particular social relationship. Adults employ a specialized way of talking with very young children (the "baby talk" register). Physicians employ a special way of talking to patients (the doctor–patient register). Adults who occupy a particular vocation often develop specialized vocabularies specific to that vocation (i.e., that register).

---

[12]See Zwicky and Zwicky (in press) for a useful discussion of the distinction between style and register. The distinction I draw is very similar to theirs.

Commercials can be divided into those that are addressed directly to viewers and those in which characters on screen talk to each other, rather than to the viewer. Many commercials employ both types of elements, of course. In Chapter 6, I discuss questions of style and register in connection with the latter type of commercial. Here I would like briefly to discuss style and register in regard to the former type of commercial.

The social context in which advertisers talk directly to consumers is, of course, an impersonal, public context. This fact has a great bearing on what products can be advertised on television, when they can be advertised, and how they are advertised. Today, douches are promoted on television, but only when young viewers can be expected not to be in the audience. A few years ago, they would not have been advertised on television at all. How products can be advertised also reflects the impersonal, public character of television as those familiar with the controversy surrounding the rather sexually explicit Brooke Shields jeans commercials of 1980 will recognize.

The type of commercial that most directly reflects the impersonal, public character of television is the fully monological, explicitly didactic commercial, spoken by an on-screen representative of the advertiser. These commercials typically employ relatively formal English, as befits the social context. However, advertisers often try to get away from this impersonal type of commercial by having the speaker engage the viewer directly (by using the pronoun *you*) or by employing some celebrity to whom viewers can be expected to react emotionally. In the latter case, the celebrity will normally employ a speech style consistent with public perceptions of the celebrity.

Whether or not there is an advertising register is difficult to say. There are certain speech patterns that recur in advertising but these alone do not suffice to constitute a register. Moreover, advertisers and viewers do not enjoy the sort of social relationship required for the emergence of a speech register, for the social relationship is not interactive in character.

As a result of the fact that viewers cannot talk back to advertisers the interpretation of interrogative sentences used in television advertising is systematically skewed. They are necessarily interpreted as rhetorical questions and their primary value to advertisers lies in what they imply. Consider the following commercial for the Reach Toothbrush.

(23)   **Reach Toothbrush** (ABC, 2/24/78, @ 8:49 a.m.)
       Type: Live action
       Setting: Studio
       Characters: Man

TEXT
Man: *The invented fluoride toothpaste to help fight cavities. Why hasn't somebody invented a better toothbrush? What if you angled it like a dental instrument to reach back teeth and concentrated the bristles to clean each tooth of material that can cause cavities and made rows of higher, softer bristles to clean between teeth? And what if they called this new brush "Reach"? The Reach toothbrush from Johnson and Johnson, to help fight cavities.*

The question *Why hasn't somebody invented a better toothbrush?* is not, of course, a question the speaker expects anyone but himself to answer. Its purpose is to imply that somebody should have invented a better toothbrush. What is interesting is that the advertiser chose to imply a need rather than asserting one, which is the sort of omission viewers ought to be sensitive to. The *what if* questions occurring in (23) are also rhetorical questions. They imply the desirability of each design feature but are careful not to assert the efficacy of any. Indeed, this commercial is a masterpiece of the art of claim avoidance in advertising.

If the context of television advertising precludes interpretation of questions directed at viewers as genuine information questions, the social relationship between advertiser and viewer precludes interpretation of imperative sentences as commands. Consider such examples as

(24)   *So use Soft Scrub for cleanser clean without all that cleanser scratch.*
         (NBC, 1/2/81, 10:20 a.m.)

(25)   *Make your team's table a training table and get Sunlite.*   (CBS, 1/2/81,
         11:46 a.m.)

(26)   *See this Sunday's paper or look in your mailbox* [for an announcement
         from *Time* magazine].   (ABC, 1/2/81, 6:15 p.m.)

(27)   *Contact an Amway distributor and get the whole story.*   (ABC, 1/16/81,
         6:13 p.m.)

Imperative sentences are, par excellance, the vehicle for giving orders, but as was noted earlier, the speaker must enjoy a superior social status relative to the listener to give a felicitous order, and advertisers do not enjoy such a social advantage over viewers. As a result, (24)–(27) will not be interpreted as orders.

Imperative sentences are widely used to make suggestions. Thus, if A is helping B fix a toy and B is having trouble getting some glue to set properly, B might say something like

(28)   Try clamping those pieces together.

by way of making suggestion

(29)   You should try clamping those pieces together.

Advertising imperatives (24)–(27) similarly make suggestions, rather than give orders.

    As we have seen, interrogative and imperative sentences directed at viewers are used to convey propositions indirectly. The advertiser who says *Why hasn't somebody invented a better toothbrush* or *Make your team's table a training table and get Sunlite* does so by way of conveying the need for a better toothbrush and the desirability of Sunlite oil indirectly. In Chater 2, we shall have much to say about this practice, arguing that the primary virtues of conveying information indirectly are, first, that indirectly conveyed propositions are rarely defended in ordinary conversation and thus advertisers are under no pressure to defend them in their advertising and, second, that indirectly conveyed propositions are perceptually less salient than asserted propositions and will less likely stimulate consumer cognitive defenses.

Language and Persuasion

    Suppose a parent wishes to stop a child from playing with a knife. Suppose further that the child is 10 or 12 years old and more or less controls the language. The linguistic options available to the parent are extraordinary. He or she might issue an order,

(30)   Stop playing with that knife.

make a request,

(31)   Would you stop playing with that knife?

give a warning,

(32)   That knife is going to cut you.

make a threat,

(33)   Play with that knife any more and I'll send you to your room.

make a plea,

(34)   You're scaring me to death.

or give advice,

(35)   That knife's very sharp.

and the like. Clearly, so long as we confine our attention solely to the intended effect, it will be quite impossible to predict what our hypothetical parent might say. Moreover, since any parent might use any one of (30)–(35) in any number of different contexts, adding information about the context to our knowledge of what the parent's intent is will not materially assist us in predicting which of (30)–(35) the parent might say. What we need to specify in order to predict what a given parent might say on a particular occasion to stop his or her child from playing with a knife is information about the **psychological means** the parent wishes to employ.

If we were to say that our hypothetical parent were to employ the psychological device of persuasion, then (32), (34), or (35) would almost certainly be the utterances of choice, rather than any of the other sentences, and which of these the parent might use would reflect the nature of the relationship between parent and child and the beliefs of the parent as to whether a speaker-oriented appeal (34) or a listener-oriented appeal (32) or (35) might be the more effective. In such a way the purpose for which language is used and the psychological means employed to accomplish that purpose can determine what someone will say on any particular occasion.

It is clear that, in advertising, the psychological means employed is persuasion. There is another term that might be used to describe the means advertisers employ to sell products and services and that is *manipulation*. Neither is particularly satisfactory. The term *manipulation* is pejorative, and the term *persuasion* focuses too much on the ratiocinative, as opposed to the affective, side of persuasion. Nevertheless, following the practice of psychologists, I shall continue to employ the term *persuasion* in most contexts. However, it is worth asking how persuasion and manipulation are alike and different.

There are a variety of theories of persuasion to which we might appeal in attempts to account for the various techniques advertisers employ in persuading consumers to purchase products and services. Of those I am familiar with, the information processing theory of persuasion (McGuire, 1969) I find the most useful, for it provides a reasonable basis for distinguishing the various techniques advertisers employ.

The information processing model of persuasion views persuasion as a process in which a source presents a message to a receiver via some communication channel in an attempt to effect either of two behavioral changes: for the receiver to believe that the message is true, or for the receiver to act upon that message. McGuire identifies six parameters necessary to the process of persuasion:

(36)   If a source S wishes to persuade a receiver R of the truth of
        some message M,

(a) S must present M to R
(b) R must attend to M
(c) R must comprehend M
(d) R must yield to M
(e) R must retain M
If the source wishes to cause the receiver to perform some action, it is additionally necessary that
(f) R must act on M.

I have only one quarrel with McGuire's formulation of the parameters governing persuasion and that is that it does not provide room for how the receiver comes to yield to the source's message. McGuire's parameters do not allow us to distinguish ordering someone to do something and persuading someone to do something, for in both cases the receiver yields. Recall our discussion of the linguistic options (30)–(35) available to a parent who wishes to cause his or her child to stop playing with a knife. Notice that were the parent to say (30) and were the child to obey, then all of McGuire's parameters are satisfied. The parent has presented the message to the child and the child has attended to it, has comprehended it, has yielded to it, has retained it (as long as necessary), and has acted upon it. However, the child has not evaluated the message at least in the sense of assessing its credibility.

Compare the parent's saying (30) with his or her saying (32). The child who hears (32) will evaluate it in the light of the fact that the parent did not employ an order, request, or threat and will therefore conclude that the option of yielding to the parent's warning is the child's. The child will yield or not depending, among other things, on his determination of the credibility of the parent's prediction. Thus, if we are to distinguish ordering from persuading, it would appear that we must allow for receiver evaluation of the source's message.

Postulation of a parameter concerned with receiver evaluation of persuasive messages allows us to distinguish between persuasion and manipulation in a reasonably straightforward way. Manipulation differs from persuasion most crucially in that in manipulation there is no conscious evaluation by the receiver of the merits of the source's message. Perhaps the clearest case in which there is no evaluation, at least no conscious evaluation, would be that in which the message is presented subliminally. A second way in which a message can be manipulative is through use of the technique of repetition, where again, the success of the message in no way depends on receiver evaluation of the message. It depends only on the receiver's remembering the name. Consider the following transcript from a television commercial for Bubble Yum bubble gum:

(37)   Bubble Yum (ABC, 12/29/79, 10:45 a.m.)
        Type: Live action
        Setting: Magic show
        Characters: Magician and children

        TEXT
        Boy 1: *It's a magic show.*
        Children, singing: *Bubble Bubble Yum, it's so much yum, yum, yum. It's
            number yum, yum, yum in bubble gum.*
        Girl: *It's yummy soft and juicy.*
        Children, singing: *Bubble Bubble Yum, it's so much yum, yum, yum. It's
            number yum, yum, yum in bubble gum.*
        Boy 2: *The yummy flavor lasts a long long long time.*
        Magician (adult male): *And now Bubble Yum introduces the only yum
            that's sugarless.* [13] *New sugarless Bubble Yum.*
        Children: *Yummy!*
        Children, singing: *Number yum, yum, yum in Bubble Yum.*

This commercial uses the morpheme *yum* no less than 24 times in 30 seconds. Although this commercial does try to be amusing, the repetitions must have the effect of causing children to remember the morpheme *yum* and, therefore, also to remember the name *Bubble Yum*. There are rational elements to this commercial. Bubble Yum is said to be soft and juicy and to have a long-lasting flavor. However, since these are quite unexceptional claims, any effectiveness this advertisement might have would surely be due primarily to the repetition of the product name.

As I am using the term, *manipulation* refers to the use of techniques that do not depend on receiver evaluation for their success. One might go a step further and argue that appeals that are nonrational in character are also manipulative. One might argue, for instance, that cereal advertisements directed at children that stress taste (e.g., in particular, sweetness) rather than nutrition are manipulative, for they exploit the (apparent) fact that children are more concerned with taste than nutrition. However, taste is relevant to anyone's choice of any food. I therefore do not see any virtue in calling such appeals manipulative. They may be nonrational or exploitative, but that is another matter. Similarly, if fear is employed in the advertising of insurance this could be argued to be manipulative, but it is difficult to see what the merit of such a claim

---

[13]This claim would be quite false, of course, if children were to construe *yum* as gum. This sort of verbal trickery serves to support my claim that those with the responsibility for monitoring children's television advertising simply don't care what advertisers say to children.

would be since we have the perfectly usable (and less pejorative) word *nonrational* to use to refer to advertising appeals that are affective, rather than rational, in nature.

The goal of commercial advertising is to cause consumers to buy products or services. The advertiser might achieve this goal simply by causing the viewer to remember the name of the product or service. He might achieve this goal by causing viewers to come to adopt a positive feeling about the product via advertisements that have great dramatic force (as in the "Mean Joe Greene" Coca Cola commercial), that are humorous (as in past Alka-Seltzer commercials), or that appeal to one's libido (as in Noxema shaving cream commercials). The advertiser might cause consumers to come to buy a product or service by providing some sort of argument for the product. In general, this study will focus on the latter, ratiocinative type of commercial.

Language can and does play an important role in the process of commercial persuasion. It is the primary vehicle for presenting messages to consumers; it is one of the tools advertisers use to get viewer attention; it is crucial to the reasoning processes by means of which consumers come to yield to advertiser's messages; and it plays an important role in facilitating consumer memory of the desirability of the product or service being promoted.

Chapter 2

Saying Things Indirectly

Although the English language provides its speakers with ample means for communicating with each other directly, it is remarkable how often we choose to communicate indirectly. Someone who wishes to make a request can do so directly by using an imperative sentence, as in

(1)   Please give me a cup of coffee.

or indirectly by using an interrogative sentence, as in

(2)   Would you mind getting me a cup of coffee?

or even a declarative sentence, as in

(3)   I would like a cup of coffee.

Similarly, someone who wishes to convey a piece of information can do so directly by using a declarative sentence, as in

(4)   John Jones married Mary Morris.

or do so indirectly by using an interrogative sentence, as in

(5)   Did you know that John Jones married Mary Morris?

In any circumstance in which language is used indirectly, the listener must draw an inference from what is said about what the speaker intended to convey. In some cases, the inference in question follows relatively directly from what is said. It is by virtue of the meaning of the verb *know*, for instance, that sentence (5) implies that John Jones married Mary Morris. A speaker cannot say (5) in good faith unless he or she has solid evidence that John Jones married Mary Morris. Use of the verb *know* signals possession of the evidence. In other cases, listeners must actually reason from what is said to what is meant. A college student who has been invited to go to a movie might refuse by saying *I've got an exam tomorrow.* To get from this sentence to the proposition that the invitee cannot go to a movie clearly requires some reasoning.

It would be surprising, I think, if advertisers were not to use language indirectly. However, several problems arise as a result. In order to bring these problems into sharp focus, it will be useful to consider the following claim made on behalf of the mythical product Wartsoff:[1]

(6)   Wartsoff contains vivaline and you know that vivaline removes
          warts instantly.

Some consumers, on reading or hearing (6), would almost certainly draw the inference that

(7)   Wartsoff removes warts instantly.

is true, whether or not they have ever heard of vivaline (which is a mythical ingredient). Such a consumer might reason as follows:

(8)   a. The claim that Wartsoff contains vivaline is relevant to my
             concerns just in case Wartsoff does what vivaline does.
        b. Since the advertiser has used the verb *know,* he must have
             solid evidence that vivaline does remove warts instantly.
        c. Therefore, Wartsoff must remove warts instantly.

Although the reasoning outlined in (8) is perfectly natural, it rests on a very shaky foundation, for Wartsoff could contain vivaline without containing a therapeutic dose.

A skeptical consumer, on hearing (6), might draw the inference that (7) is probably false. This consumer might reason as follows:

(9)   a. The claim that Wartsoff contains vivaline is relevant to my
             concerns just in case Wartsoff does what vivaline does.
        b. Since the advertiser has used the verb *know,* he must have
             solid evidence that vivaline does remove warts instantly.
        c. Therefore, it would appear to follow that Wartsoff removes
             warts instantly.
        d. But, the advertiser did not actually assert that Wartsoff
             removes warts instantly.
        e. Advertisers normally make the strongest claims they can
             defend.

[1]This example combines features of two different advertisements that we will discuss later in this chapter, a Pine Sol commercial and an Aftate commercial.

  f.   Asserting that Wartsoff removes warts instantly directly would
       be to make a stronger claim than simply implying that this
       is true
  g.   Therefore the advertiser must not be able to defend the claim
       that Wartsoff removes warts instantly.
  h.   Therefore the claim that Wartsoff removes warts instantly
       may be false.

This line of reasoning is itself not fully warranted, for (9e) could be false
in any particular case and the step from (9g) to (9h), while not unreasonable, is not valid.

Since Wartsoff could contain vivaline without containing a therapeutic dose, (6) could be true and (7) false. Nevertheless, certainly some and
probably most consumers would, on hearing (6), draw the inference that
(7) is true if they draw any inference at all. The question arises whether
or not the speaker who says (6) should be held accountable for the truth
of (7). Put more generally, we might ask whether or not advertisers
should be held responsible not only for what they assert is true but also
for what they imply is true.

In this chapter, I propose to address the question just asked. I shall
first contrast two different approaches to this question, a literalist approach and a pragmatist approach, and go on to examine the linguistic
foundations on which they rest. I shall then consider a number of cases
of the indirect use of language in contemporary advertising and offer
some conjectures about the effect of such uses of language on consumers.

The Literalist and Pragmatist Positions

As we have seen, the inferences a listener draws from what a speaker
says result in part from listener reasoning, and it is possible for different
listeners to draw different inferences from the same claim. These facts
present something of a problem for anyone who might wish to argue
that advertisers should be held responsible for all inferences consumers
draw from advertising. How is it reasonable, one might ask, to hold advertisers responsible for inferences drawn by consumers, if advertisers have
no control over consumer cognitive activities?

As a partial answer to this question let us note that there are two types
of inferences—**entailments** and **conventional implicatures**—for which
speakers (including advertisers) must unquestionably be held responsible. Let us define the concept of entailment as follows:

(10)   A sentence S **entails** a proposition P if and only if in every
        possible circumstance in which S is true, P is also true.

Given this definition, we would want to say that

(11)   John ate an egg and Mary ate some bacon.

entails

(12)   John ate an egg.

for (12) cannot be false if (11) is true. Similarly we would want to say that

(13)   It's not true that John ate an egg and Mary ate some bacon.

entails

(14)   Either John didn't eat an egg or Mary didn't eat any bacon.

for (14) cannot be false if (13) is true.

If a sentence S entails a proposition P, it does so by virtue of the
meaning of S, that is to say that any entailment of a given sentence is a
property of that sentence. Thus, even though the listener who hears (11)
may have to do some reasoning to get from (11) to (12) or from (13) to
(14), the reasoning is logically valid. It is clear then that the speaker of
any given sentence must be held responsible not only for what he or she
asserts but also for any entailment of any assertion.

The concept of entailment is straightforward enough, but is of limited
usefulness. Given the preceding definition it cannot be used to explicate
inferences we draw from questions or imperative sentences, for neither
questions nor imperative sentences can be true or false. In this light,
consider

(15)   Who killed Caesar?

Most people who hear (15) would draw the inference that

(16)   Someone killed Caesar.

is true. Since (15) is neither true nor false, we cannot say that (15) entails
(16). Nevertheless, this inference is quite sound.

Grice's term *conventional implicature* (1975, 1978) is used to refer
to this sort of inference. Conventional implicatures share one important
property with entailments. Consider[2]

(17)   *John didn't eat an egg, but John ate an egg and Mary ate some
        bacon.

---

[2]In all examples, when a proper name is repeated, the name is intended to have the
same referent in all occurrences.

(18)   *I know that no one killed Caesar, but who killed Caesar?

Both (17) and (18) are semantically anomalous. In each case, what is entailed or conventionally implicated is cancelled by the left conjunct.

Note that, given our definition of entailment, if a sentence S entails a proposition P and if S is logically conjoined with the denial of P, the result must be a contradiction, that is, a proposition that cannot be true in any circumstance. Certainly the result of conjoining (11) and the denial of (12) is a contradiction. However, the result of conjoining (15) with the denial of (16) is also a contradiction even though (15) does not entail (16). It should be clear from this that the relation of conventional implicature is logically no weaker than that of entailment.

The concept of conventional implicature is difficult to define. It is usually assumed to be different from the concept of entailment. However, the fact that neither entailments nor conventional implicatures can be cancelled suggests that they are, in fact, quite similar. For reasons that will be developed later, I shall not distinguish between these two concepts, but will refer to both as conventional implicatures. The criterion of cancellability will be used to identify cases of conventional implicature, whether or not the implicature is an entailment or conventional implicature proper.

It should be clear that if a sentence S conventionally implicates a proposition P (no matter whether the conventional implicature is an entailment or a conventional implicature proper), the speaker of S is no less responsible for the truth of P than for the truth of S. This is no less true of advertisers than it is of anyone else who uses the language.

The weakest defensible theory of truth in advertising would be one that holds an advertiser responsible for any assertion he makes and any conventional implicature that is generated by what he says. This is what I shall call the **literalist** theory of truth in advertising. It is the weakest theory because it holds advertisers responsible only for inferences that follow directly from what they say. According to this view, inferences that derive in some crucial way from listener–consumer reasoning are the responsibility of the listener–consumer, not the speaker–advertiser.

There are two types of inferences that depend crucially on consumer cognitive activities, namely **theoretical implicatures** (Böer & Lycan, 1975) and **conversational implicatures** (Grice, 1975, 1978). Theoretical implicatures are implicatures that depend for their validity on listener beliefs. Conversational implicatures are implicatures that follow from principles governing felicitous conversation.

Some of the inferences we draw from what others say depend in part on what we believe to be the case. In Chapter 8, I shall argue that young children—children below the age of 8—are disposed to believe that if a food has a fruit flavor, this is because it contains fruit or is made directly from fruit. Should a child who believes this hear that some food has a lemon flavor, he or she must draw the inference that the food is made from lemons. In some cases, of course, this inference will be false. In this example, the child's inference is based in part on what is said and in part on what the child believes. We shall refer to this sort of inference as a theoretical implicature and define this notion as follows:

(19)   A sentence S ***theoretically implicates*** a proposition P if P can be
         deduced from the logical conjunction of S and some
         empirically contingent proposition Q, which is believed by the
         listener to be true.[3]

It should be clear that a given theoretical implicature will be false or misleading, assuming the asserted proposition is true, only if the empirically contingent proposition upon which it depends is false or misleading, as in the case of the child's belief that foods can be fruit flavored only if they contain or are made directly from fruit. However, an advertiser cannot be held responsible for the theoretical implicatures consumers draw from what the advertiser says unless the advertiser is himself responsible for the belief in the proposition on which the theoretical implicature depends. One area in which advertisers, in general, could be argued to be responsible for false consumer beliefs is the area of OTC drugs, for advertisers have misled consumers over the years concerning the efficacy of OTC drugs.[4]

The second class of inferences that depend on consumer reasoning consists of conversational implicatures. Let us define this sort of implicature as follows:

(20)   A sentence S ***conversationally implicates*** a proposition P in a
         given conversation if and only if P can be "calculated" given[5]

         a. the literal meaning of S,
         b. general principles governing conversation,
         c. the context of the conversation,
         d. background knowledge shared by speaker and hearer.

Several features of this definition require elaboration.

[3]In order to distinguish theoretical implicatures from certain conversational implicatures, the condition that belief in Q is in no way dependent on the conversational context must be added. I return to this point shortly.

[4]See Clark (1943) for a discussion of the very strong claims advertisers of OTC drugs made before and during the time of World War II.

[5]I am, of course, following Grice here.

According to Grice (1975) conversation is governed by what he calls the Cooperative Principle and its attendant Conversational Maxims. He states the Cooperative Principle as

(21)   *Cooperative Principle:* Make your conversational contribution such as is required, at the stage at which it occurs, by the accepted purpose or direction of the talk exchange in which you are engaged.

According to Grice, cooperative use of language in conversation is subject to a variety of maxims, including, in particular:[6]

(22)   *The Maxim of Strength:* Say no less than is necessary.

(23)   *The Maxim of Parsimony:* Say no more than is necessary.

(24)   *The Maxim of Truth:* Do not say what you believe to be false.

(25)   *The Maxim of Evidence:* Do not say that for which you lack adequate evidence.

(26)   *The Maxim of Relevance:* Be relevant.

(27)   *The Maxim of Clarity:* Avoid obscurity of expression.

Conversational implicatures can originate from the deliberate flouting of a maxim. Thus, if someone writes a letter of recommendation for a candidate for a professorship and says only that the candidate dresses neatly, has a pleasant personality, and shows up for every lecture, he or she conversationally implicates, thanks to having flouted the Maxims of Strength and Relevance, that the candidate is not a worthy one. More commonly, conversational implicatures arise out of the assumption that the parties to a conversation are obeying the maxims.

We shall later examine a variety of cases of conversational implicatures in advertising. For the moment, let us reconsider our discussion of example (6). As I noted, some consumers on hearing (6) will draw the inference that (7) is true. This is a conversational implicature based on the Maxim of Relevance, as can be seen by examining step (8a) in the reasoning process that leads to inference (7). As we noted, however, a skeptical consumer might, on hearing (6), draw the inference that (7) may be false. This too is a conversational implicature, based primarily on the Maxim of Strength, as can be seen by considering step (9e) in the reasoning leading to the conclusion that (7) may be false.

In general the process of reasoning involved in conversational impli-

---

[6]Some of the names of specific maxims are taken from Boer and Lycan (1975), some are Grice's, and still others are mine.

catures derived from the Maxims of Strength and Parsimony (Grice's Maxims of Quantity) is based on a listener comparison of what is said with what could have been but wasn't said. Thus, since the advertiser who says (6) could have said (7) and since (7) is stronger than (6), the skeptical consumer will draw the inference that (7) may very well be false.

A crucial feature of Grice's theory concerns the relevance of context to inference drawing in general [see item (20c)] and to the drawing of inferences based on the Maxim of Relevance in particular. As was noted in the Introduction, there are four features of context that are relevant to inference drawing: the linguistic context (what has already been said); the epistemic context (background assumptions shared by the parties to the conversation); the physical context (where the conversation takes place and what is going on); and the social context (the social occasion that has brought the parties to the conversation together).

We might illustrate the role of context in conversational implicatures by reconsidering an example discussed in the Introduction. Suppose, if during a conversation about the most recent presidential election, someone were to say *Would you please pass the salt?* to the person next to him or her. In such a case, the person addressed would normally take this as a request for salt. The person addressed would note that what has just been said is irrelevant to the discussion at hand (the linguistic context), but is relevant to what is going on (the physical context). Given this and the knowledge that people often add salt to food on their plates (the epistemic context), the listener will draw the inference that the speaker must want the salt.[7]

According to the literalist theory of truth in advertising, advertisers can be held responsible for assertions and conventional implicatures, but not theoretical implicatures or conversational implicatures. The primary bases for this position are, first, that differing consumers can and sometimes surely will draw different theoretical and conversational implicatures from a given advertisement, second, that advertisers have no control over consumer beliefs and consumer reasoning and, third, that Grice's theory is too vague to measure what precisely a given advertisement conversationally implicates.

The literalist theory of truth in advertising does not satisfy critics of advertising. Dwight Bolinger (1973), in his presidential address to the Linguistic Society of America, claimed that "the most insidious of all concepts of truth is that of literalness. Advertising capitalizes on the legal

---

[7]See Searle (1969, 1975) for a discussion of how it is that an indirect question like *Would you please pass the salt?* gets interpreted as a polite request.

protection it affords [p. 542]."[8] That a linguist would object to the literalist position is not surprising for it flies in the face of how ordinary people (including very intelligent and well-educated ordinary people) ordinarily use language. Speakers of English (and of other languages as well, of course) are inferencing creatures, who are conditioned to draw inferences, invalid as well as valid ones, as part of their linguistic competence. It is this fact that militates most strongly against the literalist theory of truth in advertising. However, the question of what standards of truth should be applied to advertising is as much a legal question as a linguistic or psychological one and the burden of proof must be on those who would replace the literalist standard, which has the virtue of being relatively precise, with some pragmatically based standard.

In what follows I shall argue that the literalist theory of truth in advertising is based on a false premise, namely, that ordinary people can reliably distinguish between valid and invalid inferences, and shall go on to propose a **pragmatist** theory of truth in advertising that is based on actual, rather than ideal, human cognitive-cum-semantic skills. According to this theory, advertisers should be held responsible not only for conventional implicatures of what they say, but also for conversational implicatures of what they say. In this chapter, I shall focus primarily on implicatures that arise out of the Maxim of Relevance. I shall argue that conversational implicatures that arise out of the Maxim of Relevance [e.g., drawing inference (7) from (6)] are perceptually more salient than are the more skeptical inferences that arise out of the Maxim of Strength [e.g., drawing the inference that (7) may be false on hearing (6)].[9] According to this view, the fact that different people can and will draw different inferences from the same advertisement is something of a pseudoproblem.

A Realistic Approach to How People Understand Language

The literalist position makes a sharp distinction between inferences which can be derived wholly from the meaning of what is said and inferences which derive, if only in part, from such nonsemantic considerations as speaker and listener beliefs, and conversational principles and the context of utterance. Precisely this same distinction, the semantics–pragmatics distinction, is made by language scholars. Language scholars

[8]See Bolinger (1980) for a more recent discussion of his objections to the literalist position.

[9]In Chapter 3, I discuss implicatures arising out of the Maxims of Strength and Parsimony in some detail.

have assumed that a general theory of how people understand sentences will include a theory of sentence meaning (semantic theory) and a theory of language use (pragmatic theory). Moreover, it has been assumed that pragmatic theory must be dependent on semantic theory. Certainly Grice took this line, for he argued that the conversational implicatures we draw on hearing a sentence depend in part on the literal meaning of that sentence.[10]

In classical semantic theory it is assumed that the semantic description of any sentence must account for (at least some of) the entailments of that sentence. Thus, it might be argued that the semantic description of sentences like

(28)   John woke up in a bar.

and

(29)   John woke up at noon.

must account for the fact that both sentences entail that

(30)   John woke up.

is true. There are basically two ways in which one can account for such entailments. One could assign logical forms to (28) and (29) from which (30) can be deduced by conventional rules of inference or one can assign meaning postulates or axioms that account for these entailments. We might, for instance, postulate an axiom saying that if something happens at some place or at some time, then it must have happened.

The status of conventional implicatures proper within semantic theory is somewhat uncertain. Certainly, the fact that

(31)   John Jones married Mary Morris again.

conventionally implicates

(32)   John Jones used to be married to Mary Morris.

follows from the meaning of *again*. In the future, I shall therefore assume that semantic theory should be responsible for conventional implicatures. In the case of (31) and (32), I would assume that a meaning postulate should be assigned to the lexical representation of the word *again* that accounts for the fact that (31) conventionally implicates (32).

The practice of distinguishing entailments and conventional implicatures from pragmatic inferences is justifiable on empirical grounds for it is an empirical question whether or not a given inference is valid or not. However, it does not follow from this that language speakers control this

---

[10]See item (20a).

distinction, i.e., that an implicit or explicit knowledge of the distinction between valid and invalid inferences plays a role in how ordinary people ordinarily go about interpreting sentences. I shall argue that ordinary people do not distinguish between valid and invalid inferences and then suggest an alternative approach to the theory of how people interpret sentences. I believe this alternative approach to be empirically sounder than classical semantic theories—theories that make a sharp distinction between semantics and pragmatics, i.e., between valid and invalid inferences.

There is good reason to believe that the concept of validity is alien to speakers untutored in logic, and is even irrelevant to how speakers tutored in logic normally use their languages. Those who teach introductory logic courses, introductory linguistics semantics courses, or the like, know better than anyone else that college students—people who have mastered their native languages one would think—do not come to the first class meeting with an understanding of the distinction between valid and invalid inferences. In my experience, such students have a great deal of trouble distinguishing valid inferences from compelling, but nevertheless, invalid, conversational implicatures. Consider sentences

(33)   I'll divorce you if you don't get a job.

(34)   I won't divorce you if you do get a job.

Sentence (33) implies but does not entail (34), but it is sometimes difficult to persuade students of this fact. Indeed, until they are provided validity tests such as the previously mentioned cancellability test or a certain amount of model theory, students are often unable to draw the validity–invalidity distinction reliably.

There is solid empirical evidence that the concept of validity is alien to people untutored in logic. Wason and Johnson-Laird (1972) have made a compelling case for this. One of the experiments done under their direction is instructive. In this experiment 20 students were given ordinary-language miniarguments in which Modus Ponens

(35)   a. $P \supset Q$ If you leave, I will leave.
        b. P You left.
        c. $\therefore Q$ I will leave.

Modus Tollens

(36)   a. $P \supset Q$ If you leave, I will leave.
        b. $\sim Q$ I didn't leave.
        c. $\therefore \sim P$ You didn't leave.

the fallacy of Affirming the Consequent

(37)   a. $P \supset Q$ If you leave, I will leave.
         b. Q I left.
         c. $\therefore P$ You left.

and the fallacy of Denying the Antecedent

(38)   a. $P \supset Q$ If you leave, I will leave.
         b. $\sim P$ You didn't leave.
         c. $\therefore \sim Q$ I won't leave.

were involved.[11] There were a total of 40 decisions for each type of miniargument. In sum, there were 2 failures to recognize that Modus Ponens is valid and 21 failures to recognize that Modus Tollens is valid. There were 8 failures to recognize that Affirming the Consequent is invalid and 10 failures to recognize that Denying the Antecedent is invalid.

Although the Wason and Johnson-Laird work shows that people have difficulty with the distinction between valid and invalid inferences, there are numerous types of cases in which people routinely draw valid inferences. Adverb "stripping" cases like

(39)   a. John woke up in a bar.
         b. $\therefore$ John woke up.

(40)   a. John woke up at noon.
         b. $\therefore$ John woke up.

where verbs are "demodified," surely pose little problems. People surely also have little trouble with

Simplification:

(41)   a. John left and Bill left.
         b. $\therefore$ John left.

Disjunctive Syllogism:

(42)   a. Either John left or Bill left.
         b. John didn't leave.
         c. $\therefore$ Bill left.

and Existential Generalization:

(43)   a. John left.
         b. $\therefore$ Somebody left.

---

[11]The illustrations just given are not taken from Wason and Johnson-Laird.

If we ignore Wason and Johnson-Laird's data on Modus Tollens,[12] the following generalization would appear to be warranted: Ordinary people tend to recognize valid inferences for what they are; the problem is that they tend not to recognize invalid inferences for what they are. This asymmetry begs for an explanation.

Harris and Monaco (1978) review a variety of cued-recall experiments showing that people do not reliably make a distinction between what is actually said and what is implied by what is said. Thus, subjects in one experiment more frequently recalled the pragmatic implication of a sentence like

(44)   The angry rioter threw the rock at a window.

(i.e., that the window was broken) more often than they recalled (44) itself. It would be easy to misinterpret such results. Certainly people are capable of distinguishing what is said from what is entailed or implied by what is said. To argue otherwise would be tantamount to saying that people have no memory for sentences, i.e., for the actual words they have heard. What I think this sort of experiment shows is that in our normal mode of using language we are, as listeners, concerned with the "gist" of what others say to us. We have learned that we are expected to draw inferences (valid and invalid inferences alike) as part of our language competence and we somehow acquire the pragmatic conventions governing such inferencing—speech act felicity conventions, politeness conventions, and conversational maxims—along the way. Put in developmental terms, I would say that there is a good deal of pressure on children to maximize their inferencing abilities rather than to restrict them (as would be the case if children were expected to acquire and systematically use the validity–invalidity distinction). This perspective allows us to account for the asymmetry noted earlier—the observation that people's logical errors tend to consist of failing to recognize that invalid inferences are invalid rather than failing to recognize that valid inferences are valid. What I would like to argue is that people approach language essentially pragmatically and that, in a way I shall outline, we come to recognize that certain types of inferences are always or almost always justified. However, or so I will argue, our learning that some inference pattern based on the use of a particular word (say, Modus

[12]Failure to recognize the validity of Modus Tollens may be due to perceptual or cognitive factors. In a sentence like *If you leave, I will leave, if you leave* is the topic. In the case of Modus Ponens, the topic is affirmed, but in Modus Tollens, there is a shift of focus away from the topic to the comment, for the comment is denied. This shift of focus may present perceptual difficulties sufficient to interfere with a correct assessment of the soundness of Modus Tollens.

Ponens, which is based on *if*) is normally justified does not automatically carry with it a recognition that certain other inference patterns involving that word (say, Affirming the Consequent) are not justified.

Before continuing this line of thought, I must point out that the fact that people cannot reliably distinguish valid from invalid inferences does not prove that we do not have an implicit or tacit knowledge of the concept of validity. Indeed, linguists routinely make the assumption that speakers have linguistic knowledge which they are not, in any direct way, conscious of. Thus, for instance, we would argue that the clausal object of the verb *know* in

(45)   Everybody knows that Joe is happy.

like the object of this verb in

(46)   Everybody knows Joe.

is a noun phrase even though linguistically untutored speakers, if asked, would almost certainly not say that the clausal object of *know* is a noun phrase. We make this claim because both types of objects of *know* act alike syntactically. For example, both can be promoted to subject position by the passive transformation, as (47) and (48) show.

(47)   That Joe is happy is known by everybody.

(48)   Joe is known by everybody.

We feel justified in saying that people know tacitly that clausal objects of verbs are noun phrases because they, through how they construct passive sentences, act as if clausal objects are noun phrases. This line of reasoning strikes me as quite unobjectionable.

In the case of the validity–invalidity distinction, there is no evidence, direct or indirect, supporting the hypothesis that people control this distinction. What evidence there is suggests in fact that they do not. Moreover, it is very difficult to see wherein logically untutored speakers might acquire a tacit knowledge of this distinction. The average parent is, for instance, incompetent to teach it. Given the propensity of linguists to postulate innate human linguistic gifts of all sorts, I suppose some will be inclined to suggest that we are natively gifted with this logical skill. I can't take this sort of assumption seriously and would suggest that the burden of proof must be placed on those who can. The only other alternative is that we somehow acquire a tacit ability to distinguish valid from invalid inferences as an automatic consequence of learning our languages. There is no evidence that this is true. Again, the burden of proof falls on those who wish to maintain that we somehow do acquire this logical ability, an ability that we do not seem to be all that good at realizing at a conscious level until we somehow acquire training in logic.

I would like now to suggest an alternative theory of sentence meaning within which the relative primacy of semantics and pragmatics is reversed. I shall assume that children learn in the course of language acquisition that they are expected to maximize their inferencing abilities, i.e., that they must acquire a theory of inference drawing that warrants a wide variety of types of inferences, some valid and some not, and that at no point in the normal course of language acquisition do children acquire and use a validity–invalidity distinction of the sort standard semantic theories assume speakers control. I shall further assume that this theory is a suitably modified version of Grice's (1975) theory of conversation. According to the view I shall propose, children's semantic skills emerge out of their developing pragmatic skills.

In the course of learning their languages, children will observe that people draw inferences that are not calculable in the sense of Grice, i.e., inferences that are not warranted by Grice's Cooperative Principle and its attendant maxims, including, in particular, Grice's Maxim of Relevance. Consider, for instance, this inference pattern:

(49)   a. S_1 and S_2
        b. $\therefore S_1$

In my view, children will learn that upon hearing (49a) they are entitled to draw inference (49b) and that this inference is independent of the content of S_1 and S_2 and is independent of the context of utterance. In such a case, children must recognize that (49b) follows from (49a) wholly by virtue of the meaning of *and*. Similarly, children will learn that upon hearing (50a) they are entitled to draw the inference that (50b) is true and that this inference is also in no way dependent on the context of utterance.

(50)   a. Joe will do that again.
        b. Joe did that before.

Children will recognize that this inference follows from the meaning of the word *again*. In such a way, children will acquire a theory of word meaning. It is not difficult to see how a principle of compositionality might also be acquired. Children will learn, for instance, that if S_1 in (49) contains an occurrence of negation, Simplification will still be warranted. However, if they encounter a sentence like (51), where both conjuncts are in the scope of negation, they will come to recognize that they are not entitled to draw inference (52).

(51)   It's not true that I left and Bill left.

(52)   I left.

In short, children will learn that *not* has sentence scope and that the meaning of any sentence containing *not* depends on its position in the sentence. It is just this sort of sentence knowledge that the principle of compositionality is designed to account for.

Within the framework that I have just proposed, it is very difficult to see how children could possibly come up with the distinction between entailment and conventional implicature, a distinction that is none too simple to draw. I suggest, instead, that we follow Cresswell's (1974) view that a theory of word meaning should not draw a sharp distinction between inferences warranted by the meanings of logically central words like *and, or,* and *not* from those warranted by the meanings of logically noncentral words like *know* and *again*. Certainly there is no solid linguistic evidence to support drawing this somewhat arbitrary distinction.

I would like to propose that the distinction between inferences that are not dependent on context and those that are should replace the distinction between valid and invalid inferences. This proposal allows us to reconstruct much that has been learned about sentence meaning from the perspective of classical semantic theories without assuming counterfactually that speakers control the concept of validity. When a child comes to recognize that some type of inference is not dependent on context, but is dependent only on the meaning of a particular word, he or she will construct a meaning postulate for that word that accounts for that inference. However, learning that a particular rule of inference associated with a particular word is generally warranted does not equip the child to recognize that other commonly drawn inferences associated with that word are not generally warranted. Thus learning that Modus Ponens (which is associated with the word *if*) is warranted does not equip the child to recognize that Affirming the Consequent (also associated with *if*) is not generally warranted. Indeed, since children must learn to reason inductively, they will be encouraged, in fact, to use Affirming the Consequent quite frequently. Only when children come to study logic or science or the like will they come to find out that Affirming the Consequent is not valid.

It should be clear from what has been said that if a theory of truth in advertising is to be based on actual, rather than ideal, human cognitive-cum-semantic skills, then we must move from the literalist theory to a pragmatist theory in which advertisers are held responsible for conversational and (in some cases) theoretical implicatures of what they say as well as for conventional implicatures. Naturally, we would want to exclude from consideration, theoretical implicatures based on idiosyncratic beliefs, conversational implicatures based on idiosyncratic perceptions of the nature of the speech context, and other cases of idiosyncratic inference drawing. There remains, however, the difficulty posed by the fact that different people can and do draw different inferences as a result of considering different conversational maxims. I return to this point in the following discussion.

Conventional Implicatures in Advertising

There are a number of constructions in English with which conventional implicatures are associated. One of the more interesting is the verbal complement system, i.e., constructions in which clauses and infinitive constructions occur as subjects or objects of verbs. Consider, for instance, the "Wartsoff" claim

(53)   You know that vivaline removes warts instantly.

In this sentence, the clause *that vivaline removes warts instantly* functions as the object of *know*. As we noted, (53) conventionally implicates (54), thanks to the presence of *know*.

(54)   Vivaline removes warts instantly.

In this light, consider the following transcript of a television commercial for Pine Sol:

(55)   Pine Sol (CBS, 7/18/78, 11:18 a.m.)
         Type: Live action
         Setting: Indoors
         Characters: No on-screen characters speak

         TEXT
         Voice Over (adult male): *You know that Pine Sol liquid cleans up dirt.*
         Singers: *Pine Sol.*
         Voice Over: *You know that Pine Sol cleans up grease.*
         Singers: *Pine Sol.*
         Voice Over: *And you know that Pine Sol kills household germs that can cause odors and leaves a fresh clean scent.*
         Singers: *Pine Sol.*
         Voice Over: *But here's one thing about Pine Sol you may not know.*
         Singers: *Pine Sol.*
         Voice Over: *Pine Sol stops mold and mildew and their odors.*
         Singers: *Pine Sol.*

> **Voice Over:** *Pine Sol's more than a cleaner. It's a cleaner-disinfectant that cleans, disinfects, and deodorizes.*
> **Singers:** *Pine Sol.*

Of interest to us are the following claims:

(56)   *You know that **Pine Sol liquid cleans up dirt.***

(57)   *You know that **Pine Sol cleans up grease.***

(58)   *And you know that **Pine Sol kills household germs that can cause odors and leaves a fresh clean scent.***

(59)   *But here's one thing about Pine Sol you may not know . . . **Pine Sol stops mold and mildew and their odors*** [emphasis added].

Claims (56–(59) each conventionally implicates the truth of the (bold italic) clause occurring as the object of *know*. It is worth asking what sort of effect these implicatures will have on consumers.

The ostensible purpose of this Pine Sol commercial is to cause consumers to come to believe that Pine Sol stops mold and mildew and their odors, i.e., the bold italic proposition of (59). However, (56)–(58) are themselves of more than passing interest. Indeed, the thought occurs that conveying the bold italic propositions of (56)–(58) may have been as much the purpose of this advertisement as conveying (59). Let us look more closely at (56)–(58).

A central principle of the theory of how people understand language is that we interpret what is said in the light of what the speaker might have said but didn't. In this light compare (60) and (61).

(60)   I know that John left on time.

(61)   I believe that John left on time.

In general we use *believe* when we have evidence, but not conclusive evidence, of the truth of the proposition that occurs in object position. We use *know* only when we have conclusive evidence.[13] (I assume here that the speaker is being honest, of course.) This difference is reflected by the fact that (62) is anomalous, while (63) is not.

(62)   *I know that John left on time, but I may be wrong.

(63)   I believe that John left on time, but I may be wrong.

In sentences (60)–(63), the subject is *I*. Even more interesting are sentences like (56)–(58), where the subject is *you*. Normally, we do not make claims about other people's internal states, including what they do

---

[13]I do not mean, of course, that the evidence must actually be conclusive before a speaker uses *know*, but that the speaker must believe it to be.

and do not know. However, there are some exceptions. Consider a case where a student has failed to recognize that some proposition P is true. His or her teacher might say something like this: *You know that Q_1 is true, that Q_2 is true, and that Q_3 is true; but if Q_1, Q_2, and Q_3 are true, then P must be true.* But a teacher would say this only if he or she had very good reason to believe that the student knows that Q_1, Q_2, and Q_3 is true. Moreover before our hypothetical teacher would say this, he or she would also have to believe that the student himself or herself had good reason to believe that Q_1, Q_2, and Q_3 are true. Otherwise the teacher would have used the verb *believe* in place of *know*.

I believe that the net effect of (56)–(58) is to convey the impression that the conventionally implicated propositions are in no way controversial. It is important to note in passing that this effect is contrived wholly linguistically. No evidence is cited in support of the truth of the bold italic propositions of (56)–(58). If this commercial is credible its credibility derives wholly from a consumer assumption that the advertiser is using language in quite conventional ways, i.e., that the advertiser is obeying Grice's Cooperative Principle.

There are quite a number of verbs that work like *know*. Just a few examples, drawn from advertising, are given here. In each case the a-sentence conventionally implicates the b-sentence.

(64) a. *In 1912, while ice-fishing, Clarence Birdseye **discovered** that quick-freezing preserves freshness.*   (ABC, 2/24/78, @8:50 a.m.)

     b. Quick-freezing preserves freshness.

(65) a. *We're about to **find out** orange juice from Florida isn't just for breakfast anymore.*   (CBS, 2/24/78, @ 12:58 p.m.)

     b. Orange juice from Florida isn't just for breakfast anymore.

(66) a. *We're in the appliance department to **find out** why Sears is where America Shops.*   (ABC, 7/11/78, 10:54 p.m.).

     b. Sears is where America shops.

(67) a. *This Atra face-hugging action **keeps** twin blades at the perfect angle.* (ABC, 7/11/78, 11:40 p.m.)

     b. Atra twin blades are at the perfect angle.

(68) a. *No matter how much you relax, this* [J. C. Penney's] *shirt will **stay** looking neat and crisp because the outside is all polyester.*   (CBS, 6/2/78, 9:56 p.m.)

     b. This J. C. Penney's shirt looks neat and crisp.

In each of the preceding cases, the conventional implicature derives from the presence of the bold italic verb.

In the following line from a Gainesburger commercial, two different propositions are conventionally implicated and another is conversationally implicated.

(69)   [New improved Gainesburgers] *is still moist and meaty, but now it tastes even better than before.*   (NBC, 2/25/78, evening)

Thanks to the presence of *still*, (69) conventionally implicates the truth of

(70)   Gainesburger was moist and meaty before.

Thanks to the presence of *even*, (69) conventionally implicates

(71)   One would not expect Gainesburger to be able to taste better than before.

And, from (71), it follows (but this is a conversational implicature based on the Maxim of Relevance) that (72) is true.

(72)   Gainesburgers used to taste very good.

There is nothing inherently deceptive about (69)—implicatures (70)–(72) all represent judgments rather than matters of fact—but it should be clear that much of the effect of (69) is contrived purely verbally, by the selection of words with which conventional implicatures are associated. It is because of examples like (64)–(69) that I believe we must conclude that language is not simply a vehicle of communication in advertising but can be and sometimes is the very substance of advertising.

Perhaps the most bizarre example of a conventional implicature occurs in an advertisement for the movie *Capricorn One*.

(73)   Capricorn One [14]

> **Voice Over (adult male):** *What if man's greatest technological achievement . . . is a fraud? . . . What if something went wrong? . . . What if someone found out . . . the most important event in recent history . . . never really happened? . . . This is* **Capricorn One**. *. . . . The whole world thinks they're* [the astronauts are] *dead, and the only way the truth can come out is if they live long enough to tell it. . . .* **Capricorn One**. *. . . . How do we know this hasn't already happened? . . . How do we know it won't happen again?*

[14]This particular commercial was broadcast over the Qube Cable Television Company of Columbus, Ohio as a preview for *Capricorn One*. However, some regularly broadcast commercials for this movie used the word *again* as commercial (73) does.

On screen, we see scenes taken from the movie *Capricorn One* that make quite clear that the movie is about a manned space mission to an extraterrestial body. When I first saw this commercial I believed that the movie was about a faked manned mission to the Moon, for *man's greatest technological achievement* and *the most important event in recent history* clearly refer (in this context) to the Moon landings, and there is nothing in the text or in what is shown on screen that precludes an interpretation in which *Capricorn one* is about a faked manned moon mission. In any event, the last line in this commercial conventionally implicates that (74) is true.

(74)   A faked manned mission to some extraterrestial body has happened before.

Since the only manned space missions to extraterrestrial bodies have been the manned moon missions, (73) conventionally implicates that one of more of these was faked, a proposition I believe to be false. It would be interesting to know how many persons went to this movie because they thought it was about a real, rather than a purely fictional, event.

In all of the preceding examples of conventional implicature, the implicature was associated with the occurrence of a particular word: *know, even, again*, etc. Conventional implicatures are also associated with certain constructions. As we noted earlier, sentence (75) implicates (76).

(75)   Who killed Caesar?

(76)   Someone killed Caesar.

That (76) is a conventional implicature is shown by the fact that this implicature cannot be cancelled [see (77)].

(77)   *Although no one killed Caesar, who killed him?

This is characteristic of WH-questions, questions that begin with *who, what, where, how*, etc.

Examples of the use of WH-questions in television advertising are:

(78)   *What's great about Chuck Wagon dog food?*   (NBC, 2/24/78, evening).

(79)   *What do you love about Freshen Up gum?*   (NBC, 2/25/78, evening).

Sentences (78) and (79) conventionally implicate (80) and (81) respectively.

(80)   There is something great about Chuck Wagon dog food.

(81)   You love something about Freshen Up gum.

The instances of conventional implicatures discussed earlier fall into two classes, those associated with particular words (e.g., *know, keep, find out, even*) and those associated with questions. In commercials employing implicatures of the former type, none of the implicatures are defended in the commercial. They are simply assumed to be true. The advertiser of Atra, for instance, simply assumes the truth of the quite remarkable proposition that Atra twin blades are at the perfect angle [see (67)].

The fact that advertisers do not defend conventionally implicated propositions is fully consistent with how such implicatures work in ordinary conversation, for normally, when we use a sentence in ordinary conversation that conventionally implicates some proposition we do so in the belief that the listener also believes this proposition to be true. Thus, if A were to say (82) to B, A would normally do so only if A had some reason to believe that B believes (83) to be true.

(82)   Mary wants to keep John happy.

(83)   John is happy.

It is because A believes that B believes that (83) is true, that A would normally not defend (83) even though A is responsible for its truth. Should A's belief be mistaken, B might challenge the truth of (83), but he or she is just as likely to assume that A is speaking in good faith and simply assume that (83) is true. This fact—that a listener who does not happen to know that some conventionally implicated proposition is true may simply assume that the speaker is obeying the Cooperative Principle and accept the truth of the implicature—is crucial to understanding how conventional implicatures are used in advertising.

Since conventionally implicated propositions are rarely defended in ordinary conversation, I submit that viewers will normally not expect to find them defended in advertising. Therefore, any advertiser who wishes to convey some proposition P but does not want to defend P or cannot defend P can simply use a construction that conventionally implicates P with little fear that viewers will question P. In this light, compare (67a), repeated as (84a), with (84b).

(84)   a. *This Atra face-hugging action keeps twin blades at the perfect angle.*

        b. Atra twin blades are set at the perfect angle and this Atra face-hugging action keeps them that way.

I submit that viewers would be much more likely to challenge the truth of the proposition that the Atra twin blades are set at the perfect angle had the advertiser said (84b) instead of (84a). The advertiser does pay a small price for conventionally implicating rather than asserting a proposition, however, for assertions are perceptually more salient than are conventional implicatures.

The claim that conventional implicatures are perceptually less salient than assertions and thus tend less to arouse listener cognitive defenses than assertions is nicely illustrated by comparison of (84a) with (84b) or by comparison of the Texaco claim (85) with (86).

(85)   *We're working to keep your trust.*

(86)   We've got your trust and are working to keep it.

I submit that viewers would more likely challenge (87) on hearing (86) than on hearing (85).

(87)   We've got your trust.

What has been said about the Atra and Texaco claims holds for conventional implicatures of WH-questions. The speaker who says (75) would normally not do so unless he believes that the listener believes (76) to be true. The speaker will normally not defend his belief that (76) is true and the listener will normally not question the truth of (76) unless he or she has good reason for believing (76) to be false. How WH-questions work in conversation is nicely illustrated by the following excerpt from a Chuck Wagon dog food commercial.

(88)   **Chuck Wagon dog food** (NBC, 2/24/78, evening), excerpt.
         Man: *Mam, what's great about Chuck Wagon dog food?*
         Woman: *It's that cute little wagon, right?*
         Man: *Wrong! Chuck Wagon's great because it's crunchewy.*

The man's opening question in this commercial conventionally implicates that there is something great about Chuck Wagon dog food. Note that the woman accepts this proposition and offers an answer to the question, albeit a rather silly one.

When WH-questions are directed at viewers, they cannot, of course, be interpreted as information questions. Instead, they must be interpreted as rhetorical questions. In some cases, rhetorical WH-questions do not carry the expected conventional implicature. Observe that (89) is not intended to conventionally implicate (90).

(89)   *After all, who knows more about the taste of meat than Alpo?*   (NBC,
         7/24/78, 8:44 a.m.)

(90)   Someone knows more about the taste of meat than Alpo.

Instead, (89) conversationally implicates (91).

(91)   No one knows more about the taste of meat than Alpo.

Just why (89) implicates (91) is not completely clear. I believe it follows from the fact that being a rhetorical question, the speaker is responsible for answering (89), and, given the context, the speaker is most unlikely to promote competing products.

Theoretical Implicatures in Advertising

As we noted earlier, theoretical implicatures arise in conjunction with listener beliefs. We said that a sentence S theoretically implicates a proposition P if P can be deduced from the conjunction of S and some proposition Q which is believed to be true by the listener (whether or not it is believed by the speaker). I believe that the apparent success of the Jif line, *Choosy mothers choose Jif,* may be due to the fact this sentence theoretically implicates proposition (92) to anyone who believes that if a mother isn't choosy, she isn't a good mother.[15]

(92)   If a mother doesn't choose Jif, she isn't a good mother.

The reasoning process is given in (93).

(93)   a. *Choosy mothers choose Jif.*   (premise)
        b. If a mother is a choosy mother, she will choose Jif.
           (from a).
        c. If a mother doesn't choose Jif, she isn't a choosy
           mother.   (from b by Contraposition)
        d. If a mother isn't a choosy mother, she isn't a good
           mother.   (premise)
        e. If a mother doesn't choose Jif, she isn't a good
           mother.   (from c and d by Transitivity)

Thus to anyone who accepts proposition (93d), a not implausible proposition, (93a) actually entails (93e).

The phenomenon of theoretical implicature offers advertisers the opportunity to exploit consumer beliefs, including false beliefs. The clearest example of this arises in the advertising of fruit-flavored products to children. As we shall see in Chapter 8, television commercials directed at children abound with verbal references to fruit flavors and with visual and verbal references to fruit, whether or not the products being promoted contain fruit or are naturally or artificially flavored.

---

[15]This line employs eight fricatives (including affricates), namely [č, z, ð, z, č, z, j, f], a fact brought to my attention by Arnold Zwicky, and this could have a good deal to do with the effectiveness, especially the memorability, of this line.

In my view verbal and visual references in commercials to fruit and fruit flavors will theoretically implicate to young children (say, under the age of 8) that the products being promoted contain fruit or are made of fruit. Such children will know, of course, that fruits are fruit flavored, and will have eaten fruit-flavored foods containing fruit (e.g., applesauce, fruit juices, pies) and may have seen fruit-flavored foods made of fruit at home. It is only natural that children believe that foods are fruit flavored because they contain fruit.

Of course, these days it seems that virtually any flavor can be chemically simulated, though how successful some of these simulations are is problematic. However, it is quite likely that few young children, especially preschool children know this or, more to the point perhaps, have a substantive understanding of what is meant by the phrase *artificially flavored*. To those children the verbal and visual references to fruit and fruit flavors in advertisements for fruit-flavored foods must theoretically implicate the presence of fruit in the products being promoted.

A second area in which theoretical implicature may play an important role is in the advertising of OTC drugs. Until the FTC was empowered to stop deceptive advertising practices, OTC drug advertisers were free to say whatever they wished and, as Clark (1943) amply demonstrates, some advertisers employed deceptive claims. Consider, for instance, item (94), which is taken from Clark's study:

(94)   *Wet feet? LOOK OUT FOR A COLD—Gargle with LISTERINE QUICK*

The language of (94) conversationally implicates (Maxim of Relevance) that Listerine can prevent colds, for it is only if Listerine can prevent colds that there would be need for quick action.

To anyone who believes that an OTC drug could prevent a cold, the implicature from (94) that Listerine can prevent colds would be elevated from a conversational implicature to a theoretical implicature. Put more generally, anyone who believes falsely that a certain class of OTC drugs can prevent or cure some disease, rather than alleviate its symptoms, will be quite vulnerable to advertising of that type of drug. Where such a false belief has been created by advertising, the advertisers in question should clearly be required to disabuse consumers of such false beliefs.[16]

---

[16]The manufacturers of Listerine were ultimately (after some 40 years) compelled by the FTC to include disclaimers in their advertising concerning the efficacy of Listerine in treating colds. In the only such case I have on tape, the advertiser stated: *While Listerine will not help prevent colds or sore throats or lessen their severity, Listerine's strong formula keeps your breath clean for hours—it kills the germs that can cause bad breath.* The reader will note that this statement conventionally implicates that Listerine will not prevent colds or sore throats or lessen their severity, rather than asserts it, and thus exploits the apparent fact that conventional implicatures are perceptually less salient than are assertions.

Conversational Implicatures in Advertising

I suggested during the discussion of conventional implicature that, in general, consumer cognitive defenses will tend less to be aroused by conventional implicatures than by claims overtly asserted. This would be true not only for conventional implicatures but also for conversational implicatures.

In a magazine advertisement, the Ramada Inn corporation employed headline claim (95).

(95)   *We're building a reputation, not resting on one.*   (*Newsweek*, 2/6/78)

Claim (95) could be used to deny an allegation that Ramada Inn has been resting on its reputation. However, to virtually everyone I have discussed claim (95) with, it implies (96).

(96)   Some leading competitor of Ramada Inn is resting on its
           reputation.

In fact, most respondents go on to say that they take the leading competitor in question to be Holiday Inn.

Claim (95) by no means conventionally implicates (96). Instead, it conversationally implicates (96), the relevant conversational maxim being the Maxim of Relevance. Why say you're not resting on your reputation unless someone has said that you are or you believe someone else is resting on his reputation? The advertisement line (95) occurs in in no way defends (96) (see Photograph 2.1). This is not surprising, for implied claims are rarely defended—in conversation or in advertising. Instead, the advertisement defends only what (95) asserts, i.e., that Ramada Inn is building a reputation. In my view, consumer cognitive defenses are much less likely to be aroused by (95) than by (97), wherein (96) is claimed overtly.

(97)   Some major hotel chain is resting on its reputation, but we're
           not—we're building one.

It should be clear by now why the use of indirect means to convey claims is so attractive to advertisers (and other speakers as well): One doesn't have to defend such claims and consumers are less likely to defend against them than overtly made claims. There is another motivation for employing conversational implicatures. Since they have to be "worked out" by the listener, the listener may find them to be more persuasive than asserted claims (McGuire, 1969).

One of the best examples of the use of conversational implicature in television advertising occurs in the following commercial for Tuborg beer.

We're building a reputation, not resting on one.

"George, I think you're taking your job as a Ramada Inspector a little too seriously."

When a Ramada Quality Inspector checks into a Ramada Inn, unannounced, he examines it from top to bottom for 298 tough standards.

And, to be sure everything is just right, our managers inspect their inns daily. You see, we know that our most important inspection comes when you check in.

After all, we're building a reputation, not resting on one.

It's easy to make reservations for any of our nearly 700 inns. Call your local Ramada for Room Finder reservations and a written confirmation. Call your travel planner or 800-228-2828.

You'll find we take your comfort very seriously, by George.

Photograph 2.1

(98)   Tuborg beer (ABC, 2/25/78, @ 5:27 p.m.)
          Type: Live action
          Setting: Indoors
          Characters: No on-screen characters speak

          TEXT
          Voice Over (Male): *Triumph. Some men are content with nothing less.*
          They never go for bronze or silver—they go for the gold. The Danes
          have always been such men. Centuries ago, they set out to brew the
          world's finest beer. Today, their triumph is Tuborg Gold, the golden
          beer of Danish kings. Share with your friends the pleasure of world
          famous Tuborg. And, wherever you go, go for the Gold.

Commercial (98) makes several false claims. The Danes collectively have
not always gone for triumphs and the Danes collectively did not set out
to brew the world's finest beer. However, the truly problematic feature
of this commercial is that it conversationally implicates that Tuborg is in
some sense a Danish beer, i.e., a beer brewed in Denmark or indistinguishable from Danish Tuborg.

Commercial (98) does not actually assert that Tuborg Gold is a Danish
beer or that it is indistinguishable from Danish Tuborg, but it does
conversationally implicate (Maxim of Relevance) that this is true. The
statement that consumers should share *world famous Tuborg* with their
friends strongly implies that the Tuborg beer in question is genuine
Danish Tuborg, for it is Danish Tuborg, not American Tuborg, that is
world famous. The language of (98) is consistent with Tuborg Gold's
being brewed in the United States from a formula created by Danish
brewers. However, it is difficult to imagine many people attending carefully enough and critically enough to commercial (98) to ward off the
inference that Tuborg Gold is brewed in Denmark or is indistinguishable from Danish Tuborg.

As was noted earlier, questions occurring in advertisements which are
directed at television viewers cannot be interpreted as genuine information questions. Instead, they are interpreted as rhetorical questions. Reconsider commercial (99).

(99)   Reach (ABC, 2/24/78, @ 9:40 a.m.)
          Type: Live action
          Setting: Studio
          Characters: Adult Male

          TEXT
          Man: *They invented fluoride toothpaste to help fight cavities. Why hasn't*
          somebody invented a better toothbrush? What if you angled it like a

dental instrument to reach back teeth and concentrated the bristles to clean each tooth of material that can cause cavities and made rows of higher softer bristles to clean between teeth? And what if they called this new brush "Reach"? The Reach toothbrush from Johnson and Johnson. To help fight cavities.

As the on-screen announcer utters the *what if* questions we see him effect the suggested changes in a conventional toothbrush by way of "constructing" a Reach toothbrush.

The second sentence of commercial (99), namely (100), clearly implies that (101) is true.

(100)   *Why hasn't somebody invented a better toothbrush?*

(101)   Somebody should have invented a better toothbrush.

Item (101) is not a conventional implicature of (100), for the speaker could have cancelled (101) by going on to say (102) after saying (100).

(102)   Because nobody needed to. The best possible toothbrush has existed for years.

Thus, (101) must be a conversational implicature of (100).

In general, rhetorical questions employing the interrogative adverb *why* conversationally implicate corresponding declarative propositions containing the modal *should*. The Maxim responsible for this implicature is the Maxim of Relevance. The first step in the calculation of conversational implicature (101) is the recognition that (100) is not a genuine information question. The second step devolves on the fact that (100) asks the reason why some action has not been taken to achieve some goal, a goal (to help fight cavities) that is spelled out in the sentence that precedes (100) in commercial (99). But a question asking why some action has not been taken is relevant just in case the action is desirable, i.e., the action should be taken.

Most of the conversational implicatures one finds in advertising turn on the Maxim of Relevance. However, in an advertisement for Golden Lights cigarettes, we find the Maxim of Strength being exploited in an interesting way. In this advertisement the advertiser asks

(103)   *How low in tar can you go and get good taste?*   (*Sports Illustrated,* 9/3/79)

The advertisement provides the answer (see Photograph 2.2), 8 mg of tar, the amount contained in Golden Lights. However, (103) implicates that one can go no lower than 8 mg of tar and still get good taste. Consider the hypothetical conversation (104).

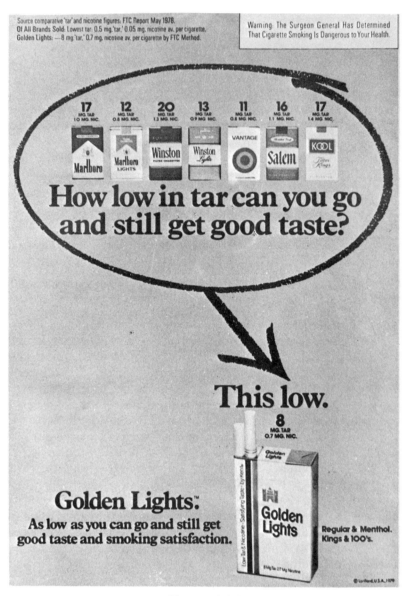

Photograph 2.2

(104)   A: "How far can you run without stopping?"
         B: "Five miles."

Suppose B can actually run 10 miles without stopping. What he or she
has said is certainly true, but it is misleading, for A will assume that B is

obeying the Maxim of Strength (i.e., is making the strongest claim he or she can justify). Similarly, the Golden Lights advertisement conversationally implicates one can go no lower than 8 mg of tar and still get good taste, a claim many competitors would surely challenge if made overtly. Pursuing the line of reasoning I have developed for indirectly communicated claims, I would predict that the Golden Lights advertisement would be less likely to stimulate consumer cognitive defenses than would be a claim like (105), and may be more persuasive.

(105)   Our cigarettes contain 8 mg of tar and you can't go any lower than this and still get good taste.

We began our discussion of indirect communication in advertising with a hypothetical product claim made on behalf of the nonexistent product Wartsoff. Consider now the advertisement on which it is primarily based:

(106)   Aftate (ABC, 7/11/78, 10:51 p.m.)
    Type: Live action
    Setting: Fancy visual effects are shown
    Characters: No on-screen characters speak

    TEXT
    Voice Over (adult male): *In the latter part of the twentieth century a medication was created that killed athlete's foot fungus on contact. This medication is found in Aftate for Athlete's Foot. Aftate relieves burning, . . . itching, . . . cracking. Aftate for Athlete's Foot, with a medication that kills athlete's foot fungus on contact.*

In this commercial, it is never asserted directly that Aftate kills athlete's foot fungus on contact, though this is clearly implied (and is actually asserted in more recent commercials). The Maxim of Relevance is responsible for this implicature. The fact that Aftate contains a medication that kills athlete's foot on contact is relevant to the consumer just in case Aftate does what this medication does, i.e., kills the fungus in question on contact. Interestingly, this claim is never actually made, and any consumer who recognizes this omission (somewhat unlikely, given the "real time" character of television advertising) would (or should) draw the inference that Aftate may not in fact kill athlete's foot fungus on contact. The principle here is that advertisers make the strongest claims they can. As noted, more recent commercials assert that Aftate kills athlete's foot fungus on contact. It would be interesting to know which commercials were the more persuasive.

In general, the Maxims of Strength and Relevance can give rise to quite different implicatures, a fact that seems to support a literalist theory of truth in advertising. How, one might ask, can advertisers be held responsible for conversational implicatures if different consumers can draw different implicatures? The answer is, I think, that in general consumers are much more likely to go with the Maxim of Relevance than with the Maxim of Strength, for in such cases the latter requires much more sophisticated reasoning than does the former. In states of idle listening, while watching television, the odds very much favor the consumer's going with the Maxim of Relevance. If it should be confirmed experimentally that the Maxim of Relevance is perceptually more salient than the Maxim of Strength when the two are in conflict, then a realistic theory of truth in advertising would hold advertisers responsible for inferences based on the Maxim of Relevance.

I have run the Aftate advertisement (106) past a number of persons (including logicians) and have asked them to spot a flaw in the reasoning. No one, in fact, drew the implicature that Aftate does not kill Athlete's foot on contact. Although this is scarcely a valid basis for saying so, I am nevertheless tempted to think that implicatures rising out of the Maxim of Relevance are perceptually more salient than are implicatures arising out of the Maxim of Strength when the two are in conflict.

Concluding Remarks

I have argued that humans are inferencing creatures, trained to maximize their inferencing capacities rather than to minimize them. According to this view, logically untutored speakers must be said to be quite vulnerable to compelling, even if invalid, inferences of advertising copy. I have gone one step further and argued that, in general, consumers will be more vulnerable to claims made indirectly than to asserted claims, whether the device (inference type) employed to convey the indirectly conveyed claims are valid or not.

In an ordinary conversation with which a conventional implicature is associated, the implicated proposition is assumed by the speaker to be believed by the listener to be true. Thus, if a speaker says *Has John Jones stopped dating Mary Morris?* to a listener, he does so in the belief that the listener knows that John Jones has at one time dated Mary Morris. In the event that the listener happens not to know this, he is more likely to accept the truth of this proposition than to challenge it, the reason being that both parties to a conversation normally assume that each is obeying the Cooperative Principle. It is precisely this fact that makes *Have you stopped beating your wife?* humorous or embarrassing if asked of someone who is not in the habit of beating his wife. We tend not to challenge conventionally or conversationally implicated propositions, for example, because we assume that the speaker has evidence not only for what he asserts but also for what he conventionally implicates (Maxim of Evidence). Moreover, I think we also recognize that people employ words and constructions with which conventional implicatures are associated not to fool each other but to facilitate conversation. Much the same is true of theoretically implicated and conversationally implicated material.

I take it to be uncontroversial that advertisers should be held responsible not only for what they assert but also for what is conventionally implicated by what they say. It is an open question whether advertisers should be held responsible for what their advertisements theoretically or conversationally implicate. On one side there is the argument that advertisers should not be held responsible for theoretical implicatures because they cannot be held responsible for consumer misinformation. One could, of course, make a distinction here between the misinformation of adults and the virtually inevitable misinformation of young children. The question whether or not advertisers should be held responsible for conversationally implicated material is more problematic.

The Gricean theory of conversational implicatures has so far resisted efforts to make it fully predictive though in most cases it is not hard to see how a given conversational implicature can be "calculated." Nevertheless, there remains a certain amount of indeterminacy in Grice's system. Moreover, different people can draw different inferences from the same claim. We saw in connection with the hypothetical Wartsoff example and the actual Aftate commercial that the Maxims of Strength and of Relevance can sometimes be in conflict. I have suggested that implicatures arising out of the Maxim of Relevance are perceptually more salient than implicatures arising out of the Maxim of Strength. If confirmed experimentally, this finding could serve as the basis of a pragmatist theory of truth in advertising. Such a theory is certainly more realistic than is the literalist theory. However, adoption of the pragmatist theory is a political and legal action. In the absence of such action consumers would be well advised to adopt what I like to call the First Law of Speech Consumption: Interpret any claim in the weakest possible way consistent with its truth. The usefulness of such a law will become even clearer in the next chapter.

Chapter 3
The Strength of a Claim

We can be reasonably sure, I think, that advertisers will normally make the strongest claims they can defend. Thus the advertiser who can justify saying (1) is hardly likely to say (2).[1]

(1)   Painaway will stop your pain.

(2)   Painaway will help stop your pain.

Similarly, the advertiser who can justify saying (3) is quite unlikely to say (4).

(3)   Most people who use Painaway get immediate pain relief.

(4)   Many people who use Painaway get immediate pain relief.

Claims (2) and (4) are not only weaker than (1) and (3), respectively, it can be argued that they are so weak as to be virtually empty. Observe that sentence (5) is fully consistent with sentence (2).

(5)   Painaway will help stop your pain, but not by very much.

Sentence (2) could be true, it seems, if Painaway provides some help in stopping pain no matter how slight this help is.

Claim (4) appears to promise that a sizeable number of people have gotten immediate pain relief. However, note that sentence (6) is consistent with sentence (4).

(6)   Many people who use Painaway get immediate pain relief, but most don't.

As sentence (6) suggests, a claim like (4) can be quite weak. Suppose the manufacturer of Painaway were to have accurate records for 20,000,000

[1]*Painaway* is not a real product name.

people concerning who has and who has not gotten immediate pain relief on taking Painaway and has discovered that 200,000 got immediate pain relief. In this circumstance it would appear that we must conclude that (4) is true, for 200,000 people is many people by anybody's standards. Note though that 200,000 is just 1% of the total sample.

In light of what has been said it is clear why claims like (2) and (4) could be attractive to advertisers. Very little need be shown to justify claims employing *help* and *many*. However, claims like (2) and (4) present a deeper problem. If (2) and (4) are as weak as our analyses suggest they are, how could they possibly be effective? Surely, or so it would seem, anyone who knows the meanings of *help* and *many* will recognize that claims employing these words are very weak.

I cannot demonstrate that advertisements employing *help* and *many* are effective. Records like this are not in the public domain, and even if they were, it would be difficult to determine whether advertisements containing claims employing these words work because they contain such claims or in spite of this fact. Nevertheless, I shall assume that advertisements containing claims employing *help* and *many* can be effective despite the apparent weakness of such claims. My reason for making this assumption is that claims employing *help* and *many* as well as other "weak" words like *may, might, can,* and *could,* occur quite frequently in advertising, and advertisers do not deliberately use advertising techniques they know to be ineffective. In my view, if claims employing *help* and *many,* as well as the other apparent linguistic weaklings just mentioned, substantially reduced the effectiveness of advertisements, advertisers would long since have abandoned them.

In this chapter, I shall examine claims employing the modal verbs *may, might, can,* and *could,* the verb *help,* and the quantifiers *many* and *most* in an attempt to measure just how strong they are and, in the process, come to an understanding of how such claims might be effective despite their apparent weakness. In some cases, or so I shall argue, claims employing such words will not be perceived by listeners as being as weak as the line of reasoning given earlier would suggest. In other cases, it appears that we must appeal to psycholinguistic principles governing how people process sentences in order to explain why such claims might be effective.

On Measuring the Strength of Claims

There exists a quite precise measure of the relative strength of claims based on the concept of entailment. Consider the following definition of logical strength.

(7)   A proposition *P* is **logically stronger** than a proposition *Q* if and
        only if *P* entails *Q* and *Q* does not entail *P*.

In the preceding chapter, I argued that the concept of entailment is alien
to the speaker of English (or any other language, of course) untutored in
logic, and thus if this argument is sound, the relevance of the concept of
logical strength to the question of how ordinary people interpret claims
must, to some degree, be regarded as being problematic. However, we
did note that people do recognize some types of inferences as being
always or nearly always valid. Thus, we would not, I think, want totally to
abandon (7).

The difficulty with (7) lies primarily in how we interpret the word
entail. Within classical logic and linguistic semantics it is assumed that if a
sentence *S* entails a proposition *P* it does so wholly as a function of the
meaning of *S*, and, further, that the meaning of a sentence can be fully
specified without reference to the nonlinguistic context.[2] Given these
assumptions, which lay at the foundation of the literalist theory of truth
in advertising discussed in the preceding chapter, it would have to be
said that claims like (2) and (4) are as weak as we suggested they may be.
Within this framework, so long as there is any linguistic context within
which a claim employing *many* must be said to be weak, then every claim
employing *many* must be said to be weak. In my view, this approach to
semantics simply cannot be accepted. Within the pragmatist theory of
language understanding outlined in the preceding chapter, we must
assume that how a given word, phrase, or sentence will be understood
will be dependent on context unless it can be proven otherwise. This
theory thus reverses the normal expectation of the relevance of context
to a theory of language understanding from that of classical logic. In the
case of claims employing *many*, as we shall soon see, context is absolutely
crucial to how such claims will be understood.

Although claims like (2) and (4) have been argued to be relatively
weak, it is clear that listeners will not always interpret them as being
weak. I believe, for instance, that readers would take a claim like (8),
taken from a Preparation H magazine advertisement, to mean that a
significant number of tests proved positive (see Photograph 3.1).

(8)   *Tests by doctors on hundreds of patients showed this* [Preparation H
        gives prompt relief for hours of hemorrhoidal pain and itching] *to be
        true in many cases.*   (*Sports Illustrated,* 8/11/80)

---

[2]Even within classical logic and linguistic semantics it was assumed that the reference of
deictic elements (personal pronouns, some time and place adverbials, etc.) could not be
determined without reference to context. However, within this framework, it was usually
assumed that context is irrelevant to the interpretation of most other types of words. This
view of semantics has been abandoned by most contemporary semanticists.

Doctors Prove You Can Help Shrink Swelling Of Hemorrhoidal Tissues Due To Inflammation. Relieve Pain And Itch Too.

Gives prompt temporary relief from hemorrhoidal pain and itch in many cases.

Doctors have found a most effective medication that actually helps shrink painful swelling of hemorrhoidal tissues caused by inflammation. In many cases, the first applications give prompt relief for hours from such pain and burning itching.

Tests by doctors on hundreds of patients showed this to be true in many cases. The medication the doctors used was *Preparation H®*–the same Preparation H you can get without a prescription. Ointment and suppositories. Use only as directed.

Photograph 3.1

In an attempt to get some idea how claims like (8) are interpreted, I ran an informal experiment in which I asked groups of students in two sections of a freshman–sophomore introduction to language course to answer the following question: *Suppose you are a medical scientist and have tested a new product on 500 patients. How many of those tests would have to be positive before you could justifiably say that this new drug worked in many cases?* In one set of 27 students, 21 gave answers from 250 to 475 and of the remaining 6, more gave figures higher than 475 than lower than 250. In another group of 28 students, 20 gave answers ranging from 250 to 450, with most of the remaining giving answers higher than 450. It is clear from this (admittedly informal) survey that some claims employing *many* will be interpreted as being relatively strong.

In cases in which sentences are interpreted in ways that are at variance with what a logicosemantic analysis would predict, it is often useful to look to Grice's theory of conversational implicatures for an explanation. We might, in particular, look to Grice's Maxims of Quantity:

(9)   a. Make your contribution as informative as is required.
        b. Do not make your contribution more informative than is
           required.[3]

As stated, the relevance of maxims (9a) and (9b) to the problem of assessing the strength of a claim is not completely clear. However, were we to replace *as informative as* and *more informative than* by *as strong as* and

---

[3]In the preceding chapter, I worked with a somewhat different formulation for Grice's Maxims of Quantity. There is no significance in this difference.

stronger than, respectively, their relevance would be quite clear. However, this alternative formulation presupposes that we have some way of measuring the strength of a claim. It certainly does not give us such a measure.

Implicit in Grice's theory of the "logic" of conversation is the principle that how we interpret any given utterance is a function of our awareness of what the speaker might have said but didn't. Given this principle, we could say that we interpret a claim like (4) in light of the fact (among other things) that the advertiser who says it did not say (3) and did not say (10).

(10)   Few people who use Painaway get immediate pain relief.

I submit that on hearing (4), we interpret it as being intermediate in strength between (3) and (10). What we require is some method for making such an analysis explicit. In the next section, I offer such a method.

Many

Suppose John Jones is known by 100 women and is interested in knowing how many of these women like him. I believe he would be more pleased to discover that (11a) is true than that (11b) is true or more pleased to discover that (11b) is true than that (11c) is true, and so on down the list.

(11)   a. Every one of the women likes John Jones.
         b. Most of the women like John Jones.
         c. Many of the women like John Jones.
         d. Some of the women like John Jones.
         e. Few of the women like John Jones.
         f. None of the women likes John Jones.

Certainly, (11a) seems stronger than (11b), which seems stronger than (11c), etc.

Can the definition of logical strength given in (7) account for our intuitions about the relative strength of (11a)-(11f)? One difficulty with this definition is that (11a) fails to entail (11b)-(11d), for the latter make an existential commitment not made by the former. Note, for instance, that (12) is true but (13) is false.

(12)   All unicorns have one horn.

(13)   Some unicorns have one horn.

However, if the set of things quantified is not empty, then a proposition containing *all* or *every* [e.g., (11a)] will entail the corresponding proposition with *some* [e.g., (11d)].

Definition (7) seems to give the right results in the case of (11a) and (11b). It is a little less clear that propositions with *most* always entail propositions with *many*. Suppose our population consisted of three women and that two like him. Clearly (11b) would be true, but would (11c) be true? If it is, then definition (7) gives us the right results. If it isn't, then this definition must be discarded. I am of the opinion that (11c) would not be true in this circumstance. However, whenever the sets ranged over by *most* and *many* are reasonably large, propositions containing *most* do entail corresponding propositions containing *many*.

The definition given earlier clearly accounts for our intuition concerning the relative strength of (11c) and (11d), for (11c) entails (11d), but not conversely. However, our definition does not account for our intuitions concerning *some* and *few*. Sentence (11d) clearly does not entail (11e) and, if we may assume that (11e) is consistent with (11f), as I think we must, (11e) does not entail (11d). In the case of (11e) and (11f), we must adjust for the fact that both are negative. On any negative scale, (11f) would asymmetrically entail (11e). Consider (14) and (15).

(14)   None of the women dislikes John Jones.

(15)   Few of the women dislike John Jones.

If (14) is logically stronger than (15), then (11e) must be said to be logically stronger than (11f).

As we have seen, only data (11d) and (11e) present a serious problem for definition (7). We could rectify the situation by assuming that we learn that (11d) is stronger than (11e) ad hoc. The question arises as to whether or not it is possible to pin down what a speaker who makes a claim like (11b) or (11c) or (11d) is committed to. I would like to suggest a procedure, according to which a ranked list like (11) is mapped onto a scale.

The principle that how we interpret any given claim is a function of our recognition of what the speaker might have said but didn't will be of use only if we can delimit with some precision the set of sentences with which we compare any given utterance for anyone who says a given sentence might have said but didn't say an infinite number of other sentences. In light of this I propose the following method for constructing what I shall call the "comparison class" for any given utterance.

(16)   The **comparison class** for any given sentence S containing
         grammatical element E (a word or phrase) is composed of

those sentences that can be obtained from S by substituting for E all members of the smallest semantic class which contains E.

Given this principle, the comparison class for sentence (11c) would consist of the sentences of (11). It would not include (17) however.

(17)   Many of the women like John Jones, but most don't.

I submit that on hearing a sentence like (11c) we assess its strength relative to the other sentences of (11), but not relative to (17). This is the most crucial assumption of my theory of how claims employing *many* will be interpreted by consumers.

Given comparison class (11) for (11c), and a ranking of the relative strength of the members of this class, we require some method for assessing to what exactly someone who says (11c) is committed. I propose the following method:

(18)   Given a scale S (say a 10 point scale plus 0) and a comparison class C formed with respect to lexical element E, assign those members of C that have absolute values to the appropriate points on S and assign all other members of C to S, giving equal space on S to each member.

Given (18), we would map the sentences of (11) into scale (19).

(19) $\begin{array}{ccccccccccc} 0 & 1 & 2 & 3 & 4 & 5 & 6 & 7 & 8 & 9 & 10 \end{array}$

none   few   some   many   most all

Given principles (16) and (18), we would be forced to say that claims employing *many* will (at least in some cases) be interpreted as being relatively strong. All things being equal, a claim like (20) will, I submit, be interpreted as claiming that something between 50% and 75% of the set of things that variable X ranges over have property P.

(20)   Many X's are P

Notice that the informal survey I did in connection with Preparation H claim (8) is reasonably consistent with the results of the analytic technique just proposed.[4]

As datum (17) suggests, *many* can range up and down a scale like (19). Were we to say that *most* is invariant in its interpretation, as I think we should, mapping (17) into a scale like (19) would give us scale (21).

---

[4] Actually, scale (19) somewhat underestimates the strength of *many* if the results of this informal survey can be trusted.

(21)

Clearly someone who interprets a claim like (11c) in the light of the fact that (17) is consistent with it would have to conclude that (11c) is very weak. However, I submit that we do not normally interpret in this way.

Context can play a very important role in how claims employing *many* will be understood. Consider how we might once have thought of our Representatives in Congress before Koreagate and Abscam and related disclosures were made. In this era, had Walter Cronkite said (22) on the evening news, I believe that we would agree that what he said was true if our morning paper ran headline (23).

(22)   CBS news has learned that a Washington grand jury will return indictments on many congressmen tonight.

(23)   20 Congressmen indicted by Grand Jury

That is, in an era in which it would be presumed that Congressmen are basically honest or too clever to get caught, it would not take a very large percentage of our congressmen to get indicted to justify a claim like (22). Suppose, however, that Walter Cronkite were to have said (24) on some evening.

(24)   CBS News has learned that many congressmen plan to run for reelection next year.

In this case, the number of congressmen who satisfied (24) would have to be quite large. As this "thought experiment" shows, the number of things or people that count as many is not fixed.

These "thought experiments" can be made consistent with the analytic technique proposed earlier. Let us assume that before principle (18) is employed, we adjust the scale to reflect our expectations. Suppose that we hear a proposition like (20) in a context in which our expectation is that something like 90% of those in the set X ranges over can reliably be assumed not to satisfy the predicate P. In this case we block off the upper 90% of the scale and apply principle (18) to the remainder of the scale. Clearly, in this case, the value assigned to *many* will be quite low. In cases in which our expectation is that very few of the members of the set that X ranges over can reliably be assumed not to satisfy the predicate P, the value assigned to *many* will be relatively high.

Let us return to the Preparation H claim (8). If what I have said concerning how *many* will be interpreted in neutral contexts is correct, then a pragmatist theory of truth in advertising, a theory which is sensitive to how people actually interpret language rather than to how they should (perhaps) interpret language, would have it that the manufacturer must demonstrate that from 50% to 75% of the tests run on the "hundreds" of patients in question were positive.[5]

The quantifier *many* also occurs in television advertisements for Preparation H. Consider advertisements (25) and (26).

(25)   **Preparation H** [6]
         Type: Live action
         Setting: Drug store
         Characters: Woman Customer and Woman Clerk

         TEXT
         Clerk (woman): *Looking for something, Betty?*
         Customer (woman): *For relief, Mrs. Rollins. Hemorrhoids again—pain, itch.*
         Clerk: *Try this.*
         Customer: *Preparation H?*
         Clerk: *Many folks tell me it temporarily relieves occasional pain and itch of hemorrhoidal tissues—fast.*
         Customer: *Really works?*
         Clerk: *Folks swear by it. Even helps shrink swelling due to inflamation.*
         Customer: *I'll try it.*
           (Later)
         Clerk: *Feeling better today?*
         Customer: *Thanks to you and Preparation H.*
         Voice over (adult male): *Preparation H . . . relieves pain and itch . . . helps shrink swelling.*

(26)   **Preparation H** (NBC, 1/2/81, 10:19 a.m.)
         Type: Live action
         Setting: Bedroom
         Characters: Two adult women

---

[5]The analytic technique can pin down how I believe *hundreds* will be interpreted. Principle (16) will give us the following comparison class.

(i)   We did thousands of tests.
(ii)   We did a thousand tests.
(iii)   We did hundreds of tests.
(iv)   We did several hundred tests.
(v)   We did a hundred tests.

If we allow (iii)–(iv) to range over the values between 100 and 1000, then, for (iii) to be true, some 500–949 persons would have to be tested. This seems to me to be consistent with how "hundreds" will normally be interpreted.

[6]This commercial was taped during recreational use of my videotape machine.

TEXT
Woman 1: *Of all times to get hemorrhoids.*
Woman 2: *I got 'em when I was expecting, sis.*
Woman 1: *What'd you do?*
Woman 2: *Used Preparation H. Many found it gives temporary relief for hours from flare-ups. Combines active ingredients to relieve pain and itch.*
Woman 1: *Sounds like real medicine.*
Woman 2: *Even helps shrink swollen inflamed hemorrhoidal tissue.*
Woman 1: *I'll try it.*
Woman 2: *Since you're expecting, check with your doctor before using any medicine.*
        (Later)
Woman 2: *Hi, sis, How goes it?*
Woman 1: *Great, thanks to Preparation H.*
Woman 2: *Ahh.*
Voice over (adult male): *Preparation H relieves pain and itch, helps shrink swelling.*

In commercial (25), claim (27) occurs.

(27)   *Many folks tell me* [Preparation H] *temporarily relieves occasional pain and itch of hemorrhoidal tissues—fast.*

This use of *many* is very different from those of (8), (11c), (22), and (24) for in this case the size of the set *many* ranges over is not fixed and, furthermore, there is no suggestion that opinion, pro and con, was solicited. All (27) appears to claim is that a significant number of people—significant in the eyes of the speaker—got temporary relief from occasional pain and itch of hemorrhoidal tissues. Thus, claim (27) makes no very strong claim. Claim (28), however, taken from commercial (26), appears to report on some prior survey.

(28)   *Many found it gives temporary relief for hours from flare-ups.*

As a result, I believe *many* in (28) has essentially the same interpretation as in (8), (11c), (22), and (24). However, this claim is rather hopelessly vague. Consumers would do well to discount such a claim.

The quantifier *many* occurs in two other commercials on my tapes. Consider (29) and (30).

(29)   **Fresh Start** (NBC, 1/8/81, 8:22 p.m.)
        Type: Live action
        Setting: Studio
        Characters: Man

TEXT

Man: *Try any powder. Try any liquid. No leading detergent does more for your wash than Fresh Start. Fresh Start combines the best dirt 'n stain fighters of powders with the best grease fighter of liquids in one concentrated granular detergent. It works effectively on dirt, grease, and many common stains. And just a quarter cup does your whole wash. Fresh Start, the best of powders and liquids in one.*

(30)   **Massengill** (NBC, 1/8/81, 10:19 p.m.)
         Type: Live action.
         Setting: Dress designer's
         Characters: Two women

TEXT

Woman 1: *No more vinegar and water douches for me. They're such a bother.*

Woman 2: *Jane, look Massengill has a vinegar and water disposable douche. It's convenient.*

Woman 1: *Vinegar and water?*

Woman 2: *The ingredients many doctors recommend. But this is premixed, premeasured, sanitary. No more bother. Look how cleverly it's designed. Only Massengill has this special design.*

Voice over (adult female): *The vinegar and water disposable from Massengill is specially designed.*

In my view, the word *many* of commercial (29) will be interpreted in essentially the same way as in commercial (26). Thus, however many "common" stains there are, Fresh Start must work effectively on some 50–75% of them. In the case of (30), no fixed number of doctors appears to have been sampled, thus *many* is quite vague, much as it is in (27).

I have argued that some, but by no means all advertising claims employing *many,* will be interpreted as being relatively strong. There are claims in which the variable *many* operates on ranges over a set of fixed size where we have no particular expectations about how many in the set will or will not satisfy the predicate of the sentence. It should not be surprising if such claims were to be effective, for they are relatively strong. In other cases, such as the claims of commercials (25) and (30), no very strong claim is made, and I would predict that ordinary speakers of English will not perceive such claims as being very strong.

Most

In addition to *many, most* also occurs in advertising. Consider, for instance, the following claims:

(31)   *It* [Freedent gum] *can't stick to most dental work.*   (ABC, 2/24/78,
          @ 8:56 a.m.)

(32)   *And we* [Allstate] *settle most damage claims on the spot.*   (CBS,
          6/2/78, 11:04 p.m.)

(33)   *Light 'n Easy, it weighs a lot less than most irons.*   (NBC, 2/24/78,
          evening)

(34)   *Phillips' Milk of Magnesia liquid works with your body as you sleep,*
          using your body's water to lubricate and soften. Next morning, most
          people get gentle relief.   (NBC, 2/24/78, evening)

(35)   *It's* [Loving Care's] *not like most hair colorings: it's gentler because it*
          has no peroxides.   (NBC, 2/24/78, evening)

Given the preceding analytic technique, we would be forced to say that
an advertiser making a claim like (36) must show that between 75% and
100% of the set X ranges over has property P.

(36)   Most X's are P.

According to this view, claims employing *most* are quite strong.

We saw that *many* can range up and down scales depending on the
context. Is *most* equally variable? In my view it is not. Certainly, it could
never range below 51%. I say this because any analysis of *most* must
account for the fact that (37) is a contradiction.

(37)   *Most women like John Jones, but most don't.

The question arises whether or not (36) could be said to be true if the
percentage of X's which satisfy the predicate P of an example like (36)
was as low as 51%. I don't think it can.

Suppose that a presidential candidate C were to get 60% of the popu-
lar vote. In such a case, would (38) be true?

(38)   Most voters pulled the lever for C.

I believe (38) would be false in the circumstance in question, but there
may be some who would disagree. What is needed is solid empirical
evidence concerning how logically and linguistically naive speakers
would interpret such a claim. The analytic technique proposed during
the discussion of *many* predicts that somewhere between 75% and 100%
of the set ranged over by X in a proposition like (36) must satisfy the
predicate P. This seems correct to me.

Modal Verbs

I would like to turn now to claims employing modal verbs like *may, can,* and *could.* They are of interest because given classical logical or linguistic semantic analyses, i.e., literalist analyses, such verbs substantially weaken the claims they occur in. Note, for instance that (39) makes perfectly good sense and, as a result, it would appear that we must say that claims employing *may* are very weak indeed.

(39)   Painaway may relieve your pain, but probably won't.

A claim like (40) shows that *could* also very much weakens the force of claims containing this verb.

(40)   Painaway could relieve your pain, but probably won't.

Claims employing *can* have the interesting property that they can be true even if no test of the claim has ever been positive. Thus (41) could be true even if Painaway had never once relieved anyone's pain.

(41)   Painaway can relieve your pain.

For (41) to be true, all that need be shown, it appears, is that Painaway has the biochemical potential to relieve pain.

If the literalist or classical semantic approach to sentences containing modal verbs like *may, can,* and *could* were correct as an analysis of how people ordinarily interpret such claims, then no such claim should ever be effective. There are two possible explanations of why they might be effective. The first explanation is that these claims are simply not as weak as the literalist point of view suggests. I shall argue in favor of this view in certain cases. Another possibility is that in certain cases in which we hear claims containing modal verbs like *may, can,* and *could,* we simply ignore the modal verbs. Miller and Johnson-Laird (1976) have argued that in states of idle listening, the normal state of those watching television commercials, we for all practical purposes do just this. Presumably the same would hold of states of idle reading as well. These two explanations of the effect of claims employing *may, can,* and *could* are not, of course, mutually exclusive.

May

As noted, according to the literalist analysis of sentences containing *may,* such sentences are phenomenally weak. A sentence like (42) would have to be said to be true, according to a literalist perspective, if it is possible in principle that Painaway relieves somebody's pain.

(42)   Painaway may relieve your pain.

However, I do not believe that English speakers will in fact interpret a claim like (42) in the way that the literalist theory would suggest that we should.

Consider the following examples of the use of *may* in television advertising:

(43)   *It* [a Curtis-Mathes television set] *may be the best set you can buy.*   (ABC, 2/25/78, @ 5:41 p.m.)

(44)   *There's been a lot published about fiber lately. It may be more important than we've realized.*   (Kellogg's All Bran cereal, ABC, 7/30/78, 12:01 p.m.)

(45)   *With Comtrex, you may almost forget you have a cold.*   (NBC, 1/8/81, 10:07 p.m.)

(46)   *Introducing what just may be the first small wonder of the world, Starlet, a Toyota born small to give you what no other gas powered car can deliver.*   (CBS, 1/11/81, 2:12 p.m.)

From the perspective of the literalist, claims (43)–(46) are so weak that it is difficult to understand why an advertiser would bother to make them. Note that each of the claims made by (43)–(46) is consistent with its denial.

(47)   A Curtis-Mathes television set may be the best set you can buy and, then again, it may not.

(48)   Fiber may be more important than we've realized, and then again, it may not.

(49)   With Comtrex, you may almost forget you have a cold and, then again, you may not.

(50)   Introducing what just may be the first small car wonder of the world, and what may not be the first small car wonder of the world.

Suppose that you very much wish someone to come to a party. I believe you would much prefer that he or she say (51a) instead of (51b), or (51b) instead of (51c), or (51c) instead of (51d).

(51)   a. I will come to your party.
         b. I may come to your party.

      c. I may not come to your party.

      d. I won't come to your party.

Certainly, (51a) seems stronger than (51b), which seems stronger than (51c), etc. How can we account for these intuitions?

The definition of relative logical strength [see (7)] suffices to account for the relative strength of (51a) and (51b), for (51a) asymmetrically entails (51b). However, this concept will not assist us in connection with (51b) and (51c) for neither entails the other. We might therefore resort to some sort of conversational explanation after the manner of Grice. We might, for instance, argue that a claim like (51b) is virtually empty; a speaker would not burden a listener with a sentence like this unless he or she meant to express something more than the mere possibility of his or her coming to the party. Such an explanation presupposes the Maxim of Strength.

As we have already seen, the Maxims of Strength and Parsimony— Grice's Maxim of Quantity—do not assist us at all in ranking the members of a comparison class [see (16)], and as we have seen, the concept of logical strength will not assist us in this regard in connection with (51b) and (51c). I submit that principles (16) and (18) accurately predict how the claims of (51) will be interpreted.

Suppose we have heard (51b). In my view, its force will be assessed relative to the force of the other sentences of (51), but not relative to a sentence like (52) which denudes *may* of almost all force.

(52)   I may come to your party but the odds against it are 100 to 1.

Given Principle (16), we would set up (51) as the comparison class of (51b).[7] I suggest in connection with (51b) and (51c) that English speakers have accepted by convention that *may* is stronger than *may not*. Given this assumption, Principle (18) would map (51) into scale (53).

(53)   0 1 2 3 4 5 6 7 8 9 10

        will not   may not   may   will

This analytic technique thus predicts that a sentence like (51b) conversationally implicates that there is an even or better chance that the speaker will come to the party.

In my view the analytic technique proposed in this chapter, a technique that simply makes more precise the predictions of Grice's Maxims of Quantity, accurately measures how speakers who can be assumed to

---

[7]Principle (16) must be revised to allow for relevant negations, including in particular negations in the scope of the element E of the statement of this principle.

be obeying Grice's Cooperative Principle will interpret a claim like (51b). However, as noted, there is another quite credible explanation of why claims like (43)–(46) might be successful. As noted, Miller and Johnson-Laird (1976) argue that in states of idle listening, certain modal elements may or may not be fully attended to. If one can argue that people are normally or often in states of idle listening while watching television commercials, as I think one can, then the proposal of Miller and Johnson-Laird that we in some sense ignore the presence of *may* could account for any effectiveness that claims like (43)–(46) might have. Consider, in particular in this connection, commercial (54), from which the Comtrex claim (45) was taken.

(54)   Comtrex (NBC, 1/8/81, 10:07 p.m.)
        Type: Live action
        Setting: Various settings
        Characters: Woman, man, male announcer

        TEXT
        Voice over (adult male): *With Comtrex, you may almost forget you have a cold.*
        Setting: Clothing store.
        Woman: *I know my cold is still there. But thanks to Comtrex, I almost feel like it's gone.*
        Setting: Office.
        Man: *I still have a cold. But thanks to Comtrex, I almost don't feel like I do.*
        Setting: Bathroom.
        Male Announcer: *These are some of the things you can take for a cold. But for one with nasal congestion, aches, sneezing and coughs, Comtrex Multi-Symptom Cold Reliever does more. It even relieves coughs. So all by itself, it gives more kinds of relief than Dristan, or Contac or Bayer. Try Comtrex, in tablets, liquid, or capsules.*

Observe that claim (45) is very much weaker if viewed from the literalist perspective, than is (55), for (55) does not contain *may*.

(55)   *I still have a cold, but thanks to Comtrex, I almost don't feel like I do.*

Advertisers may take *almost* to be a "weasel" word of indeterminate force, but this would be very wrong indeed. Claim (55), even from a literalist perspective, is extremely strong, promising virtual total relief of nasal congestion, aches, sneezing, and cough. The manufacturer might argue that the opening statement by the announcer, namely claim (45), serves to qualify all following statements. However, this cannot be taken seriously, for (45) and (55) are said by different speakers. Moreover, if what Miller and Johnson-Laird have said about how we cope with modal verbs in states of idle listening, then some consumers may not even assess the impact of *may* on claim (45) itself.

The analytic technique based on principles (16) and (18) will clearly overestimate how some uses of *may* will be interpreted. If I were to invite you to a party that you did not want to go to, you might say (51b) to spare me the embarrassment of rejecting the invitation directly. However, I believe you would elaborate on (51b), perhaps by saying (56).

(56)   I may come to your party, for I want to, but I fear that my wife may already have booked us for that night.

Notice that the second occurrence of *may* must be interpreted as being relatively strong if the first is to be interpreted as being relatively weak. Clearly *may* like *many* can move up and down a scale like (53) depending on context. However, in "neutral" contexts, I believe scale (53) reasonably accurately measures how we will interpret a claim like (51b).[8]

It should be clear that my proposal concerning the neutral context *may*, and the Miller and Johnson-Laird proposal are by no means mutually exclusive. Indeed, both may be correct.

Can

The modal *can* appears to occur with a good deal more frequency in advertising than does *may*. Consider examples (57)–(63).

(57)   *Even when you can't hold up any longer, your hair can with Final Net.*   (CBS, 2/24/78, 12:35 p.m.)

(58)   *Like so many women, I have two kinds of skin. Dry skin here, where some soaps can make it drier. And oily skin here, where some creams can make it oilier. So I wash with Phisoderm. Phisoderm gets out grease and dirt from oily places, while it moisturizes dry places.*   (CBS, 5/8/78, 1:22 p.m.)

(59)   *Campho-Phenique gently penetrates skin injuries to kill germs that can cause infection, helps speed healing.*   (CBS, 7/18/78, 10:55 a.m.)

(60)   *Use Breck Shampoo, Brecks Instant Conditioner, so your hair can take the heat of hot irons, hot rollers, and blow dryers without drying out.* (NBC, 7/24/78, 8:34 a.m.)

[8]Academics use *may* with some frequency. I believe that when we do, unless we are criticizing another's point of view, we mean for the claims to be significant ones. However, when criticizing another's point of view, if we acknowledge that the other's point of view may be correct, *may* would be meant to be very weak in force.

(61)   *With my arthritis, getting in and out of the tub can be frightening. But*
         with Arthritis Strength Bufferin, I can ease the minor pain for hours,
         move better. It gives me extra strength when the arthritis first flares up.
         But Arthritis Strength Bufferin adds extra protection from stomach
         upset ordinary aspirin can cause.   (CBS, 1/2/81, 11:54 a.m.)

(62)   *Winter colds and flu can trigger bronchial asthma attacks.*   (Primatine
         Mist, NBC, 1/8/81, 10:32 p.m.)

(63)   *It* [Oil of Olay] *can help you look younger too.*   (CBS, 1/15/81, 6:58 p.m.)

Advertisers appear to think that *can* means merely 'be possible' in examples like (57)–(63). Were this true, then claims like (57)–(63) would have to be said to be quite weak. However, this view of the meaning of *can* cannot be correct as an analysis of the meaning of *can*. Compare (64) and (65).

(64)   I can lift 400 lb.

(65)   I can possibly lift 400 lb.

If *can* meant 'be possible', then *possibly* would be redundant in (65) (which it is not) and (64) and (65) would be logically equivalent (which they are not).

A sentence like (64) is a bit tricky. Were it said in a context in which some 400 lb object needed to be moved, it would count as a promise that the speaker would be able to lift the object if asked. However, in a discussion among weight lifters, someone who cannot now lift 400 lb because he or she is not in training, could still say (64) in good faith if he or she has lifted 400 lb. In this context, (64) would mean something like 'I can lift 400 lb under certain circumstances.' However, (64) could not legitimately be said if the speaker has never lifted 400 lb but believes he has the potential to do so. Thus, while (64) does not commit the speaker to being able to lift 400 lb under every circumstance, it does commit the speaker to being able to lift 400 lb in some circumstance. Thus, *can* is not equivalent to *be possible* though *can* does entail *be possible*.

As we have seen, in some cases a sentence like (64) would count as an absolute promise (as when a 400 lb object needs to be moved) and in others as a conditional promise (as when weight lifters are talking about their past performances). In this light, (62) would have to be said to be quite legitimate if in certain circumstances winter colds or flu have triggered bronchial asthma attacks. It does not commit the advertiser to the proposition that every winter cold or flu will trigger such an attack.

Claim (63), on the other hand, is quite problematic. The speaker who says (66) could, of course, have said (67) and speakers will interpret (66) in the light of this fact.

(66)   Oil of Olay can help you look younger, too.

(67)   Oil of Olay might help you look younger, too.

Claim (66) is significantly stronger than (67). Moreover, it is not a conditional promise. That is, (66) is not as weak as (68).

(68)   Oil of Olay can help you look younger, too, under certain
         circumstances.

What we must conclude is that (66) unconditionally promises every person some degree of help in looking younger. It would be interesting to see the evidence for this.

Could

Claims employing *could* are significantly weaker than claims employing *can*. Consider

(69)   *Fact is, until I found Freedent, I'd forgotten how fresh and clean my
         mouth and breath could feel anytime.*   (ABC, 2/24/78, @ 8:56 a.m.)

(70)   A: *Sir, what's the hurry?*
         B: *Gonna rent a car.*
         A: *Well, you don't have to run.*
         B: *Gotta run.*
         A: *Oh, no. If you had an Avis wizard number, you could walk.*   (CBS,
         6/2/78, 10:10 p.m.)

(71)   *If you need six passenger space . . . if you need a roomy trunk . . . if you
         want mileage like this . . . then the full size 1978 Ford LTD could be
         just the car for you.*   (ABC, 2/25/78, afternoon)

Note that *could* occurs in explicitly conditional sentences in (70) and (71). And, in general, *could* differs from *can* in that *could* is intrinsically conditional in meaning while *can* is not. In essence, *could* means no more than *be possible*, i.e., (69) is no stronger than (72).

(72)   Fact is, until I found Freedent, I'd forgotten how fresh and
         clean it is possible for my mouth and breath to feel anytime.

If claims like (69)–(71) are effective, I suspect we would have to appeal to the proposal by Miller and Johnson-Laird concerning how modal elements are dealt with in states of idle listening to account for this, for claims employing *could* are very weak.

Help

By far the most frequently occurring modal element in advertising is *help*.[9] Consider the following examples:

(73)   *I hate roaches, but now I've got something that helps me get rid of roaches for a long time—New Raid Roach Tape.*   (CBS, 5/8/78, 3:15 p.m.)

(74)   *Calgon helps detergents get laundry up to 30% cleaner.*   (CBS, 7/18/78, 10:47 a.m.)

(75)   *Pampers stay dry lining stays drier to help keep your baby's skin stay a lot drier.*   (CBS, 2/24/78, @ 12:34 p.m.)

(76)   *And, remember, AC filters help protect your engine from dirt and rust.*   (CBS, 6/2/78, 9:32 p.m.)

(77)   *Dawn helps keep grease away from my pans, my glasses, even away from my roasting pan.*   (CBS, 5/8/78, 3:07 p.m.)

(78)   *It* [Phisoderm] *helps keep my whole face in perfectly balanced 5.5 pH condition, like normal skin.*   (CBS, 5/8/78, 1:22 p.m.)

(79)   *It* [A & H baking soda] *even helps prevent septic tank odors.*   (CBS, 5/8/78, 1:30 p.m.)

(80)   *Skin Quencher is the soft, fragrant skin lotion, drenched with moisturizers to help skin feel younger.*   (ABC, 2/24/78, @ 8:56 p.m.)

(81)   *When your child has a stuffy nose and fever from a cold, it's time for St. Joseph Cold Tablets for Children. It helps with two kinds of relief; an effective nasal decongestant plus the same aspirin in St. Joseph's Aspirin for children.*   (WUAB, Cleveland, 2/24/78, @ 12:01 p.m.)

(82)   *It's* [One-A-Day Plus Iron's] *the only leading brand with the exact 18 mg recommended for women to help build red blood cells plus 10 essential vitamins.*   (NBC, 2/25/78, evening)

(83)   [Super Poli-Grip] *helps form a seal between your dentures and gums . . . helps keep food out, dentures in.*   (CBS, 1/2/81, 11:53 a.m.)

[9]*Help* is not, strictly speaking, a modal verb, but many advertisers use it as if it were.

(84)   [Prudential Life Insurance] *will help pay for things.*   (CBS, 1/5/81, 9:01 p.m.)

(85)   *And the extra income* [from being an Amway distributor] *helped buy this car.*   (ABC, 1/6/81, 6:25 p.m.)

(86)   *Vaseline Intensive Care Lotion helps heal roughness, dryness—helps heal tightness, flaking, lets the healing begin in seconds.*   (CBS, 1/6/81, 8:25 p.m.)

(87)   a. *Dexatrim helped me lose all those middle-age pounds I couldn't lose before.*

         b. *Just one time release capsule works all day to help you diet and lose weight.*

         c. *Dexatrim has definitely helped me lose weight and I love it.*   (CBS, 1/6/81, 9:01 p.m.)

(88)   *Bayer or Tylenol help these six symptoms, Contac these six, but Dristan relieves all twelve of these cold symptoms.*   (NBC, 1/8/81, 8:54 p.m.)

(89)   *Control is helping me to suppress my appetite in order to help me to lose weight.*   (NBC, 1/8/81, 10:19 p.m.)

(90)   *Moisture Wear actually helps skin over 25 look younger.*   (CBS, 1/15/81, 6:46 p.m.)

(91)   *It* [Oil of Olay] *can help you look younger too.*   (CBS, 1/15/81, 6:58 p.m.)

(92)   *Dentu-Cream denture toothpaste has a powerful antistain formula that helps brush away tough stains, leaving your dentures feeling fresh and clean.*   (ABC, 1/16/81, 6:25 p.m.)

(93)   *Fixodent helps fix loose spots, fills those tiny gaps between dentures and gums with ingredients that give added dimension to holding.*   (NBC, 1/18/81, 6:39 p.m.)

In most of the cases above, *help* occurs generically. Before considering these uses of *help*, it will be helpful to consider more conventional uses of this verb.

In cases in which *help* is used to describe a past or future event, it commonly occurs with a direct object. Consider (94) and (95).

(94)   John helped Bill carry out the sofa.

(95)   John will help Bill carry out the sofa.

There are two crucial features of a sentence like (94). First, (94) entails that both John and Bill performed part of the task at hand and it entails that the task was completed. Sentence (95) entails that both John and Bill will perform part of the task at hand and that the task is expected to be completed.

In the case of a sentence like (94), John need not have done part of the carrying. However, he must have done something (e.g., clear Bill's path) that facilitated Bill's completion of the task. A sentence like (94) at least implicates that the task John performed was essential to the completion of the overall task. Does (94) entail that this is so? Consider

(96)   John helped Bill carry out the sofa, but what John did was totally unnecessary.

I find (96) to be very peculiar at best and as a result am inclined to believe that for (94) to be true, what John did must have been essential to the completion of the task of carrying out the sofa. That what Bill did was essential to the carrying out of the sofa is quite clear. Let us summarize what has been said as follows:

(97)   A sentence of the form *A helped B to P* entails
         (a) P was accomplished.
         (b) A did something that was essential to the accomplishment of P.
         (c) B did something which was essential to the accomplishment of P.

Sentences containing *help* in which there is no direct object also occur, as (98) and (99) show.

(98)   John helped carry out the sofa.

(99)   John will help carry out the sofa.

Such sentences entail the existence of someone (or perhaps something) that John did assist (98) or will assist (99) in carrying out the sofa. Thus, sentences like (98) and (99) are no different in principle from (94) and (95).

Consider examples (87a) and (87c), examples taken from a single commercial. Sentences (87a) and (87c) entail that the speaker did lose the weight in question and that Dexatrim played an essential role in this process. Thus, both entail that Dexatrim was effective. Sentence (85) also uses *help* in the past tense and commits the Amway company to the view that being an Amway distributor generated non-negligible amounts of income for the speaker.

Claims (85), (87a), and (87c) are modest because they recount individual personal experiences. Of much greater interest are cases in which *help* is used generically, by far the most common way in which *help* is used. Consider (73), which makes claim (100).

(100)   New Raid Roach Tape helps me get rid of roaches for a long time.

Claim (100) is like those we have already discussed, for *help* occurs with a direct object. The question we must address is how strong claim (100) is.

Generic sentences have the virtue from the literalist perspective, of sounding good while saying relatively little. Consider (101).

(101)   New Roachaway gets rid of roaches for a long time.

Claim (101) could be true even if Roachaway were not to work always or even very often. Suppose that there were 10 types of roaches and that Roachaway gets rid of only 1 type. We would nevertheless have to say that (101) is true or so it would seem. Suppose further that Roachaway gets rid of these roaches only when they are 1 week old. Again, we would apparently have to say that (101) is true. Suppose, still further that Roachaway were to work only when the relative humidity is 95% or higher. Again, we would apparently have to say that (101) is true. Note, though, that under the circumstances, Roachaway would rarely be effective.

Generic sentences express inductive generalizations. The lawlike statements of science, which are normally generic, are arrived at in this way. In science and in any other context in which people can be assumed to obey Grice's Cooperative Principle, a generic statement will be used only when it expresses a statistically significant generalization. It is this assumption from which the apparent strength of generic sentences arises.

A claim like (101) implicates that Roachaway can get rid of all types of roaches in all circumstances. Since the speaker who says (101) could have said (102), he or she implicates by not saying the weaker sentence (102) that Roachaway can get rid of more than just most types of roaches.

(102)   New Roachaway gets rid of most roaches for a long time.

Similarly, someone who hears (101) will further assume that there are no other significant exceptions since there was no mention of such exceptions, and the listener would normally have no reason to suspect their existence.

There is no doubt that qualifying a claim by adding the generic verb *helps* weakens the claim. However, the manufacturer of Raid Roach Tape [see (73)] is nevertheless committed to the position that what this product does is essential [see (97b)], i.e., that consumers cannot expect to get rid of roaches without somehow causing the task that Raid Roach Tape performs to be performed. No less important is that a claim like (73) entails that the combination of the use of Raid Roach Tape and other possible consumer actions (e.g., keeping one's kitchen scrupulously clean) can accomplish getting rid of roaches for a long time [see (97a)]. This latter fact is of great importance to the evaluation of advertising claims employing *helps*.

In this light, consider claim (74), repeated here as (103).

(103)   *Calgon helps detergents get laundry up to 30% cleaner.*

In the next chapter, it will be argued that the most natural interpretation of the elliptical comparative of (103) is shown in

(104)   Calgon helps detergents get laundry up to 30% cleaner than would be the case were Calgon not used.

It is clear, from (103) that Calgon plays an essential role in accomplishing the advertised task—getting laundry up to 30% cleaner. Since Calgon is said to help the detergent to accomplish this task, (103) entails that Calgon causes detergents to perform more effectively. This is, of course, credible. Now consider (80), repeated as (105).

(105)   *Skin Quencher is the soft, fragrant skin lotion, drenched with moisturizers to help skin feel younger.*

Claim (105) entails that Skin Quencher facilitates our skin's work of making our skin feel younger. Assuming that it makes sense to suggest that skin could feel as if it were younger, which is anything but obvious, claim (105) entails that our skin performs some essential task in the effort to make itself feel younger. It is anything but clear what this task might be.

Consider now, claim (106), taken from the Preparation H advertisement (25).

(106)   *Preparation H . . . helps shrink swelling.*

Claim (106) entails that Preparation H is efficacious, i.e., that what Preparation H does is essential to the task of shrinking swelling [see (97b)]. Moreover, (106) entails that shrinking swelling is accomplishable through the use of Preparation H [see (97a)]. The question arises as to what, if anything, Preparation H assists?

In my view, the verb *helps*, when it does not have a direct object, has some sort of understood direct object. However, what this is in the case of (106) is not clear. In the case of (106), it could be the listener or the listener's body or some other medication (i.e., Preparation H assists some other product in the task of shrinking swelling). We can dismiss the third alternative because the need to use Preparation H in conjunction with some other product is, in no way, hinted at in this or any other Preparation H advertisement. In my view, for (106) to be true, either (107) or (108) must be true.

(107)   Preparation H assists the body in the body's effort to shrink swelling.

(108)   Preparation H assists people in their efforts to shrink swelling.

Should (107) be what the manufacturers of Preparation H have in mind, then they could be required to identify the bodily function that Preparation H assists and how it assists this bodily function. Should (108) be what the manufacturers have in mind then, if this is to make sense, it must be the case that there is something else besides taking Preparation H that we can do that, combined with what Preparation H does, results in the shrinking of swelling. It would be interesting to know what this is.

I suspect that advertisers often add *helps* to claims by way of simply weakening these claims enough to protect them from the FTC and others. That is, I suspect that *helps* is used as if it were a strength weakening modal operator, which it is not. This would explain how relatively incoherent claims like (106) might arise. Why though are claims employing *helps* as effective as the frequency of use of *help* would suggest? There are two possible answers. I believe we might appeal to an explanation along the lines of Miller and Johnson-Laird's proposal concerning modals, i.e., that in states of idle listening, we ignore the presence of *help*. Another explanation is that sentences containing generic *help*, like other generic sentences are normally assumed to express statistically significant inductive generalizations. According to this latter view, advertising claims employing *help* are impressive because they are indistinguishable from the lawlike generic claims of scientists. If this is correct, then advertisers should be held to the same standards of proof as scientists, that is, an advertiser who claims that his product helps to achieve some desired goal should be required to show that the action the product performs is essential to achieving this goal.

Chapter 4
Comparatives

Comparative constructions abound in advertising, and for good reason. They are used to say that some product is better than it used to be, or that it is better than competing products, or that consumers will be better off if they use some product than if they don't. Comparatives are also used in price advertising to say that consumers can get more of something for their money than they used to be able to, or to get more of something than before for less money than they used to have to pay. The fact that comparatives are used so frequently in advertising makes them of interest to the study of the language of advertising, but it is how they are used—and abused—in advertising that makes them most interesting.

In the simplest sort of case, a comparative sentence compares two individual objects or two types of objects along some dimension. In sentence (1), for instance, oranges and lemons (types of things) are compared along the dimension of sweetness.

(1)   Oranges are sweeter than lemons.

In sentence (2), two sets of oranges—the oranges the speaker used to have and the oranges he or she now has—are compared along the dimension of sweetness.

(2)   Our oranges are sweeter than they used to be.

Sentences like (1) are used in advertising in which one product is compared with a competing product. Sentences like (2) are used in product improvement advertising. A sentence like (3) is used in what we might call "better than nothing" advertising claims.

(3)   You'll live longer if you eat oranges.

In this case, what are being compared are the life spans of listeners who do not eat oranges with the life spans they would have if they were to eat oranges.

Competing products comparatives like (1) can be used in price advertising, i.e., in cases in which cost is the dimension along which objects are compared. "Product improvement" comparatives like (2) also occur where the dimension along which older and newer versions of a product are compared is cost. The most interesting cases of this are "more for less" claims in which it is asserted that one can get more of some product than before for less money than before. Comparatives like these are frequently more than a little problematic as we shall see.

As surely everyone is aware, many of the comparatives which are used in advertising are elliptical in that the object terms of comparatives like (1) and (2) are not identified. The result is something like (4).

(4)   Our oranges are sweeter.

Elliptical comparatives like (4) are quite vague. Sentence (4), for instance, could be interpreted as in (5) or (6).

(5)   Our oranges are sweeter than our competitor's oranges.

(6)   Our oranges are sweeter than they used to be.

Still other types of interpretations of elliptical comparatives are possible in special contexts.

Even subject terms of comparatives are sometimes not identified. A magazine advertisement for Kent cigarettes headlines claim (7).

(7)   *25% less Tar.*   (*Newsweek*, 3/6/78)

It is reasonably clear that the implicit subject of (7) is intended to be *Kent cigarettes.* I have yet to see a comparative with no subject term in which the implicit subject is not the product being promoted.

The primary advantage of elliptical comparatives to advertisers becomes clear on consideration of (7). Some consumers may take it to be claiming (8), a proposition I believe to be false.

(8)   Kent's have 25% less tar than competing brands.

However, if pressed to defend (7), the advertiser might argue that what he meant to be claiming was (9).

(9)   Kent's have 25% less tar now than before.

Clearly, (8) is the more remarkable claim, but (9) is the more easily defended. In my view, however, advertisers who make ambiguous or vague claims should be held responsible for all of their linguistically defensible interpretations. According to this view, the manufacturer of Kent cigarettes would be held responsible for both (8) and (9).

In what follows, I shall take up three topics. First, we shall consider an important felicity condition of comparatives, namely, that the things compared be genuinely comparable. We shall then take up the phenomenon of elliptical comparatives. Finally, we shall consider multiple comparatives including, in particular, "more for less" claims.

A Felicity Condition of Comparatives

In order to be felicitous, a comparative must compare genuinely comparable things. A sentence like (10) violates this condition rather dramatically.

(10)   The idea that Reagan is President is better than this orange.

Sentence (10) is clearly syntactically well formed. There is even a sense in which (10) is well formed semantically for *goodness* can be predicated of both ideas and oranges. Nevertheless, (10) is extraordinarily odd, for the idea that Reagan is President and oranges are not genuinely comparable. In this case, we might argue that the sense in which ideas can be good and the sense in which oranges are good are different, i.e., that the dimensions along which these two things are measured are different.

In order to be felicitous in advertising, a comparative must involve genuine alternatives. Baker (1968) cites an advertising claim of the Armour company that went like this: *1 pound of Armour Star franks is as nourishing as a 1 pound steak.* The problem with this claim is that while a hungry person might eat a 1 lb steak, it is a great deal more difficult to imagine someone putting away 12 hot dogs, with or without buns. This is clearly not a felicitous comparison.

Perhaps in response to growing criticism of the sugar contained in presweetened breakfast cereals, General Mills, Inc. raised the question *Which has more sugar, an apple or a bowl of Trix?* on the back of a cereal box (see Photograph 4.1).[1] Below this headline, we find a photograph of an apple and a bowl of Trix, which is followed by General Mills' answer to its question: *an apple!*

There are three words and phrases in the General Mills question of interest: *sugar, an apple,* and *a bowl of Trix. Sugar* normally refers to

---

[1] I am indebted to Chris Farrar for bringing this advertisement to my attention.

Which has more sugar, an apple or a bowl of Trix?

An Apple!

Mother Nature sweetens apples for two good reasons—to make them taste good and to make them a source of energy. That's why she puts 15 grams of sugar in a medium-sized apple.

We sweeten Trix for the very same reasons. But a 1 oz. serving of Trix has only 10 grams of sugar (about 2 rounded teaspoons) — sugar that comes from natural sources like sugar cane and beets. And our bodies use the sugar in Trix the same way they use the apple's sugar . . . for energy.

But Trix is more than a good tasting source of energy. One ounce of Trix provides 25% of the U.S. Recommended Daily Allowance of seven essential vitamins and iron.

Delicious Trix. Nutritious. Convenient. Economical. And less sugar than an apple!

Behind the good taste is a very good cereal.

General Mills

For more information about sugar and nutrition, please write to us at:

General Mills, Inc.
Nutrition Department
Box 6, Dept. 865
Minneapolis, MN 55460

Photograph 4.1

sucrose and in this light it is worth pointing out that on boxes of Trix we find both sugar (second) and corn syrup (fourth) in their list of ingredients. A question that needs answering is whether *sugar* in the General Mills advertisement is meant to refer to sugar alone or to both sugar and corn syrup?

The terms *an apple* and *a bowl of Trix* are both indefinite noun phrases of indeterminant reference. Obviously, if one is free to choose whatever size apple and whatever size bowl of Trix one wishes one can make either *an apple* or *a bowl of Trix* the correct answer to the General Mills question. It is clear from the text of this advertisement that General Mills has drawn the comparison rather unfairly. The advertisement goes on to say:

(11)   a. *Mother nature sweetens apples for two good reasons—to make them taste good and to make them a source of energy. That's why she puts 15 grams of sugar in a medium-sized apple.* [2]

        b. *We sweeten Trix for the very same reasons. But a 1 oz. serving of Trix has only 10 grams of sugar (about 2 rounded teaspoons)—sugar that comes from natural sources like sugar cane and beets. And our bodies use the sugar in Trix the same way they use the apple's sugar . . . for energy.*

Quite unwittingly, General Mills has made an excellent case in its own terms for choosing to eat a medium-sized apple over a 1-oz bowl of Trix: The apple has more sugar and therefore, or so General Mills would have it, children should like the apple better and they will receive a greater energy supply from it. Both of these factors are desiderata in foods according to General Mills itself. Indeed, General Mills takes the very curious position of extolling the virtues of sugar [see (11a)] while stressing how little sugar Trix has in it [see (11b)].

The phrase, *a medium-sized apple,* as noted, is indeterminant in reference. Just how big is a medium-sized apple? I asked the produce manager of a central Ohio supermarket to identify which of several packages containing apples contained medium-sized apples. He singled out a package containing 12 apples, the total weight of which was 3 3/16 lb. The average apple in this package therefore weighed 3¼ oz, that is 3.25 times as much as the 1 oz bowl of Trix. Thus, comparison of equal quantities by weight of apples and Trix would have given the result that Trix has not less, but a little more than twice as much sugar as a medium-sized apple.

---

[2]Everything claimed in (11a) is false, of course, for there is no such thing as Mother Nature.

Following passages (11a) and (11b), the General Mills advertisement goes on to say:

(12)   a. *But Trix is more than a good tasting source of energy. One ounce of Trix provides 25% of the U.S. Recommended Daily Allowance of seven essential vitamins and iron.*

         b. *Delicious Trix. Nutritious. Convenient. Economical. And less sugar than an apple.*

One wants to ask why General Mills makes so much of its comparison of apples and Trix. I suspect the answer is that General Mills wants to persuade parents that if they do not object to their children's eating an apple, then, as far as sugar content is concerned, they shouldn't object to their children's eating Trix. Another possibility is that General Mills is trying to persuade parents and children alike that they should eat Trix instead of apples. Sugared cereals are eaten as snacks without milk by some children and the child who encounters the General Mills advertisement might believe that on grounds of sugar content alone he is better off eating Trix than eating an apple, which would not be true if the child ate much more than an ounce of Trix. In any event, it can be argued that the comparison of apples and Trix is infelicitous, for these things are not genuine alternatives.

Elliptical Comparatives

As we have noted, comparatives normally contain two term expressions naming objects or types of objects that are compared along the dimension named by the comparative adjective. However, as I have noted, one also finds elliptical comparatives, especially in advertising, that contain only a one term expression. Sentences (13) and (14) illustrate two quite different types of cases.

(13)   Thinner people live longer than fatter people.

(14)   New Dirtaway gets clothes cleaner.

Both (13) and (14) are clearly elliptical. In (13) the elliptical comparatives occur as prenominal modifiers and are interpreted along the lines of (15).[3]

---

[3]Alternatively, one might argue that (13) has an interpretation like (i).

(i)   People who are thin to some significant degree live longer than people who are fat to some significant degree.

(15)   People who are thinner than average live longer than people
         who are fatter than average.

Comparatives of this sort are quite common in advertising. In a issue of
Cosmopolitan (4/80), I found (16)–(18).

(16)   *Carlton. The lighter 100's.*

(17)   *The Limited Edition Regal Sommerset. If there is such a thing as a better
         looking Buick, this is it.*

(18)   *The Higher High Potency Vitamin.* (for Super Plenamins)

The Carlton phrase, *the lighter 100's* means 'the 100's which are lighter
than average'. The comparatives of (17) and (18) are interpreted in a
similar way. Examples (16) and (18) are of special interest, for each
conventionally implicates that the product is the **only** product possessing
the property named by the comparative adjective. Thus, the phrase *the
lighter 100's,* conventionally implicates that Carlton 100's are the only
100's that are lighter than average and the phrase, *the higher high potency
vitamin,* conventionally implicates that Super Plenamins are the only high
potency vitamins that are higher than average for high potency vitamins.
These are extraordinarily strong and surely quite false claims.

Comparatives like (13) all seem to be interpreted in the same sort of
way. However, there are no hard and fast rules for interpreting comparatives like (14). We might use (14) to say essentially the same thing as
(19), but we could also use (14) to say what (20) says.

(19)   New Dirtaway gets clothes clearner than old Dirtaway did.

(20)   New Dirtaway gets clothes cleaner than do competing products.

Although there is a sense in which interpretations like (19) and (20) are
especially natural, other interpretations are possible. Note, in particular,
that (14) is consistent with an interpretation along the lines of (21).

(21)   New Dirtaway gets clothes cleaner than they would get if no
         detergent were used.

Just how a given elliptical comparative like (14) will be interpreted will,
as we have noted, depend on the context in which it is used. However, it
is commonly the case that context does not fully disambiguate the elliptical comparatives of advertising.

Examples of comparatives that have interpretations along the lines of
(19)—we might call these *reflexive comparatives*—occur frequently,
primarily because product improvements are quite frequent. Consider
the following commercial for the 1978 Chevrolet:

(22)   1978 Chevrolet (CBS, 6/2/78, @ 9:21 p.m.)
        Type: Live action
        Setting: Outdoors
        Characters: Man

        TEXT
        Chorus (voice over): *See what's new today, in a Chevrolet.*
        Man: *To the more than 600,000 people who bought the new Chevrolet
        during its very first year, thank you. You've made it the most popular
        car in America. For the rest of you a simple reminder: with its
        advanced design,* **the new Chevrolet has more headroom, more rear
        seat legroom, more trunk room.** *So drive it. The new Chevrolet. Now
        that's more like it* [emphasis added].

The elliptical comparative of (22) can be interpreted along the lines of
(23) or along the lines of (24).

(23)   The new Chevrolet has more headroom, more rear seat
        legroom, more trunk space than did the previous model.

(24)   The new Chevrolet has more headroom, more rear seat
        legroom, more trunk space than competing automobiles.

Our knowledge that the new Chevrolet is not the first Chevrolet allows
an interpretation of the elliptical comparative of (22) as a reflexive comparative, i.e., as having the same meaning as (23). However, an interpretation like that of (24) is clearly possible. Clearly, (24) is the more interesting claim, but (23) is the more easily defended. The advertiser
should, of course, be held responsible for both interpretations.

If the comparative of commercial (22) is unclear, the comparatives of
the following commercial for Ty-D-Bol are bizarre.

(25)   Ty-D-Bol (WUAB, Cleveland, 2/24/78, @ 12:01 p.m.)
        Type: Live action
        Setting: Bathroom
        Characters: Adult male

        TEXT
        Man: *Now there are two great ways to help this part of your bathroom be
        clean and fresh. There's famous blue Ty-D-Bol automatic bowl
        cleaner with lemon-fresh borax. And now there's new green Ty-D-Bol
        with pine-scented borax. Both have the power of borax to clean and
        deodorize.* **So both are even tougher on stains, tougher on odors.** *Get
        Ty-D-Bol with borax. In original lemon-fresh blue or new pine-scented
        green Ty-D-Bol* [emphasis added].

The elliptical (bold italic) comparative of (25) is a discourse nonsequitur. In prefixing this statement by the word *so*, the advertiser signals that an inference is being drawn. However, the premises leading to this conclusion are missing. What is needed is a statement to the effect that both Ty-D-Bol products have somehow been improved over original blue Ty-D-Bol. How will it be interpreted? An inattentive viewer might fail to notice that the elliptical comparative of (25) is a nonsequitur and may, as a result, simply assume that premises supporting it have been established, i.e., that the products are superior to original blue Ty-D-Bol. According to this view (26) would have the same meaning as (27).

(26)   *So both are even tougher on stains, tougher on odors.*

(27)   So both blue and green Ty-D-Bol are even tougher on stains, tougher on odors than was blue Ty-D-Bol.

Viewers who do interpret (26) along the lines of (27) would, of course, be drawing what appears to be a false inference.

I believe viewers must either assign interpretation (27) to (26) and be misled or assign no interpretation, for (26) cannot, I think, be interpreted as being either a "competing products" comparative [see (28)] or as a "better than nothing" comparative [see (29)].

(28)   So both are even tougher on stains, tougher on odors than competing products.

(29)   So both are even tougher on stains, tougher on odors than plain water.

Explicit product comparisons used to be quite rare in television advertising, but are very common today. In some cases, precisely what the product being promoted is better than is made explicit. In others, it is not. Consider the following commercial for Ultra-Slim Lipstick.

(30)   Ultra-Slim (CBS, 1/6/81, 8:54 p.m.)
        Type: Live action
        Setting: Outdoors, in convertible automobile
        Characters: Woman

        TEXT
        Voice over (adult male): *Your lips are gonna drive people wild . . .*
        Woman: *. . . with this sleek design in lipstick. Ultra-Slim by Maybelline.
        Ultra-Slim lipstick is long and slim, with a slant tip for easy control **to
        go easier around the curves, easier around the corners,** to shape
        beautiful lips in racy creamy colors* [emphasis added].
        Voice over (adult male): *Your lips are gonna drive people wild. Ultra-Slim
        lipstick by Maybelline.*

The elliptical comparatives of (30) seem only to be interpretable as competing products comparatives. The same is true of the elliptical comparative of (31).

(31)   Raintree (ABC, 1/2/81, 6:17 p.m.)
        Type: Live action
        Setting: Movie set
        Characters: Natalie Wood

        TEXT
        Voice over (adult male); *Natalie Wood in* **West Side Story** *nineteen years ago. You should look at her now.*
        Natalie Wood: *I loved working* **West Side Story** *but I wouldn't go back. Today's what counts and Raintree helps you make the most of it.*
        Voice over (adult male): **Raintree moisturizer is different.** *It has natural protein complex, smooths dry skin lines even around your eyes and it's never greasy [emphasis added].*
        Natalie Wood: *If you're like me, you don't want to go back in time. You want to stay ahead of it.*
        Voice over (adult male): *Raintree keeps your age your secret.*

It is clear that Raintree is not being said to be different from what it was but that it is different from competing products.

In some cases an elliptical comparative can be interpreted as a competing products comparative even when the advertiser could argue that it is merely a reflexive comparative. Consider the following commercial for Ford vans:

(32)   Ford vans (ABC, 2/25/78, @ 5:30).
        Type: Live action
        Setting: Outdoors
        Characters: No on-screen characters speak

        TEXT
        Voice over (adult male): *There are more Ford vans on the road than any other make. And now your Ford dealer has a wide selection of vans, all with Ford's outfront van design,* **all with a more forward engine that gives you more room to move around inside** *them all, from hard-working business vans to Ford's free-wheeling vans and cruising vans that come already customized. There are more Ford vans on the road today than any other make, and a wide selection to choose from, at your Ford dealer [emphasis added].*

It is not clear here whether the *more forward engine* that gives consumers *more room to move around inside* is more relative to previous Ford vans or relative to competing vans. The reference in the first and last lines to other makes of vans might lead consumers to draw the inference that the Ford vans offer *more room to move around* than do competing types of vans. On the other hand, the advertiser might argue that he did not actually say this and that the comparative is meant to be a reflexive, product improvement type of comparative. It is clear from this why elliptical comparatives are attractive to advertisers. Reflexive comparatives are easier to defend than competing products comparatives, but are not nearly so impressive as competing products comparatives. An advertiser whose elliptical comparatives are sufficiently vague can imply that his product is better than competing products but argue that all he need defend is the claim that his product is better than before. Actually, the advertiser should be held responsible for both interpretations, for any other position would be linguistically indefensible.

Although elliptical comparatives will normally be either reflexive, product improvement comparatives or competing products comparatives, other interpretations are possible as I noted earlier. Consider (33).

(33)   Signal (NBC, 1/8/81, 9:06 p.m.)
        Type: Live action
        Setting: Two settings
        Characters: Two men and three women

        TEXT
        Setting: Kitchen
        Man 1: *Kiss me, I just tried the onion dip.*
        Woman 1: *Onion?*
        Man 1: *Come on, kiss me, I got the Signal.*
        Woman 1: *Nice.*
        Voice over (adult male): *Signal mouth wash fights strong mouth odors.*
        Setting: Band stand
        Woman 2: *Kiss me, I just had spaghetti with garlic.*
        Man 2: *Garlic?*
        Woman 2: *Go ahead, kiss me, I got the Signal.*
        Man 2: *Minty.*
        Voice over (adult male): **Signal fights strong mouth odors, even garlic, even onions, gives you fresher, cleaner breath.** *Clinical tests prove it, a kiss will prove it* [emphasis added].
        Woman 3: [To viewers]: *Kiss me, I got the Signal.*

The elliptical comparative of (33) could be interpreted as a competing products comparative, but a more likely interpretation is that it has the same meaning as (34).

(34)   Signal fights strong mouth odors, even garlic, even onions, gives

you fresher cleaner breath than you would have if you used
no mouth wash at all.

We have, then, the third possible interpretation for elliptical comparatives, a "better than nothing" interpretation.

Elliptical competing products comparatives are of special linguistic
interest, for in suggesting that some product is better than competing
products it is not clear whether the competing products are just some
competing products or all competing products. Reconsider the elliptical
comparative of (31), repeated as (35).

(35)   *Raintree Moisturizer is different. It has natural protein complex, smooths
         dry skin lines even around your eyes and it's never greasy.*

Claim (35) conversationally implicates (Maxim of Relevance) that Raintree differs from competing products in that it contains natural protein
complex (whatever that means), smooths dry skin lines, and is never
greasy. But is Raintree being said to be different from just some competing products in these respects or from all competing products? In my
view, the comparative in (35) conversationally implicates (Maxim of
Strength) that the product being promoted is different from all competing products in having all three properties mentioned, for a weaker
interpretation is in no way hinted at.

In some cases, as in the Ty-D-Bol commercial, elliptical comparatives
are quite meaningless if examined carefully. A good deal more puzzling
is commercial (36).

(36)   **Nu-Maid Margarine** (CBS, 2/24/78, @ 12:59 p.m.)
         Type: Live action
         Setting: Indoors
         Characters: No on-screen characters speak

         TEXT
         Voice over (adult male): *If you're not putting Nu-Maid margarine on top of
         all your favorite foods, you're letting your taste down because
         Nu-Maid has a rich, full flavor all its own. And that rich, full Nu-Maid
         flavor has a uniquely delicious way of really raising the taste of
         a raisin muffin, or lifting the golden taste of corn right off the cob.
         **And when Nu-Maid's on the top, the taste of green beans sprouts up
         even higher.** So don't let your taste down. Put Nu-Maid on top*
         [emphasis added].

The comparative of commercial (36) is very difficult to interpret. The
presence of *even* is the complicating factor, for it suggests that putting
Nu-Maid on top of green beans makes the taste of green beans sprout up

higher than does putting it on a raisin muffin or corn on the cob. However, given the imperfect recall of real time television messages by
viewers, the odds are very good that viewers will interpret it as a competing products imperative.

It should be clear that the enterprise of placing precise meanings on
elliptical comparatives can be fraught with difficulties. In some cases, I
suspect that copywriters may toss elliptical comparatives into commercials without having any very clear meaning in mind. Certainly, the
comparative of (36) is anything but· clear. Of course, the real time
character of television commercials will have the effect of leading consumers to fail to recognize vague or even nonsensical comparatives for
what they are.

I have claimed that advertisers should be held responsible for all
linguistically defensible interpretations of vague or ambiguous claims.
The advertiser who makes a claim C which has interpretations I_1 and I_2,
where I_1 is false and I_2 true, might try to wriggle out of the charge of
false advertising by saying he didn't actually make false claim I_1. However, he didn't make true claim I_2 either. What he did was make two
claims, I_1 and I_2 and he should be held responsible for both I_1 and I_2.
Adoption of this perspective on ambiguous or vague claims would have
the saluatory effect of forcing advertisers to be explicit.

Multiple Comparatives

The very best possible commercial offer from the point of view of the
consumer, is to be offered something for nothing. Although "something
for nothing" offers are not infrequent, especially in retail advertising,
there is usually some sort of catch. Thus, most "something for nothing"
sales are "two for one" sales or "three for two" sales, etc. But a "two for
one" offer is not a "something for nothing" offer. It is a "more of something for the same amount of money" offer. A genuine "something for
nothing" offer would be a case in which a retailer opens his doors and
invites consumers to come in and take what they want. The manufacturer who gives out free samples is as close to making a "something for
nothing" offer as American consumers are ever likely to see.

Second only to a genuine "something for nothing offer" in strength is
a "more for less" offer, wherein the advertiser increases the amount of
product the consumer gets while decreasing the amount of money the
consumer has to pay. In a 1978 television commercial, General Motors
made the following "more for less" offer:

(37)   **Chevrolet Chevette** (NBC, 2/25/78, evening)
         Type: Live action
         Setting: Studio
         Characters: Man

TEXT

Singers: *See what's new today.*
Man: *Chevrolet announces "A lot more Chevette for a lot less money."*
New Chevette standard equipment includes a radio, reclining bucket
seats, white wall tires, console, sports steering wheel, a 1.6 litre
engine: 18 new standard features in all. Plus a wide hatch, carpeting,
front disc brakes, rack and pinion steering, and more. The '78 Chevy
Chevette. A lot more car for a lot less money.

Toward the end of this commercial, a printed disclaimer is shown on
screen, which reads as follows:

(38)   *Comparison of manufacturer's suggested retail prices for a '77 Chevette*
         with features now standard on '78 Chevettes. Except Scooter.

Let us begin our analysis of this commercial with its oral text, item
(37). Someone who hears (37) and does not read (38) must draw the
inference that General Motors is offering the standard 1978 Chevette,
which is an improvement on the standard 1977 Chevette, for less money
than the standard 1977 Chevette cost. However, it is clear from the
disclaimer that what General Motors means to be comparing is not the
standard 1978 Chevette and the standard 1977 Chevette but the standard 1978 Chevette and a comparable 1977 Chevette, i.e., a 1977
Chevette with all of the features of the standard 1978 Chevette. I don't
mean to be saying that either the oral or written texts is ambiguous on
this point, but that they are actually inconsistent with each other.

Before going on to assess the truth of the General Motors "more for
less" claim, we will do well to consider whether or not the average television viewer will have been able to read the printed disclaimer. The
disclaimer (see Photograph 4.2) contains three lines, each of which uses
3.7% of the vertical height of the television screen. The disclaimer appears on screen for just 5 seconds and presupposes a reading speed of
228 words per minute. Finally, and this is very important, the printed
disclaimer competes with a very different oral message for the viewer's
attention. I have shown this commercial to four college graduates and
they, like me, reported being unable to read the disclaimer in the time it
was on screen even though they were asked to ignore the oral message.
In short, the odds against the average viewer's being able to read this
disclaimer are very high.

In order to assess the truth of the Chevette "more for less" offer, we

Photograph 4.2

must know the price of the standard 1978 Chevette, the price of the standard 1977 Chevette and the price of a 1977 Chevette equipped with those features that were made standard in 1978. The problem in so doing is that General Motors uses the word *feature* in (37) not *option*. A car option is normally understood to be a car property that can separately be added to a car for a certain price. A car feature is any car property whatsoever. The ability of a car to be driven in reverse is a car feature but has never, to my knowledge, been offered as a car option. The specific difficulty of the use by General Motors of the term *feature* is that sources of information generally available list the prices of car options not car features. As a result, although I consulted the sales manager of a Columbus, Ohio, dealership, Edmund's buyer's guides, and material graciously supplied me by Consumers Union, I was never able to confirm that 18 features that were optional in 1977 were made standard in 1978. I don't question General Motors' claim, for given the vagueness of the term *feature* it would not be hard for General Motors to "justify" it (e.g., by splitting one or more features up into several separate features). However, I was unable to determine precisely what a 1977 Chevette, equipped in the same way as the standard 1978 Chevette, would have cost.

Let us grant that a 1978 Chevette cost less (even a lot less) than a comparable 1977 Chevette would have cost. Is the "more for less" claim true? In fact, there are two "more for less" claims as we noted earlier. According to the oral text, what is being claimed is that a standard 1978 Chevette is more car than and cost a lot less than a standard 1977 Chevette. The claim of the disclaimer is that a 1978 is more car than and cost a lot less than a comparable 1977. The following table summarizes the facts.

	a lot more Chevette	for	a lot less money
Standard '78 versus Standard '77	True	False	False
Standard '78 versus Comparable '77	False	False	True

In order for *a lot more Chevette for a lot less money* to be true, both halves of the claim must be true of some pair of cars. Consider, first, the comparison class of the oral text, namely, standard 1978 and standard 1977 Chevettes. I am willing to concede that the standard 1978 Chevette is a lot more car than the standard 1977 Chevette. However, according to 1977 and 1978 Edmund's buyer's guides, the standard 1978 Chevette cost $3354 and the 1977 Chevette cost $3225. Thus, the 1978 Chevette did not cost a lot less than the 1977 Chevette, it cost more. Thus the "more for less" claim is false on this interpretation. What of the other interpretation? I have conceded that the standard 1978 Chevette may have cost a lot less than a comparable 1977 Chevette, but the 1978 Chevette is not a lot more car than a comparable 1977 Chevette. They are precisely the same car. Thus, the "more for less" claim of the disclaimer is also false.

I do not know what role the deceptive "more for less" campaign had on the success of the 1978 Chevette. However, the 1978 Chevette did become the best selling small car in America, if one can believe subsequent television advertisements. Moreover, there is some reason to believe that General Motors had great confidence in this campaign, for the next year General Motors used it for two automobile lines, the 1979 Pontiac Sunbird and the 1979 Chevrolet Monza. Interestingly, two-page "more for less" advertisements appeared for each car in a single issue of *Sports Illustrated* (9/25/78) (see Photographs 4.3 and 4.4.)

In the Pontiac Sunbird advertisement (Photograph 4.3) the "more for less" claim is *MORE SUNBIRD . . . FOR LESS! $3781!.* The similarities of this

Photograph 4.3

Photograph 4.4

advertisement and the television advertisement for the 1978 Chevette
are remarkable. Compare (39) with the oral text of the 1978 television
commercial, which I repeat as (40).

(39)   *What better way to* **announce** *1979 than by announcing more Pontiac
         Sunbird Coupe.* **Now,** *this sporty little machine comes with more*
         standard features *than ever before. Delco AM radio, custom wheel
         covers, whitewall tires, body side molding, tinted glass all around.* **All
         newly standard for '79. Plus** *Delco Freedom battery, new deep
         contour bucket seats, front disc brakes, a kicky 2.5 litre four-cylinder
         engine, four-speed manual shift. Body by Fisher* **and more. More
         Sunbird value. For less money** [emphasis added].

(40)   *Chevrolet* **announces** *"a lot more Chevette for a lot less money."* **New**
         Chevette **standard equipment** *includes a radio, white wall tires,
         console, sports steering wheel, a 1.6 litre engine: 18* **new standard
         features in all. Plus** *a wide hatch, carpeting, front disc brakes, rack
         and pinion steering,* **and more.** *This '78 Chevy Chevette.* **A lot more
         car for a lot less money** [emphasis added].

It is clear that the 1979 Pontiac Sunbird advertising campaign was closely
modeled on that for the 1978 Chevette, and within the advertising industry, only successful advertising campaigns are likely to be repeated.

The text of (40) makes reasonably clear that what follows *plus* are
features that were standard in 1977, which does appear to be true. The
advertisement for the 1979 Sunbird is a little less clear on this point.
The previously mentioned 1978 Edmund's publication suggests that the
radio, custom wheel covers, whitewall tires, body side moldings, and
tinted glass are all optional in 1978. What of the features named after
the word *plus*? If the Delco Freedom battery is what Edmund's calls a
heavy duty battery, then this also was optional in 1978. However, Edmund's publication lists a heavy duty battery as a 1979 option also. Thus,
I conclude that the Delco battery was standard in 1978. However, the
phrase *new deep contour bucket seats* suggests that this feature was optional in 1978, or did not exist. However, the 1978 Edmund's publication
lists bucket seats as standard equipment in 1978. Thus, the remaining
features after *plus* were standard in 1978.

The total cost of the 1978 options that were made standard in 1979
had they been purchased in 1978 appears to have been $297. Given this
figure, we can now evaluate the "more for less" claim. Edmund's publications give the manufacturer's suggested list price for the 1978 two-door
coupe as $3540 and a figure (that agrees with the Pontiac advertisement)
of $3781 for the 1979 version of this car. Thus, the price of a 1978
Sunbird that was comparable to the 1979 Sunbird was $56 **more** than the

price of the 1979 Sunbird. But, this does not make the "more for less" claim true because the 1979 Sunbird is not more car than a comparable 1978 Sunbird. It is the same car. Thus the 1979 "more for less" Sunbird advertising campaign is predicated on precisely the same false comparison as was the 1978 Chevette advertising campaign.

What then of the 1979 Monza *More car, more kicks, less money* campaign? The cost of the optional features that were said in this advertisement to have become standard in 1979 (tinted glass, AM radio, sport steering wheel, shift console, and body side moldings) was $259 in 1978 according to the Edmund's publication. This publication gives $3609 as the price of the 1978 2 + 2 Hatchback Coupe. Therefore, the price of a 1978 Monza with the designated options was $3868. According to Edmund's 1979 publications, this same car cost $3970 in 1979, which is not **less** than a comparable 1978 Monza, but $102 **more.** Thus, considering just these figures, we must conclude that the 1979 Monza was not more car than a comparable 1978. It is the same car, and it does not appear to have cost less, but to have cost more.

There is a passage in the Monza advertisement that may explain the apparent discrepancy in the relative cost of the 1979 Monza and a comparable 1978 car: *More kicks with its new higher output standard 2.5 litre 4-cylinder engine (or available in V6 or V8). Even more kicks with an upgraded level of quality in vinyl interior trim, and newly designed high-back front bucket seats.* It could very well be that these improvements would have cost more than $102 had they been available in 1978. However, if these improvements were not available in 1978 then there was no 1978 Monza including the designated options that was identical to the 1979 Monza. This fact, if it is a fact, very badly complicates the analysis of the *more car, more kicks, less money* claim.

If certain features of the 1979 Monza were not actually available as options in 1978, then General Motors could argue that the 1979 Monza was more car than the 1978 Monza. However, the claim that the 1979 Monza cost less than a comparable 1978 Monza becomes meaningless, for a genuine price comparison depends on the existence of a 1978 Monza that did not exist, namely a 1978 Monza with the *new higher output* engine, the *upgraded* vinyl trim, and the *newly designed* seats. However, if we were to grant, for the sake of argument, that this hypothetical car would have cost more than the 1979 Monza, the *more car, more kicks, less money* claim would cease to be meaningless: It would become false, for this hypothetical 1978 Monza would not be less car than the 1979 Monza. It would be the same car.

General Motors is not, of course, the only firm to use the "more for less" type claim. On October 31, 1979, I received a flyer in the mail from the Bonanza restaurant chain which stated, *Get More Meal for Less Money at Bonanza* and *More Steak Dinner for Less!* This "more for less" campaign consisted of two sirloin strip dinners for more than the normal price of one such dinner and less than the price of two such dinners. As we shall see, this turns out not to be a "more for less" offer but a "less for less" offer.

The advertisement in question consisted of a business letter sized sheet of paper folded into a rectangular envelope shape, reading *More Steak Dinner for Less!* on the front and *Get More Meal for Less Money at Bonanza* on the back. On the "inside" there was a headline claim (41), a photograph of a sample dinner, coupons, and additional copy.

(41)   *A Special Sirloin Strip Dinner for 2 plus all the salad you can eat!*

On my first reading of this advertisement, I assumed that what made the *Special Sirloin Strip Dinner for 2* more meal than two regular Sirloin Strip Dinners was the offer of *all the salad you can eat*. This interpretation follows from the fact that for a proposition of the form *X plus Y* to be true, *Y* cannot be part of *X*. Ten plus 5 is equal to 15, not 10. In fact, unlimited salad is part of regular Bonanza dinners. That the Bonanza definition of dinner includes unlimited salad, contra claim (41), is in fact made clear in the following passage from this advertisement:

(42)   *No one wants to get ripped off, especially in today's economy. That's why you can't afford to pass up a real old-fashioned value—a Sirloin Strip Dinner for 2 for only $5.99!. That includes (at no extra charge) a baked potato—a thick slice of Texas toast—and all the salad and fixings you can help yourself to at our famous Discovery Salad Bar.*

It is clear then that claim (41) is quite misleading.

The phrase *Special Sirloin Strip Dinner* was accompanied by *Chef's Special Cut—limited time only* in small print at the side of the photograph of the sample dinner. I asked an employee at a Columbus, Ohio, Bonanza restaurant how the "special" sirloin strip differed from the regular one and was told that it was 1 oz smaller than the regular steak. This use of special is clearly misleading, for the word special in a commercial offer normally indicates a benefit to the consumer. For instance, the phrase, *on special,* is equivalent to *on sale.*

Is the Bonanza "more for less" offer true? At the time of this offer, a regular sirloin strip dinner sold for $4.09, so two such dinners would have cost $8.18, which is $2.19 more than the two "special" sirloin strip dinners. However, two "special" sirloin strip dinners is not more meal than two regular sirloin strip dinners; it is less meal. Thus, this Bonanza "more for less" offer would appear not to be genuine.

One last "more for less" advertising campaign is worth brief mention here, for, although a bit tricky linguistically, it is not deceptive in the ways the General Motors and Bonanza "more for less" offers, are. The advertising claim, made on behalf of Gentle Spring Disposable Douche, was *More solution ... costs less ... you'll love new Gentle Spring* (*Cosmopolitan*, 7/79). The specific claim of interest is that *Gentle Spring actually holds a full 12 ounces ... twice as much as Summer's Eve and Massengill.*

Gentle Spring consists of a water-soluable powder in a disposable bag to which the user adds 12 oz of water. The products Summer's Eve and Massengill, on the other hand, are ready to use and contain 4½ oz and 6 oz of solution, respectively. Thus, once water is added to the Gentle Spring bag it does contain twice as much (or more) than the competing products. Moreover, the claim that Gentle Spring costs less than Summer's Eve and Massengill appears to be true as well.

The "more for less" type claim is a multiple comparative, for it contains two comparatives. So also are "more for your money" type claims, for these amount to a "more product for the same amount of money" claim and *same* is a comparative. Consider the following commercial for the Continental Insurance Company.

(43)   Continental Insurance (CBS, 6/2/78, 9:20 p.m.)
        Type: Live action
        Setting: Outdoors
        Characters: *Man*

        TEXT
        Man: *If this were your home, that delivery man could sue you for everything you've got. And if most of your liability coverage was on your car instead of your home, you'd be in big trouble. That's why Continental invented the PCP car and home policy. It gives the same high liability coverage on your car, and your home.* **That's more protection for your money** *and one more reason why nobody spells "protection" like the Continental Insurance companies* [emphasis added].

Commercial (43) is rather vague. Let us assume that Continental offers liability coverage to degree D on both one's home and car for price P. For the claim *That's more protection for your money* to be true, it must be the case that other insurance companies will either charge more than P for degree of coverage D (on both home and car) or that other insurance companies do not offer as much coverage as D (on both home and car) but still charge P or more. The advertisement suggests these situations exist but doesn't actually defend this suggestion. It is entirely possible

Photograph 4.5

that all that is being claimed is that the "*D* for *P*" offer is better than a "less than *D* for *P*" offer would be, but this is a tautology.

General Motors' fondness for multiple comparatives extends to its 1979 *More Pontiac to the Gallon* campaign (*Sports Illustrated*, 5/28/79). This is a multiple comparative, for two models of the Pontiac are compared—the 1979 and 1976 Catalinas—with respect to both size and gas mileage (see Photograph 4.5.).

The sense in which the 1979 Catalina was said to be *more Pontiac* than tbe 1976 Catalina was that the former had more headroom, more legroom and more overall passenger and luggage volume. Moreover, the 1979 Catalina was said to get better mileage than the 1976 Catalina did. Consider

(45)   *What's more, the estimated MPG figures is 38% better than just a few years ago. (Percentage increase less in California). That's comparing '76 and '79 Catalinas equipped with standard engines. Rather impressive.*

The key phrase in this passage is *standard engine,* a phrase that has a constant meaning ('the engine that comes with an automobile at no extra charge'), but can vary in reference from year to year. In fact, General Motors achieved its better gas mileage in 1979 in part by radically decreasing the size of its "standard engine" from 400 cu. in. in 1976 to 231 cu. in. in 1979. Thus, while the 1979 Catalina may have gotten 38% better mileage over the 1976 Catalina, it did so, in part, by reducing the engine size by 42% and the horsepower of the engine by 20% (from 170/4000 rpm to 135/4000 rpm).

Nowhere in the General Motors advertisement for the 1979 Catalina does General Motors reveal that the reference of the phrase *standard engine* changed from 1976 to 1979. As a result, the unwary reader might not realize that while the 1979 Catalina might be "more car" along one dimension (passenger and luggage volume) it is clearly "less car" along another (engine size).

One might go one step further and raise the question: How much can a car model (or any other product) change before it ought to be given a different name? This question involves both meaning and reference distinction. General Motors would very probably take the position that the "meaning" of any particular General Motors car model name is defined relative to the other models General Motors makes. According to this view, Pontiac cars remain in the same position relative to Cadillacs, Buicks, Oldsmobiles, and Chevrolets, for all have changed in essentially the same ways in recent years. I have no real quarrel with this line of reasoning, but consumers should be aware that while the "meaning" of

Pontiac Catalina may not have changed in recent years, the reference has changed a good deal.

Conclusion

As we have seen, comparatives in advertising present a variety of problems of a nontrivial character for consumers. Elliptical comparatives are often hopelessly vague and are sometimes quite meaningless if examined carefully. When they occur in television advertising the problems posed become virtually insurmountable, for remembering exactly what actually was said in a television commercial is normally very difficult if not impossible. I would be the last to suggest that elliptical comparatives be banned on television. Our First Amendment rights would surely preclude such a move anyway. However, when an advertiser uses an elliptical comparative that is ambiguous, he should clearly be held responsible for all linguistically defensible interpretations.

Consumers would do well to examine "more for less" claims very closely for, as we have seen, some are quite false. The difficulty here is that evaluating "more for less" claims is none too easy to do. In my view, those responsible for monitoring advertising should routinely examine all such claims, for, in my experience, they are more often false than true.

Chapter 5

Some Words and Phrases
of Advertising English

William Shakespeare once claimed that a rose by any other name would smell as sweet. If what Shakespeare meant is that the things of this world have the physical properties they have irrespective of the names we give them, then what he said is true enough. However, if what he meant to claim is that the words we use to refer to things have no influence on how we perceive these things, then what he said is very far from being true. The name *horse mackerel* was once used to refer to a large, relatively easily caught and easily processed fish, and fish packers wanted very much to market it. Unfortunately, it seems that few people wanted to eat horse mackerel. This marketing problem was solved once the name of this fish was changed to *tuna*. Tuna, it seems, tastes better than horse mackerel did.

Human perception is selective and the language we use to refer to things and to describe these things can influence how we perceive them and the judgments we make about them. In this chapter, I propose to examine a variety of lexical and phrase level phenomena in an attempt to shed light on how advertisers use language to shape consumer perceptions. We shall take up the use of descriptive terms in brand names, terms used by OTC drug advertisers to refer to the symptoms such drugs are designed to treat, and the use of explicit and implicit similes in advertising.

Product Names

Advertisers do not share Shakespeare's apparent disdain for names, and for good reason. Some product names are miniadvertisements in

their own right. The name *Groom and Clean* (hair gel for men) suggests
that the product will assist in grooming and cleaning one's hair, the latter
property being a quite remarkable one if true. The name *The Dry Look*
(men's hair spray) suggests that use of the product will result in dry
looking hair. It further suggests (conversationally implicates through the
Maxim of Relevance) that use of other hair sprays will result in wetter
looking hair. The name *Nice 'n Easy* (hair colorer) suggests that the
product is easy to use. And so on.

Product names are an integral feature of product packages and can
assist in attracting attention to a product at the point of sale. This would
be especially true of those product names that serve as miniadvertisements and those that attract attention by virtue of being unusual in some
way. It is difficult not to be attracted to a product name like *Small Miracle*
(hair conditioner) or *Vanquish* (pain reliever) or *Easy to Be Me* (panty
hose) or *I can't believe it's a girdle* (girdle).

From the perspective of advertising, the fact that a product name is
itself a miniadvertisement or an attention-getting device would be quite
important, of course. However, the primary function of the product
name in a context like television advertising is to serve as a link between
advertising and sales. The average large supermarket contains around
10,000 different items and, as a result, it would hardly be surprising if a
shopper were not sometimes to simplify the choices he or she must make
by going with products that he or she is familiar with. Thus, an advertisement that simply plants a product name in consumer's minds may be
reasonably effective. Certainly, some television commercials seem to be
designed primarily with this purpose in mind. Recall, for instance, the
Bubble Yum commercial discussed in Chapter 1.

Although product names are noun phrases, virtually any linguistic
construction can be used as a product name. Consider

(1)   a. Names with nouns as heads
        1. *Secret* (deodorant), a noun
        2. *Good News* (razor), adjective plus noun
        3. *The Dry Look* (hair spray), a conventional article, adjective,
            noun sequence
        4. *Fruit Stripe* (gum), a noun compound
        5. *Head and Shoulders* (shampoo), compounded nouns
        6. *Body on Tap* (shampoo), a noun-prepositional phrase
            sequence
       b. Names with adjectives as heads
        1. *Sure* (deodorant), a simple adjective
        2. *More* (cigarette), a comparative adjective

3. *Most* (cigarette), a superlative adjective
4. *Naturally Dry* (deodorant powder), an adverb–adjective sequence
5. *Short and Sassy* (shampoo), compounded adjectives
6. *Easy to Be Me* (panty hose), complex adjective phrase

c. Names with verbs as heads
  1. *Rave* (home permanent), a verb
  2. *Groom and Clean* (hair gel), compounded verbs

d. Names consisting of prepositions
  1. *Off* (insect repellant)

e. Names consisting of sentences
  1. *I can't believe it's a girdle* (girdle)

I have not yet come across product names consisting of prepositional phrases or adverbs, etc., but it doesn't take much imagination to think up such possibilities.

Proper names present a very interesting semantic problem of great importance to the understanding of how consumers will interpret them, and this is true whether or not they have meaning. Certainly, proper names have reference. Their primary function is to refer to or designate or pick out some individual object in the world, some thing (*The White House*) or place (*Washington*) or person (*Ronald Reagan*). In this respect, proper names are like definite descriptions, i.e., noun phrases that (usually) consist of the article *the*, some common noun, and one or more adjectives or restrictive relative clauses, etc., such as *the official residence of the President of the United States*. The definite description *The official residence of the President of the United States*, like the proper name *The White House*, refers to a particular building in Washington. However, there is a fundamental difference between these two constructions. The definite description, *the official residence of the President of the United States*, refers to the White House in virtue of its meaning, which is a compositional function of the meanings of the words that comprise it. On the other hand, if a proper noun like *The White House* has meaning, it is certainly not a function of the meanings of the words it is composed of. We might continue to refer to the White House as *The White House* even if Nancy Reagan were to have it painted pink. Similarly, the name *Crazy Horse* does not pick out the American Indian it refers to in virtue of the (conventional) meanings of *crazy* and *horse*. Crazy Horse was presumably not crazy and was certainly not a horse.

Consider the names *Fruit Stripe* (gum), *Froot Loops* (cereal), and *Fruit Roll* (rolled up sheets of dried fruit). Fruit Stripe gum contains no fruit and is artificially flavored. Froot Loops cereal contains no fruit but is naturally flavored. Fruit Roll, as noted, consists of fruit. Clearly, whether or not these products contain fruit cannot be determined from the names they have. The question arises whether or not the use of the word *fruit* in the name *Fruit Stripe* and perhaps also in *Froot Loops* is misleading.

If proper names do not have meaning, then it's difficult to see how one could reasonably object to a name like *Fruit Stripe*. Moreover, even if it could be shown that proper nouns do have meaning it would not necessarily follow that descriptive terms in product names have conventional meanings when used in such names. If we concede that *The White House* would continue to designate the White House even if Nancy Reagan had it painted pink then surely we must concede that the word *fruit* in *Fruit Stripe* need not have its conventional meaning to be used legitimately in this product name.

There is reason to believe that proper names must have meaning in some sense of the word. Note that if proper nouns do nothing but refer, then any two or more names that refer to the same thing must be completely equivalent semantically. It should then also follow that if one of these names were to occur in a true (false) proposition then it should be the case that one can substitute any referentially equivalent proper name for it in this proposition without changing its truth value. Observe in this connection that (2) and (3) are logically equivalent.

(2)   Mark Twain wrote *Tom Sawyer*.

(3)   Samuel Clemens wrote *Tom Sawyer*.

There are contexts in which referentially equivalent proper names are not mutually substitutable. Compare (4) and (5).

(4)   John Jones believes that the man who is married to Nancy
         Reagan is president.

(5)   John Jones believes that the man who preceded Jerry Brown as
         governor of California is president.

Clearly, John Jones could know that the man who is married to Nancy Reagan is president but have no idea who preceded Jerry Brown as governor of California. Given this scenario, we would have to say that (4) is true and that (5) is false. Since *the man who is married to Nancy Reagan* and *the man who preceded Jerry Brown as governor of California* are referentially equivalent, we must attribute the difference in truth value of (4) and (5) to some difference in the meanings of these phrases. This seems reasonable, for the two phrases do not have the same meaning.

Observe that if John Jones has never heard of Samuel Clemens, but has read *Tom Sawyer* and knows it was written by Mark Twain, then (6) would be true and (7) false.

(6)   John Jones believes that Mark Twain wrote *Tom Sawyer*.

(7)   John Jones believes that Samuel Clemens wrote *Tom Sawyer*.

Given that *Mark Twain* and *Samuel Clemens* are referentially identical, it would appear that these two proper nouns must differ in some other respect, namely in meaning.

What we might say is that proper nouns do have meaning but that the meanings they have are not directly a function of the meanings of the words that comprise them. Moreover, we would also want to say that the meanings of proper nouns can vary idiosyncratically from person to person in a way that the meanings of common nouns do not. We might say that the meaning of a proper noun consists of some set of properties satisfied by what the proper noun refers to. Any of the following properties might apply, for instance, to Ronald Reagan.

(8)   a. The president of the United States.
       b. A former governor of California.
       c. The man who preceded Jerry Brown as governor of California.
       d. The husband of Nancy Reagan.
       e. The man who played The Gipper in a movie about Knute Rockne.

Clearly, different people can and will know a person or thing by different properties, and it is this that accounts for failure of substitutability. One of the properties of the person referred to by *Mark Twain* is that he is Samuel Clemens and one of the properties of Samuel Clemens is that he wrote under the pseudonym of *Mark Twain*. Someone who does not know Mark Twain or Samuel Clemens by these properties would be said to attribute different meanings to *Mark Twain* and *Samuel Clemens* than would someone who does know these things. Thus, it is quite reasonable that (6) and (7) could have different truth values.

One of the more interesting properties of names like *Fruit Stripe*, *Froot Loops*, and *Fruit Roll*, all of which are noun compounds, is that the head nouns (*Stripe*, *Loops*, and *Roll*) can be interpreted more or less literally, that is, *Stripe*, *Loops*, and *Roll* could be said to have something like the same meanings as *stripe*, *loops*, and *roll: Fruit Stripe* gum has stripes on it; *Froot Loops* consist of doughnut-shaped cereal; and *Fruit Roll* consists of rolled up sheets of dried fruit. On the other hand, the "modifying" noun of noun compounds used as product names are sometimes much less closely related semantically to the corresponding common nouns. *Fruit Roll* consists of fruit, but *Fruit Stripe* and *Froot Loops* do not. *Froot Loops* is naturally flavored and *Fruit Stripe* is artificially flavored, so the relationship they bear to fruit is having a flavor like that of fruit. Certainly, *Fruit Stripe* and *Froot Loops* do not consist of stripes of fruit and loops of fruit, respectively.

Surely most adults have learned not to trust the implicit promises of product names. However, names like *Fruit Stripe* and *Froot Loops* cannot help but mislead children who have not developed sufficient market wisdom or cynicism to realize that manufacturers sometimes take certain liberties with the words they use in product names. This problem is compounded for children by the fact that numerous products do deliver on the impliict promises of their names. In the interests of fair business competition and of truth, especially in the area of children's products, a requirement that there be some substantive connection between the ordinary meanings and referents of the words used in a product name and the product itself would not be unreasonable for at least some products, including, in particular, the names of foods and drugs.

Some Phrases Characteristic of OTC Drug Advertising

Although physicians themselves sometimes prescribe OTC drugs for use by patients, such drugs are normally not taken under the supervision of physicians. In general, consumers determine a need for some OTC drug as a result of self-diagnosis. In the best of circumstances, a consumer's self-diagnosis will be accurate and he or she will select only drugs that are consistent with the diagnosis.

Language can play an important role in consumer choice of OTC drugs. Suppose someone who has never had athlete's foot contracts this malady. Suppose further that the consumer observes that the areas between some of his or her toes are inflamed and that they itch and burn. Such a consumer will surely have heard of the term *athlete's foot* and may suspect that this is his or her problem. On examining packages of athlete's foot medication, he or she will, on at least one such package, find reference to the capacity of the medication to relieve burning and itching between the toes. It is the coincidence of the consumer's language for referring to symptoms and the language of OTC drug labels that would be the primary criterion for selection of an OTC drug in cases like the one just cited where the consumer does not know precisely what ails him or her and has not received competent advice.

In recent years, as a part of a general review of the effectiveness of OTC drugs, the Federal Drug Administration (FDA) has made the decision that some of the language used on OTC drug labels has been inaccurate in various ways and now requires that the language used on OTC drug labels be medically sound. It has established or is still in the process of establishing a vocabulary appropriate to "indications for use" that is not only medically sound, but is also understandable to consumers. Interestingly, the OTC drug industry objected very little to this FDA effort.

In late 1975, the FTC announced its intention to promulgate a rule prohibiting claims made by OTC drug advertisers in their advertising that would not be approved by the FDA. Since the phrases used to refer to "indications for use" are central to the import of claims containing these phrases, much of the attention of the FTC has been focused on such phrases. Although the OTC drug industry did not put up much of a fuss at the FDA decisions affecting drug labeling, it vigorously objected to the FTC rule. From this, I draw the inference that the OTC drug industry itself recognizes that it is the language of drug advertising, not the language of drug labels, that sells drugs.

The concern of the FDA and FTC has been that language should be medically sound and understandable to consumers. Naturally there is room for disagreement on what phrases are medically optimal and are understandable to consumers. One of the real difficulties of satisfying these two criteria is the virtually inevitable tension between the language of science (in this case, medicine) and ordinary language. Scientists construct technical language because there exist no ordinary language equivalents or because ordinary language terms are inadequate in that they are too vague to be usable, too broad in meaning, or too narrow in meaning. The FDA and FTC have found fault with terms used on OTC drug labels or in OTC drug advertising on such grounds.

The least defensible terms used in OTC drug advertising are terms describing maladies or symptoms that do not exist. Geritol's now discredited term *tired blood* is such an example. The phrase *tired blood* entails that blood can somehow "wear out" or "get tired." Since this product was targeted at older people (note the name), some consumers must have assumed that blood or our capacity to regenerate blood can degenerate as we age. To people not knowledgeable about biology, this must have seemed quite plausible. One could also include in this category the term *irregularity,* used in the advertising of drugs designed to treat constipation. The problem here is with the implication that having irregular bowel movements is or should be a cause for concern. As noted in an

FTC Staff Report (FTC, 1979), there was concern within the FDA that this term could lead people to take medication on a regular basis in order to achieve regularity.

Advertisers of OTC drugs have also used terms that are so vague that no clear referent can be specified. The linguist Charles Fillmore cited *the blahs, out of balance,* and *fizzled out* (FTC, 1979) as instances of this. To some degree, use of such terms could work to the disadvantage of advertisers, for if consumers are unclear about what a term used in an OTC drug advertisement refers to, they will not know when they might need the drug.

During the FTC hearings on OTC drug advertising, three issues arose of real linguistic and medical interest: These are (*a*) the use of terms that are overbroad in meaning; (*b*) the use of terms that are overspecific in meaning; and (*c*) the question whether "synonyms" for FDA approved terms should be permitted in OTC drug advertising. Linguists, including Fillmore in particular, played an important role in the adjudication of these issues. Although it appears that the FTC commissioners will reject the proposed FTC rule, these issues are nevertheless important and worthy of discussion.

The potential harm in the use of terms that are overbroad in meaning is clear. Consider, for instance, the term *upset stomach.* The range of problems that might lead a consumer to believe that he or she has an upset stomach includes among other things, heartburn, acid indigestion, stomach gas, hiatus hernia, stomach ulcers, and stomach cancer. There is no drug that can relieve symptoms of all these maladies. The problem with advertising that claims that a particular OTC drug can relieve an upset stomach is that consumers may use the drug when such use is inappropriate. In this light, consider the following commercial for Pepto-Bismol.

(9)   Pepto-Bismol (ABC, 1/2/81, 6:16 p.m.)
        Type: Live action
        Setting: Outside tent
        Characters: Napoleon

        TEXT
        Napoleon: *Hello, I'm Napoleon Bonaparte. It's been like this all winter. Eat and run, eat and run, Look, a new cannon.* [Cannon has been destroyed.] *When I finally get 5 minutes to eat, what do I eat: wet snow and cold beans. It's enough to give even an emperor an upset stomach.*
        Announcer: *Upset stomach, Pepto-Bismol. It coats, soothes, relieves.*
        Napoleon: *I hope the food is better at Waterloo.*

The Pepto-Bismol commercial employs the term *upset stomach,* which the FDA has determined is overbroad in meaning. Even more problematic is the language used to characterize the cause of Napoleon's distress. The word *it* in line (10) could be construed as referring back to eating wet snow and cold beans, as in (11).

(10)   *It's enough to give even an emperor an upset stomach.*

(11)   Eating wet snow and cold beans is enough to give even an emperor an upset stomach.

However, I believe *it* in (10) could also be interpreted as referring back to the situation Napoleon faces as a whole, i.e., both eating and running, and eating improperly.

The attempt at humor in this commercial suggests that the advertiser did not mean the scenario to be taken completely seriously. However, it is not clear which aspects of the scenario are not to be taken seriously: the idea that eating and running can cause a type of upset stomach of which Pepto-Bismol can relieve the symptoms, or the idea that eating poorly (note the reference to the quality of food at the end of the commercial) can cause a type of upset stomach of which Pepto-Bismol can relieve the symptoms. Or both. In my view, consumers, if they draw any inferences from this commercial at all, will draw the inference that eating and running and/or eating poorly can cause an upset stomach and that Pepto-Bismol can relieve the symptoms of this sort of upset stomach. It would be interesting to see the medical evidence in support of such a causal link.

In this commercial there is a vague reference to a coating action of Pepto-Bismol. Since in other commercials it is claimed that this product coats the stomach, this must be what the advertiser has in mind here. The FDA has rejected the claim that Pepto-Bismol can "coat" the stomach (FTC, 1979), and adoption of the FTC rule would have precluded the use of such a claim in advertising.

The following features of the Pepto-Bismol commercial would, I believe, be prohibited had the FTC rule been adopted: use of the term *upset stomach;* the suggestion that eating and running is enough to cause an upset stomach; the suggestion that eating poorly is enough to cause an upset stomach; and the claim that Pepto-Bismol "coats" the stomach.

There can be no serious doubt that the use of overbroad terms like *upset stomach* to characterize maladies and symptoms of maladies can lead consumers to use OTC drugs inappropriately. Somewhat less clear is the view of the FDA and FTC that harm can come to consumers as a result of the use of overspecific terms. Let us turn to consider this question.

On my tapes, there is a commercial for Doan's Pills that is advertised for use in the relief of backache, a commercial for Bayer aspirin saying that it should be taken for the relief of "minor arthritis pain," and a commercial for Bufferin urging use of this drug to "fight fever." Each of these drugs contains aspirin (or, as in the case of Doan's Pills, a very closely related drug). Similarly, there are commercials for Sinutab advocating its use to treat "sinus headache" and a commercial for Co-Tylenol urging its use to treat "aches, pains, fever," as well as other cold symptoms. These latter two products contain acetaminophen. What concerned the FTC staff is, first, that although aspirin and acetaminophen are general purpose pain relievers, an advertisement claiming that one of these drugs should be used to treat some very specific pain such as a backache or a sinus headache suggests that the drug is especially formulated to treat the specific kind of pain in question. Certainly, the manufacturers of Doan's Pills and Sinutab appear to be trying through their advertising to promote just such a view. Even the name *Sinutab* furthers such an inference.

The practice of using overspecific terms to refer to maladies and symptoms of maladies can be objected to on three grounds. First, the implication that some symptom-specific OTC pain reliever consisting of aspirin or acetaminophen is required for each specific type of pain is false. Second, the drugs promoted for the treatment of some very specific type of pain are sometimes more expensive than garden variety aspirin and acetaminophen, and thus consumers who are misled by such promotions may spend more than they need to, to get relief. Third, consumers suffering from several symptoms may be led by the advertisements in question to take several different but chemically identical drugs at the same time with potentially dangerous consequences for their health. This latter consideration is much the most important one, of course.

The question is this: Will someone who suffers from chronic arthritis, who contracts a cold, and who has a back sprain be led by overspecific advertising claims to take three different aspirin or acetaminophen products, or, even more likely, a combination of aspirin and acetaminophen products in order to treat these different medical problems? The FTC staff took the position that this sort of thing can happen. In my view, there can be no doubt that when there exists three such different symptoms as a back pain, a sinus headache, and fever the most natural assumption is that three different medications must be used to treat them. Advertising that uses highly specific terms to refer to these symptoms would certainly reinforce this assumption.

Part of the problem of potential overdose with aspirin and

acetaminophen products derives from the fact that these products can be used to treat such seemingly different ailments as back pain, a sinus headache, and fever. In general, one would not expect a drug to be able to treat such disparate symptoms. Thus, it is in the best interests of the consumer to be informed that general purpose pain relievers can treat these specific maladies and advertising is one of the ways this information can be transmitted to consumers. Thus, it would be misguided to prohibit use of highly specific names of ailments and of symptoms of ailments in OTC drug advertising. In my view, the problem of overdose derives not from this practice, but from another one.

A common practice in the promotion of OTC drugs is failure to disclose drug ingredients. This is characteristic of the advertising of acetaminophen products generally, and commercials for Anacin never, in my experience, say what Anacin consists of. In my view, were disclosure of the presence of aspirin or acetaminophen mandatory in advertisements consumers would be much less likely to take two or three different aspirin products or two or three different acetaminophen products. The problem of combining these two drugs could be dealt with by a warning on labels and in advertising about the dangers of this practice.

The linguistic issue involved in this dispute is that where there are different names for things speakers will normally infer that the things the names name are different. In the case at hand, the inference is correct, and, thus, the FTC staff seems to have taken the quite remarkable position that advertisers should be prohibited from making true claims. If the manufacturer of aspirin product A claims that A will reduce fever and the manufacturer of aspirin product B claims it relieves back pain, then nothing false has been said. Moreover, the inference that fever and back pain are different (because they have different names) is also true. Any problems that arise, arise out of the fact that aspirin (the same could be said of acetaminophen) has the remarkable ability to treat such different ailments. It would be more sensible (and more constitutional) to allow OTC drug manufacturers to make true claims concerning specific benefits of taking a drug and to require disclosure of drug ingredients, than to prohibit advertisers from making true claims.

The problem of aspirin and acetaminophen overdose derives in no small part from the fact that all sorts of drugs, prescription and nonprescription alike, contain aspirin or acetaminophen or both, and the problem of overdose can arise no less from prescription drugs than from OTC drugs. The possibility that a consumer will take two or more prescription drugs containing aspirin as well as aspirin itself is surely as real as the possibility that someone might take Doan's Pills (for backache),

Bufferin (for arthritis), Anacin (for fever), and Bayer (for a headache), all at the same time, and the FTC staff proposal did not consider the former possibility.

The problem of OTC overdose arises in other medical areas. However, I see no reason to object on linguistic grounds to the making of true symptom-specific advertising claims so long as ingredient disclosure and appropriate warnings are made. I may be oversimplifying the problems, but the FTC proposal covering symptom-specific claims was not only of questionable constitutional merit but also offers a rather simplistic solution to the problem of accidental overdose.

A third problem of linguistic interest that arose in the FTC hearings concerned a drug industry proposal that they be permitted to use language that is equivalent to FDA approved language. The FTC staff report devoted some 70 pages to this issue, but it is possible to discuss the linguistic issues involved more briefly.

The FTC considered three senses of language equivalence: *perfect synonyms*—pairs of terms that are in all respects identical semantically; *functional synonyms*—pairs of terms that are "identical in meaning as to all important components of meaning, and in all relevant contexts [FTC, 1979, p. 85]"; and a third sense, not given a name, in which pairs of terms merely share aspects of meaning. This last "Roget's Thesaurus" sense of similarity of meaning was rejected, quite rightly, as providing much too weak and too vague a sense of a language equivalence as a measure of the suitability of language presented as an alternative to FDA approved language.

The FTC staff, as well as the presiding officer, accepted the view of language scholars, including Charles Fillmore in particular, that perfect synonyms are very rare in language and that, furthermore, while there are procedures for establishing differences in meaning, there are no procedures for establishing identity of meaning. And, as Fillmore observed, even where there might be perfect synonyms at some point in a language's history, there is a tendency for speakers to differentiate them over time (FTC, 1979, p. 89).

Clearly, if there are no synonyms, then, language proposed as an alternative to FDA approved language must, therefore, never be identical to the FDA language. However, it would, of course, be absurd to prohibit alternative language on such a ground, for there are hosts of pairs of terms that are virtually identical in meaning, where the differences in meaning are much too subtle to be of any practical consequence in most contexts. In recognition of this, the FTC staff considered the suitability of the weaker concept of functional synonymy as a measure of the appropriateness of language presented as an alternative to FDA approved language.

The staff report discussion of the suitability of functional synonymy is long on theory and short on relevant examples. As the FTC notes, a term A which is close in meaning to a term B might be perceived as different in meaning since, as noted earlier, semantic differentiation is an extremely common consequence of differences in form. This could lead to a false differentiation between products should advertisements for one product use only term A and advertisements for the other use only term B. The difficulty with this line of reasoning is that this possibility already exists within the FDA approved language. The FDA has approved *heart burn, sour stomach,* and *acid indigestion* for use in the case of antacid labels (FTC, 1979, p. 134). Surely, if the FTC is to object to novel terms proposed by the drug industry on the grounds that this could lead to specious product differentiation, it must no less strenuously object to the existence of alternative terms in the FDA's list of approved terms. Should advertisements for antacid A use only *heartburn,* advertisements for antacid B use only *sour stomach,* and advertisements for antacid C use only *acid indigestion,* then, according to the line of reasoning of the FTC itself, a specious product differentiation could result.

A more serious basis for objecting to the use of terms that are functionally synonymous with FDA approved terms is that the differences in meaning, though subtle and unlikely to be noticed by consumers, might be medically significant. The FDA rejects *indigestion due to excess stomach acid* as an alternative to *acid indigestion,* apparently on the grounds that the former asserts an unproved causal link between indigestion and excess stomach acid that the latter term does not assert. The problem with this line of reasoning is that *acid indigestion* implies such a causal link and, as I noted in Chapter 2, the distinction between asserting something and implying it is, to a very large degree, a distinction without a difference. Nevertheless, since some language or other must be chosen for use on drug labels and in advertising, it is surely preferable to choose the least misleading language. *Acid indigestion* does appear to be a preferable choice to *indigestion due to excess stomach acid.*

It will come as no surprise that the FDA has approved language that the average person does not understand, including *antiflatulent, antiemetic, antitussive,* and *hypersomatic.* However, it seems that more comprehensible alternatives—sometimes noun phrases rather than nouns—have also been approved for use by the FDA in each case. So advertisers would not have been restricted to using these obscure terms.

In sum, the FTC staff appears to have been on solid linguistic grounds in objecting to terms that describe nonexistent conditions (*tired blood* and *irregularity*), vague terms (*the blahs*), and overbroad terms (*upset stomach*). It is less clear that the use of symptom-specific language in OTC drug advertising is undesirable so long as ingredient disclosure and appropriate warnings (e.g., do not take separate medications containing aspirin and acetaminophen) are made. Also somewhat suspect was the FTC staff position that OTC drug advertisers should be prohibited from using terms that are "functionally synonymous" with terms approved by the FDA. In my view, so long as what one might want to say can be demonstrated to be true, and it is not seriously misleading, then it ought to be unconstitutional to prohibit saying it.

To some degree, the problems the FDA and FTC have been trying to remedy result from the attempt to use language that is medically sound language and understandable by consumers. The difficulty with this is that colloquial English rarely serves the interests of science which is, after all, the reason scientists create technical language. As a result, a completely satisfactory language for describing symptoms that OTC drugs are designed to treat is surely unattainable.

Similes

If someone says that something is butter, it would be easy enough to determine whether or not this thing is in fact butter, for whether or not something is butter can be decided based upon objective empirical grounds. But if someone says that something is buttery, there is no objective empirical basis for determining whether or not what is said is true. All that is being claimed is that the thing in question is like butter in some respect, and this sort of claim usually does not admit of objective analysis. What is buttery to one person may not be buttery to another.

The adjectivalization process that converts *butter* into *buttery* creates the equivalent of a simile. Note that (12) and (13) are equivalent in meaning.

(12)   Margarall has a buttery flavor.

(13)   Margarall has a flavor like that of butter.

Semantically, the adjectivalization process that converts *butter* into *buttery* effects a shift of reference from the thing *butter* refers to to a property of this thing.[1] Thus, (12) claims that Margarall has a property that butter has, namely a buttery flavor. Similarly, (13) amounts to saying Margarall shares a property with butter, namely flavor.

Alongside sentences like (12), which contains a noun phrase consist-

---

[1]An adjectivalization process is a grammatical process that turns something else (e.g., a noun or verb) into an adjective. Associated with such a syntactic change is a semantic change, in meaning and reference.

ing of an adjectivalized noun modifying another noun, we have sentences containing noun compounds, as in (14).

(14)   Margarall has a butter flavor.

To someone who knows that Margarall is not butter, (14) will doubtless be interpreted in essentially the same way as (12). However, in (15), *butter flavor* will be interpreted along the lines of *flavor that fresh butter has*, rather than *flavor like that of fresh butter*.

(15)   Our butter has a fresh butter flavor.

The vagueness of noun compounds like *butter flavor* is exploited in product names, as we saw earlier in this chapter. The same also holds true for other uses of such noun compounds.

Explicit Similes

Many years ago, the guardians of grammaticality rose up in protest against the Winston cigarette claim *Winston tastes good like a cigarette should,* on the grounds that it employed *like* rather than *as.* The net result was to make this claim all the more well known and memorable. Quite rightly, advertisers continue to use *like,* rather than *as,* in similes on the very solid gound that colloquial English better serves those who communicate to the public at large than does the conservative dialect of the language "purist."

The guardians of grammaticality might better have objected to claims employing similes in advertising on the grounds that they are, on the whole, empty. A commercial for Alpo dog food begins with Lorne Greene saying

(16)   *Heh, heh! Look at her. She thinks* [sic] *she's still a puppy, and she looks like one too. But she's 14 years old! That's 98 to you and me.*   (CBS, 5/8/78, @ 1:05 p.m.)

The emptiness of the simile in (16) is clear. The older dog does look like a puppy in that she has four legs, two ears, a tail, a dog shaped body and head, etc. One might reply that this is not what the simile claims, for it speaks to characteristics of puppies, specifically, as opposed to dogs generally. However, it is difficult, if not impossible, to see how a 14-year-old dog could actually look like a puppy unless it had oversize paws, much puppy fat, etc.

A simile like *A is like B* or *A looks like B* or *A tastes like B* conversationally implicates that A is not B (Maxim of Strength). If something is a puppy then it would violate Grice's Maxim of Strength to say that it is like a puppy. In short, in cooperative conversation, one should never assert a similarity relation when one can assert an identity relation. This fact makes similes potentially treacherous. Thus, for example, the manufacturer of an instant coffee who says it tastes like real coffee might cause consumers to doubt that it is real coffee.

Similes constitute one of the areas in which "puffery" abounds. Alongside the simile of (16), one might also cite such cases as (17) and (18).

(17)   *There's no lipstick quite like Lip Quencher.*   (ABC, 2/24/78, @ 7:47 a.m.)

(18)   *Hey, I know this taste. There's nothing else like it.*   (Hawaiian Punch, CBS, 5/8/78, 2:27 p.m.)

The claim that there is no lipstick quite like Lip Quencher is palpably false as is the claim that there is nothing else like the taste of Hawaiian Punch.

The puffery involved in (16)–(18) strikes me as rather harmless, at least in advertising directed at adults, for I can imagine no one taking these claims very seriously. Each is very much a transparent exaggeration. How children will react to similes is another matter, of course. Will a child interpret a claim like (19) as being a substantive one?

(19)   [Cookie Crisp] *tastes like little chocolate chip cookies.*   (ABC, 1/10/81, 10:54 a.m.)

To my knowledge, no research has been done on the question of how young children might interpret similes, but I would be surprised if a good many, on hearing (19), were not to conclude that Cookie Crisp differs only negligibly from chocolate chip cookies.

Perhaps the zaniest use of simile in advertising occurs in the following commercial for A-1 Steak Sauce.

(20)   **A-1 Sauce** (CBS, 11/12/79, 6:49 p.m.)
         Type: Live action
         Setting: Dinner table
         Characters: Two men and two women

         TEXT
         Woman 1: *A-1 Steak Sauce . . .*
         Man 1: *. . . on your hamburger?*
         Man 2: *My friends, what is hamburger? Chopped ham? It's chopped steak! And what's better on steak than A-1?*
         Voice over (adult male): *A-1 makes hamburgers taste like steakburgers.*

> **Man 1:** *This I gotta try.*
> **Man 2:** *A-1's herbs and spices blend with the meat's natural juices, make it juicy and tastier.*
> **Woman 2:** *It is tastier.*
> **Woman 1:** *Best hamburger I ever had.*
> **Man 2:** *Sure, A-1 makes every bite count.*
> **Voice over:** *A-1 makes hamburgers taste like steakburgers.*

The simile employed in (20) is (21).

(21)   *A-1 makes hamburgers taste like steakburgers.*

As noted earlier, a simile of the form *A is like B* conversationally implicates that A is not B. But note that if hamburger is chopped steak, as this commercial falsely claims, and if steakburger is chopped or ground steak, as seems reasonable, then (22) must be true.[2]

(22)   Hamburger is steakburger.

But recall that (21) conversationally implicates (23).

(23)   Hamburger is not steakburger.

Commercial (20) boils down to a contradiction, and a very puzzling one. If hamburger is steakburger, then A-1 Sauce need do nothing to make hamburger taste like steakburger. Thus, the falsehood that hamburger is chopped steak would appear to work against the claim that A-1 makes hamburgers taste like steakburgers.

Commercial (20) appears to have been successful nevertheless. It was followed by second generation commercials like (24), and, at this writing, the advertiser is running a third generation commercial along the same lines as (20).

(24)   **A-1 Sauce** (CBS, 1/15/81, 6:41 p.m.)
        Type: Live action
        Setting: Kitchen
        Characters: *Two men and two women*

        TEXT
        Man 1: *You're not mixing A-1 Steak Sauce into your ground beef?*
        Woman 1: *A-1 and ground beef?*

[2]The term *steak* refers not to a body part of steers, but to slab-shaped cuts of meat. The claim that hamburger is chopped steak entails that it be made from slab-shaped cuts of beef that could be sold as steaks and that are chopped as opposed to ground. Neither is normally true of hamburger. The point of this (transparent) deception is clearly to suggest that steak sauce can do for hamburger what it does for steak by confusing the distinction between hamburger and steak.

Man 1: *My dear sister, what is ground beef but ground steak? And what brings out the flavor of steak better than A-1? Here it is. A-1's herbs and spices make it juicy and tastier.*
Woman 2: *Hamburgers and meat loafs taste really special.*
Woman 1: *I'll try it.*
Woman 2: *Just add 3 tablespoons for every pound of ground beef.*
Man 2: *Joanie, this tastes terrific.*
Man 1: *Sure does. A-1 makes every bite count.*

Commercials like (20) and (24) cannot be successful because they provide persuasive arguments. I suspect that some viewers will find these commercials amusing, or will fail to detect the contradiction and decide that claim (21) is a substantive one. Still another possibility is that these commercials, which have been broadcast quite frequently, work only because they have drummed the product name in viewers' minds.

In colloquial English, *like* can also be used in essentially the same way as writers use *e.g.* or *for example*. Consider line (25).

(25)   [C. W. Post Cereal's] *got hearty ribsticking things like crunchy rolled oats, rice, whole wheat: good tastin' natural things that are good for them* [my family].   (CBS, 7/18/78, 10:46 a.m.)

Although (25) has the form of a simile, this is not the intended interpretation. Rather, what is intended is that the list of grains be interpreted as being examples of what is contained in C. W. Post cereal. This use of *like* is rather common in contemporary English.

y-Adjectives

Adjectives formed from nouns by adding *y* occur frequently in advertising. Dog foods are said to be chewy or crunchy or crunchewy or to have a meaty taste. Margarines have buttery aromas and flavors, or so we are told. Foods are said to have chocolatey or fruity or spicy flavors. Soaps have bubbly lathers. And so on. This type of word is rather interesting. In many cases, *y*-adjectives are meant to be interpreted as similes. Consider (26).

(26)   *Gaines' Gravy Train. We've got meaty taste in the bag.*   (ABC, 2/24/78, @ 8:55 a.m.)

Clearly, (26) is intended to be interpreted along the lines of (27).

(27)   Gaines' Gravy Train. We've got a taste like that of meat in the bag.

Gaines' doesn't tell us what meat (as opposed to particular meats like beef or pork or lamb) tastes like.

Claims employing *y*-adjectives used as similes are like similes in what they imply. Thus, (26) implies that Gaines' Gravy Train dog food does not consist of meat (though it may have meat or meat by-products in it). However, in many cases *y*-adjectives are meant to be taken literally. Many foods that are said to have a chocolatey flavor actually contain milk chocolate or cocoa. In many cases, one's knowledge of the type of product being promoted suffices to determine how a given *y*-adjective should be interpreted.

A commercial for Blue Bonnet margarine is interesting, for it confuses the distinction between margarine and butter, in part through the use of the word *buttery*.

(28)   **Blue Bonnet** (CBS, 5/8/78, 3:22 p.m.)
        Type: Live action
        Setting: Kitchen and dining room
        Characters: Two women and a man

        TEXT
        Woman 1: *Who left you a million dollars?*
        Woman 2: *What?*
        Woman 1: *You've gone back to using butter.*
        Woman 2: *It's not butter.*
        Woman 1: *Oh, but these potatoes have a special kind of fresh, creamy, buttery aroma.*
        Woman 2: *It's not butter. It's new improved Blue Bonnet margarine.*
        Woman 1: *Blue Bonnet!*
        Voice over (adult male): *New improved Blue Bonnet is made to have more buttery flavor, more buttery flavor and more buttery aroma than ever before.*
        Man (Woman 2's spouse): *Ah, this is my kind of eating: a baked potato smothered in butter.*
        Voice over: *New improved Blue Bonnet, more buttery flavor, more buttery aroma. Try it on your hot potatoes.*

The initial topic of this commercial is Woman 2's apparent use of butter. The topic is then shifted to Blue Bonnet margarine, or, more precisely, to Blue Bonnet's *buttery* characteristics. There is a second topic shift back to butter in Woman 2's husband's comment, followed by a shift back to Blue Bonnet's *buttery* characteristics.

The topic shifts from butter to Blue Bonnet's *buttery* characteristic, a point–counterpoint type of device, that assists in the effort to blur the distinction between butter and Blue Bonnet margarine. Clearly, what is intended is to persuade viewers that in regard to flavor and aroma, the difference between Blue Bonnet and butter is negligible. Whether or not viewer's will be persuaded is another matter, of course.

Noun Compounds

In food advertising, such noun compounds as *fruit filling, cheese flavor,* and *orange juice* can be interpreted in several ways. In some cases, a phrase like *lemon flavor* has an interpretation as a simile, that is *lemon flavor* has a meaning like 'flavor like that of lemons'. In other cases, they appear to be intended to be interpreted literally, as when *lemon flavor* has a meaning like 'flavor that lemons have'. In general, when a noun compound has as its head a noun that refers to a property of a thing, as in *cheese flavor* or *butter flavor,* the noun compound can be interpreted in either of the two ways just mentioned. Such phrases are therefore quite useful in advertising, for they blur the distinction between the product and the thing named by the "modifying" noun. Thus something can have a cheese flavor without containing cheese. However, when the head noun refers to the product (*peanut cookies* or *orange juice*) or a component part of a product (*almond topping*) the modifying noun often can be taken literally. The exceptions to this latter rule arise when such a noun compound refers by convention, to an ersatz product, as in *orange drink.* In the latter case, *orange drink* contrasts with *orange juice,* which by definition contains 100% juice of oranges.

We might conclude our discussion of similes and simile-like constructions by noting that they are quite useful in advertising for they allow the advertiser to make claims that "sound good," but that often allow for interpretations that are subjective or empty. In either case, the advertiser has a "good sounding" claim that is rather easy to defend.

Count Nouns as Mass Nouns

In the case of similes, where something A is said to be like B there is a shift of reference from B to properties of B. Another device that achieves this effect is the use of a count noun as a mass noun. Consider (29) and (30).

(29)   More tomatoes for your money.

(30)   More tomato for your money.

Claim (29) is quite clear in meaning. In order for it to be true there must be a set of tomatoes T at cost C and a set of tomatoes T' at cost C', where T is smaller than T' and C is greater than C', and the speaker must be offering T' at cost C'. Furthermore, someone must once have offered or now be offering T at cost C.

The truth conditions for a sentence like (30) are anything but clear. Sentence (30) does not speak to the quantity of tomatoes, but to their quality. Using the terms just established, T' must be better than T in some respect and C' must be less than C. Set of tomatoes T' might be juicier, or firmer fleshed, or redder, or more or less acidic, etc. Thus, we have a shift of reference from tomatoes to properties of tomatoes (as in the case of y-adjectives and some noun compounds). There is an attendant increase in vagueness, and whether or not (30) is true is a matter of subjective judgment. It should be no surprise then that advertisers might find this linguistic device useful.

Advertisers commonly use count nouns as mass nouns in "more for less" claims, as was noted in Chapter 4, but this device is not restricted to such constructions. In a commercial for the AMC Concord VL (NBC, 2/24/78, evening), the copywriters have a woman saying, *I'm really surprised at that much car for that price.* This claim "sounds good" but is so hopelessly vague and subjective that it is difficult to see how it could be falsified. The contrast between use of a count noun as a count noun and as a mass noun comes out clearly in a Mazda GLC commercial (NBC, 2/24/78, evening) that concludes with *It's a great little car; it's a great lotta car.* This contrast was central to the overall Mazda GLC advertising campaign in which it was used.

The subjective character of claims using count nouns comes out quite clearly in the *More Pontiac to the gallon* campaign, discussed in Chapter 4. What General Motors had done was to increase the size of the passenger and luggage compartments of the 1979 Pontiac Catalina over that of the 1976 Catalina and increase its fuel efficiency. Thus, clearly, the 1979 Catalina was *more Pontiac* than was the 1976 Catalina in some respect. However, General Motors increased the fuel efficiency of the 1979 Catalina in part by radically decreasing engine size and engine power. It hasn't been so many years since engine power was a primary desideratum in automobiles, including Pontiacs. Thus, some people would surely take the position that the 1979 Catalina was less car than the 1976 Catalina. However, General Motors is, of course, fully within its rights in picking the property of Catalinas it means to be comparing. The result is a claim that "sounds good," but is quite subjective in character.

Perhaps the vaguest use of a count noun as a mass noun occurred in a

1981 advertisement on behalf of Spain in which it was claimed that consumers could get a lot more vacation for a lot less money in Spain. Unfortunately, this commercial did not spell out which country's vacation possibilities were being compared to Spain's or what counts as "more vacation." Spain could surely find some country somewhere that offered less vacation possibilities than Spain but in which prices were higher.

Conclusion

In this chapter, I have tried to identify some lexical and phrasal phenomena that have interested me, and, in the case of the language of OTC drug advertising, other linguists as well. I have touched only the surface of this topic, for there are numerous other similar phenomena that could have been discussed. I would like to conclude by making the following generalization: In general, advertisers tend to prefer vague language rather than language with explicit empirical consequences and to prefer subjective claims to objective claims, for, in both cases the claims that result, though they may "sound good," are very difficult if not impossible to falsify. What is interesting is that such vague, subjective claims could be effective. I fear that consumers may not bother to think through such claims.

Chapter 6

The Sociolinguistics
of Television Advertising

Much of the advertising that appears on television consists, at least in part, of conversation. In some cases, the conversation consists of some sort of interview, as in "taste-test" commercials in which an interviewer causes a shopper in a supermarket to sample two or more different brands of some product. In others the conversation is part of a mini-drama in which "ordinary people" (or, more likely, professional actors playing this role) are placed in some "natural" environment, as when a customer solicits advice from a pharmacist or clerk in a drug store or two women discuss the relative virtues of a dish detergent in a kitchen. Let us refer to these two types of commercials as "Interviews" and "Mini-dramas," respectively.

As I am using the term, a *Minidrama* presents a "slice of life" in which the characters are engaged in (relatively) normal activities in naturalistic settings. It is characteristic of a Minidrama that the bulk of the conversation is not directed primarily to the viewing audience. In an Interview, there is normally a person—the Interviewer—whose primary function is to represent the product.[1] He (very rarely she) conducts some sort of product test, questions a Consumer about why he or she prefers a particular product, or "lectures" a Consumer on the virtues of a product, etc. Since commercials are not constructed according to rigid rules, there is a certain amount of overlap between these two types of commercials.

---

[1] I shall capitalize initial letters of names referring to roles. An *Interviewer* is someone representing a product who solicits endorsements from *Consumers*, characters represented as being ordinary people. *Product Representatives* are like Interviewers in representation of products but differ from Interviewers in that they "lecture" Consumers. *Consumer Authorities* are Consumers (i.e., ordinary people) who are represented as having special consumer expertise. *Celebrities* are celebrities.

We might illustrate Interviews with the following commercial for Dristan Long Lasting Nasal Mist.

(1)   Dristan Long Lasting Nasal Mist (ABC, 1/5/81, 8:12 p.m.)
        Type: Live action
        Setting: Indoors
        Characters: Adult male Interviewer and adult female Consumer

        TEXT
        Interviewer: *Sinus cold congestion? Try this breathing bag test.*
        Woman: *I'm trying as hard as I can.*
        Interviewer: *What's happening?*
        Woman: *No air is coming through.*
        Interviewer: *Try Dristan Long Lasting Nasal Mist.* [She does.] *Now let's try the breathing bag again.*
        Woman: *It's fantastic.*
        Interviewer: *Think it will last all day?*
        Woman: *I'll let you know.* [Time elapses.] *Dristan Long Lasting lasted the entire day.*
        Interviewer: *Try the breathing bag again.* [She does.] *All day and you're still clear.*
        Woman: *Absolutely terrific.*
        Voice over (adult male): *Get Dristan Long Lasting. Relieves virtually all day or all night.*

In this commercial, the function of the Interviewer is to conduct the product test and solicit an endorsement. The function of the Consumer is to test and endorse the product being tested.

The language of commercial (1) is fully consistent with the context in which it occurs and with the relationship that exists between the Interviewer and Consumer. The Interviewer and Consumer are strangers, as is reflected in the highly impersonal character of what the Interviewer says. Note, in particular, the Interviewer's use of imperatives (e.g., *Try this breathing bag test*) to give instructions. This is very much like how an experimental scientist might talk to the subject of an experiment, the "real world" activity that the commercial tries to simulate. The conversation is also relatively natural, given the context. The sentences are relatively short, as is characteristic of ordinary conversation, and there is a certain amount of ellipsis (e.g., *Think it will last all day?* versus *Do you think it will last all day?*), as is characteristic of informal speech.[2] Moreover, instead of repeating the product name in full every time reference to it is made (as sometimes happens in television commercials for rather obvi-

---

[2]See Akmajian, Demers, and Harnish (1979) for an illuminating discussion of this sort of ellipsis.

ous reasons), some references are pronominal in form (e.g., *It's fantastic* versus *Dristan Long Lasting Nasal Mist is fantastic*). This too is characteristic of informal conversation. One of the strengths of the Interview-type commercial is that it is fully consistent with the inclusion of explicitly didactic elements. The Interviewer is presented as and is surely perceived as a representative of the company advertising the product and, as a result, it is only natural that he (very rarely she) make a pitch for the product. The inclusion of didactic elements in Minidramas can present a problem. In a case in which a customer in a drug store solicits advice from a pharmacist, it is quite natural that the pharmacist "lecture" the customer about the virtues of a drug. However, when two "ordinary persons," playing the role of Consumer act out some real life consumer problem, didactic elements can be quite intrusive. And, the more natural the conversation, the less natural, and, hence, the less seemingly authentic, will be the inclusion of explicitly didactic messages.

Normally, when two Consumers appear in a commercial Minidrama, one will be established as a Product Authority and the didactic elements will be put in his or her mouth. For the most part, advertisers employ stereotypes in order to establish one of the Consumers as a Product Authority. Examples of typical stereotypes are that store clerks know more about the products they sell than do customers, mothers and mothers-in-law know more about household affairs than do daughters and daughters-in-law, wives know more about household affairs than do husbands, and so on.

We might illustrate the Minidrama-type commercial with the following advertisement for Liquid Plumr.

(2)   Liquid Plumr (NBC, 1/8/81, 8:54 p.m.)
       Type: Live action
       Setting: Bathroom
       Characters: Husband and Wife

       TEXT
       Husband: *Give me a break, a plumber's wife using Crystal Drano.*
       Wife: *Liquid Plumr's more convenient but this hair clog's tough.*
       Husband: *Liquid Plumr works best on tough hair clogs. Watch Crystal Drano versus Liquid Plumr on identical clogs.*
       Wife: *You used Crystal twice . . .*
       Husband: *. . . Liquid Plumr only once.*
       Wife: *Ah, Liquid Plumr's penetrating.*
       Husband: *Yep, and Liquid Plumr worked better. No mess either.*
       Wife: *On real tough hair clogs, . . .*
       Husband: *. . . use Liquid Plumr. Just pour it in, and it works . . .*
       Wife: *. . . better.*

This commercial is unusual in that normally "wives" are presented as more knowledgeable about household affairs than "husbands." However, the husband's expertise as a plumber overrides this advertising convention.

The conversation of (2) is unnatural in several respects. First, note that on several occasions, one of the characters completes sentences started by the other. Although this phenomenon does sometimes occur in ordinary conversation, it would rarely occur as it does in (2). Second, each character who refers to Liquid Plumr uses its full name rather than a pronoun on its first mention in a given "turn" in the conversation. In informal conversation, for instance, the husband would almost certainly have said *Yep, and it worked better,* rather than *Yep, and Liquid Plumr worked better.* However, the most unnatural features of this commercial are the abrupt verbal transition from a conversation between the husband and wife to statements by them directed to viewers and the "magical" appearance of two clogged drains in what is otherwise a naturalistic setting (compare Photographs 6.1 and 6.2). One of the questions we shall want to entertain is to what degree these non-natural elements work against the persuasiveness of such a commercial.[3]

In the conversations that comprise Interviews and Minidramas, the rationale for the product emerges in the conversations, and I submit that the credibility of such commercials depends in no small measure on the authenticity of these conversations. I shall argue that the authenticity of such conversations can be measured in sociolinguistic terms—in terms of the appropriateness of the language used in the conversation to whom the conversants are, to the relationship that exists between the conversants, and to the social context in which the conversants are placed. The concepts of "speech style" and "speech register" are central to measuring the appropriateness of conversation in these respects.

Styles and Registers in Advertising

In any circumstance in which we wish to achieve some end there will be a variety of options available to us. Consider, for instance, how a

---

[3]One aspect of this commercial that is worth special mention is the conversational implicature of the husband's first remark that a plumber's wife should know better than to use Crystal Drano. The inference I drew on hearing this is that plumbers know Crystal Drano to be harmful to plumbing. Others might draw the inference that plumbers know Drano to be ineffective. The former inference is not defended in the commercial. The latter is.

Photograph 6.1

Photograph 6.2

parent might attempt to stop a child from playing with a knife. The parent might act nonverbally by giving the child a stern look or by taking the knife out of the child's hand. Or the parent might say something. He or she might give an order,

(3)   Stop playing with that knife.

make a request,

(4)   Please stop playing with that knife.

make a threat,

(5)   If you don't stop playing with that knife, I shall send you to your room.

give a warning,

(6)   That knife might cut you.

and so on.

In general, what someone says and how he or she says it reflects the topic of conversation, the purpose of the conversation, the context in which the conversation takes place, and the social relationships that exist among the parties to the conversation. There are four aspects of the context of a conversation worth special mention: the **linguistic context** (what has already been said), the **epistemic context** (background assumptions that the parties to the conversation believe are shared by all), the **physical context** (what is present in and happening in the environment), and the **social context** (the social occasion that brings the parties to the conversation together) (see Chapter 1 in this volume for further discussion). The linguistic, epistemic, and physical contexts can play important roles in determining the content of linguistic communications. The social context plays an important role in determining the form of linguistic communications.

Two important concepts to the study of conversation are speech style and speech register. Joos (1967) identified five different speech styles: frozen (speech that consists of verbal formulas), formal (speech of the sort one might use in giving a public lecture), consultative (speech characteristic of strangers talking to each other), casual (speech among friends and acquaintances on nonformal occasions), and intimate (speech of the sort intimate friends might use). Each of these speech styles will be appropriate in some social contexts and inappropriate in others. Speech style has much to do with where the speaker and listener are, i.e., with the social context.

The concept of speech register has less to do with where the speaker and listener are than with who the speaker and listener are and the social relationship that exists between them.[4] Speech registers are speech varieties associated with particular kinds of social relationships. Compare how a husband and wife might talk to each other with how they might talk to their 3-year-old child, or how a social superior (army sergeant) might talk to a social inferior (army private) with how the latter might talk to the former. Among social equals, how people talk typically reflects the situationally salient affinity group with which the parties of the conversation are associated.

The concepts of speech style and speech register are very closely intertwined. Two business men who are members of the same firm but of unequal status in it might talk to each other rather differently about a given business problem at work than they would after a hard game of tennis. This is due in part to the fact that these are different social contexts and to the fact that in these two contexts they participate in different social relationships. In the former case, the inequality in social status will be maximized; in the latter case it will be minimized.

Speech style and speech register have an impact on every level of linguistic structure. In formal speech, what we say is more carefully articulated than in casual speech. Thus in a formal speech context, a speaker who wishes to say *Let's go* might say [lĕts gów]; in casual speech, he would more likely say [lĕs ków]. As this example illustrates, casual speech is marked by greater application of ellipsis and assimilation processes. At the syntactic level, casual speech is also more elliptical than is formal speech. In formal speech contexts, someone who wishes to say, *Are you going to the lecture tomorrow?* would say that, but in casual speech contexts he would probably say *Gonna go to the talk tomorrow?* As this latter example illustrates, we also choose different lexical items when using different speech styles. The word *lecture* is formal; *talk* is casual.

Speech registers have a differential effect at all levels of structure as well. In talking to a very young child, an adult might adopt carefully articulated speech, morphologically simple lexical items, and simple, straightforward syntactic structures. He or she would not talk this way to a spouse. Perhaps the greatest consequence of differences of speech register is reflected in word choices. Associated with any affinity group is a specialized vocabulary for referring to the things and activities associated with that group. To another academic I might refer to an academic lecture as a *lecture*, a *talk*, or a *paper*. To a nonacademic I might use the word *speech* or *lecture* or *talk*, but would be unlikely to use the word

---

[4]See Zwicky and Zwicky (in press) for a useful discussion of style and register. My own views differ very little from theirs.

paper. The sentence *I'm going to hear a paper tonight* might be incomprehensible to a nonacademic.

In a number of the commercials on my tapes that contain conversations, one of the particpants also addresses the viewing audience. As one might expect from what has been said, the language used to address viewers can differ a great deal from that used by participants in advertisement–internal conversations. Since these "asides" to the viewing audience occur within advertisement–internal conversations, as we noted in connection with the Liquid Plumr commercial, it is necessary to consider, if only briefly, how advertisers talk to viewers.

The social context of talk by advertisers to viewers is a public one and the social relationship is closer to that of strangers than to anything else. As a result one would expect the speech style employed in talk to viewers to be consultative (i.e., relatively formal) in character. This is largely the case.

In the vast majority of cases in which a Product Representative talks directly to viewers, the speech style is relatively formal, not unlike how a college professor might talk to his or her students. For instance, one often finds sentences of great syntactic complexity and the use of technical terms. Consider the following commercial for the Bell telephone system.

(7)   Bell (CBS, 1/11/81, 2:01 p.m.)
        Type: Live action
        Setting: Fancy visual effects are shown
        Characters: No on-screen characters speak

        TEXT
        Voice over (adult male): *At this very moment, you have access to the world's most advanced information management system, the Bell Network, managing complex voice, data, and visual communications. Use it for telemarketing, to systematically buy and sell more efficiently, to open new markets, to manage more productively. Put our knowledge to work for you. The information management network from Bell.*

The first two sentences of (7) are syntactically quite complex. The first sentence contains the quite complex phrase *the world's most advanced information management system* as well as the two appositives, *the Bell Network* and *managing complex voice, data, and visual communications.* The second sentence employs compounding resulting in a rather complex sentence. These are the sorts of constructions one might hear in a public lecture but not during conversation among friends at the dinner table.

This commercial also uses technical terms, e.g., *telemarketing* and *information management system.*

Whether or not there is a special advertising register that is used to address viewers is difficult to say. In my view, the answer to this question is a qualified "no." It is characteristic of a register that a social relationship of a fairly specific sort exist among the parties to a conversation, but no such relationship exists between advertisers and viewers. This militates against the development of a specialized vocabulary. The fact that so many different types of products are promoted on television further militates against the existence of a specialized advertising vocabulary.

However, there are uses of language that occur so commonly in advertising that one might argue that there is something akin to advertising English, including the use of count nouns as mass nouns (*a lot more Chevette for a lot less money* —NBC, 2/25/78, evening); the use of elliptical comparatives (*the new Chevrolet has more headroom, more seat and legroom, more trunk room* —CBS, 6/2/78, @ 9:21 p.m.); the use of adjectivalization processes (*buttery, creamy, crispy,* etc.); the use of imperatives to make suggestions (*Try Ex-Lax pills, the overnight wonder* —ABC, 1/6/81, 6:13 p.m.); the use of rhetorical questions (*Ever wonder what Oscar Meyer has in store for you?* —CBS, 1/5/81, 9:12 p.m.); using *introducing* and *announcing* as attention getters (*Introducing the first roast beef sandwich big and tasty enough for Burger King* —NBC, 1/5/81, 8:55 p.m.); the use of parentheticals (*Dristan Tablets, relieves all 12 cold symptoms* —NBC, 1/8/81, 8:54 p.m.); the use of vocatives (*Working hands of America, let the healing begin* —Vaseline Intensive Care, CBS, 1/6/81, 8:25 p.m.); and so on. However, these phenomena have more to do with style than with register.

The conversations of television Interviews and Minidramas normally contain either or both of two ratiocinative elements. One is the presentation of explicitly didactic elements (e.g., claims made about the products, what is said during product demonstrations, and the like). The other is the endorsement by a Consumer of the reasoning employed in didactic passages or of the quality of the product as revealed in a product test of one sort or another. However, the effectiveness of commercials employing conversation is presumably also a function of the authenticity of the conversation itself. This is especially true of Minidramas in which Consumers act out some "real life" consumer problem (e.g., what sort of coffee or diaper or toilet paper one should buy).

We have all seen commercials featuring Consumers in which what the Consumer says doesn't "ring true," as when a Consumer talks overly enthusiastically about the goodness of some quite mundane product. The question arises as to what factors govern the authenticity of what the characters of commercial Interviews and Minidramas say to each other. I would like to suggest that the appropriateness of the speech style and registers employed in the conversations of Interviews and Minidramas can be crucial to the authenticity of what is said, and, thus also, to some extent, to the effectiveness of such commercials.

Interviews

Interviews employing Consumers who do product "tests" or who are invited by an Interviewer to say good things about a product depend, for their credibility, on what they say, and no less important, on how they say what they say. Since all such Consumers can be expected to say quite favorable things about a product, the manner of speaking becomes all the more important. All of us have seen commercials in which the featured Consumer's voice is unusually high pitched and/or whose rate of speech is faster than normal, rather like that of an excited child at Christmas. I find such commercials unconvincing for people normally don't talk about most consumer products with such enthusiasm.

In Interviews, there are basically two types of settings, naturalistic settings and studio settings. In the case of naturalistic settings, the Consumer is placed in a context he or she might normally be found in, such as a store or a home. In general it is the Interviewer who is "out of place" in such cases. In studio settings, we find the Interviewer and Consumer in an indeterminate location. In general, these locations are more like stage sets than anything else. In these commercials, it is the Consumer who is "out of place."

It is useful to distinguish two types of Interviews. In one type, the primary roles of the Interviewer are to solicit opinions from the Consumers that appear and to sum these opinions up in the form of punch lines. In this type of commercial the Consumer plays a crucial conversational role. In the other type of Interview, the Interviewer promotes a product to the Consumer. In this type of commercial, the Consumer plays a supporting role. He or she is there to facilitate the Interviewer's pitch for the product and to endorse this pitch.

In general, Interviews take place between strangers and the resultant conversation between Interviewer and Consumer will be relatively impersonal, i.e., consultative in style, as in the previously discussed Dristan commercial [commercial (1), p. 132]. Such a style is fully consistent with the explicitly didactic character of Interviews. However, such conversations need not be impersonal in style. This is especially true of Interviews using a naturalistic setting. Since the more candid the Consumer's conversational contributions are, the more authentic or genuine they will seem; Interviews sometimes employ a relatively casual speech style as a sign of candidness.

We might begin our examination of Interviews with the following commercial for Sears.

(8)   Sears (ABC, 7/11/78, @ 10:52 p.m.)
        Type: Live action
        Setting: Interior of Sears store.
        Characters: Two Consumers (a young married couple) and an adult male
        Interviewer

        TEXT
        Husband: *My mom is truly one of the tightest 'n one of the most
            shop-around ladies that I've ever seen, 'n if she buys Sears appliances,
            they've gotta be good.*
        Interviewer: *We're in the appliance department of a Sears store to find out
            why Sears is where America shops.*
        Wife: *They have a large selection of appliances and Sears service men
            will come to your home.*
        Husband: *And when you buy an appliance, you want something you can
            count on—something from Sears.*
        Voice over: *Sears—where America shops.*

Although this commercial is dialogical, it is only marginally conversational. The Interviewer speaks to the viewing audience, not to the husband and wife on screen. However, the husband's first comment sounds like it might have been a response to some Interviewer question like *Why does your wife shop at Sears?*

The husband and wife do not give the appearance of being professional actors. Moreover, the remarks of the husband and wife give the impression of being candid in certain respects. The husband uses contractions of *and* and *got to* in his first turn, which are characteristic of casual speech, as is the use of the slang word *tightest* and the homemade word *shop-around* (rather than the more formal word *discriminating*). The phrase *my mom,* used to refer to the husband's wife, is very puzzling. One sometimes hears a man refer to his wife as *mother* (if, of course, she is one), but rarely would one hear a husband refer to his wife as *mom,* to say nothing of *my mom.* Indeed, were it not for visual evidence to the contrary (see Photograph 6.3), use of this phrase would lead most viewers to assume that the woman in question is the husband's actual mother.

There are linguistically discordant features of the husband's first statement that suggest that what the husband says is "coached" if not

Photograph 6.3

actually scripted, namely use of *truly* and *ladies,* words more characteristic of formal rather than casual speech. The husband's use of the Equative Construction (symbolized in the transcript by the dash) in his second turn is quite inconsistent in style with his earlier statement, for the Equative Construction is normally restricted to relatively formal speech.

I would like now to turn to an Interviewer-type commercial in which the language is relatively natural. In this commercial, the Interviewer is off screen. His first and last turns are directed at viewers.

(9)   Blatz beer[5]
        Type: Live action
        Setting: Bar
        Characters: Consumer (young adult male) and off-screen male
        Interviewer

        TEXT
        Interviewer: *John Greene just took a Blatz taste test against his regular beer. Listen.*
        J. Greene: *I chose the Blatz over the Lite because of the taste. Blatz jus' tastes better than Lite.*

[5]This commercial was taped during recreational use of my videotape machine. I have no record of when it aired.

Interviewer: *Why should someone believe you?*
J. Greene: [ãyõno] (I don't know). *I have no idea. Just take my word for it or do the test themself, compare the beer themself.*
Interviewer: *What did you say before about that television—the Blatz beer commercial?*
J. Greene: *I didn't believe it.*
Interviewer: *And now?*
J. Greene: *I believe it now.*
Interviewer: *Be a Blatz believer. Taste test your beer against Blatz.*

The language of this commercial strikes me as being as close to natural conversation as any I've seen in a television commercial. The style is casual. Note, in particular, the highly reduced *I don't know* [ãyõno] of Mr. Green's second turn, the false start of the third turn of the Interviewer, and use of the singular form of *themselves* on Mr. Greene's second turn, and the Interviewers elliptical question *And now?*

This commercial goes to extraordinary lengths to seem candid. First, as John Greene is introduced, we see *John Greene, Graduate Student* on screen. The purpose of this identification is to establish Mr. Greene as a Consumer, as opposed to an actor, and, perhaps also as being of above-average intelligence. What Mr. Greene studies isn't identified. Second, as the first Interviewer message closes we see *Hidden Camera Interview— Milwaukee* on screen. The relatively poor film quality of this and other Blatz taste-test commercials I have seen supports the contention that filming was done under difficult circumstances. However, the commercial does not say whether or not Mr. Greene knew that a camera was present. The fact that the camera is hidden doesn't mean that Mr. Greene doesn't know it's there. Third, as the second voice over message is said, we see *Signed Affadavit on File* on screen. The purpose of placing the message at this point is presumably to provide the answer to the question *Why should someone believe you?* Fourth, reference to previous Blatz commercials enables the advertiser to establish that Mr. Greene was once skeptical but has become a *Blatz believer*. These efforts to establish the credibility of this commercial strike a false note, suggesting that there may be good reason for consumers not to find them believable. And there is.

The Blatz taste-test commercials, like many other product test commercials, give the appearance of being like scientific tests, but they are very far from being that. I do presume that Mr. Greene made a "blind" test of Blatz and Lite beers and that he chose Blatz. However, any single outcome of a behavioral test of this sort is totally meaningless. A second disquieting feature of this commercial is that, in general, the subject of a taste test used in a commercial knows in advance that his or her test is being filmed for use as a commercial and knows that he or she will be paid handsomely if the test is used. I do not know whether or not Mr. Greene was in possession of this knowledge, but it is clear that saying that the interview was a *Hidden Camera Interview* does not establish that he didn't know he was being filmed. It just establishes that Mr. Greene couldn't see the camera. It is clear that taste-test commercials in which the consumers tested know the purpose of the tests, and know they will be paid well if they choose correctly and look and sound convincing enough to justify use of their tests in commercials, are far from being scientific tests. Viewers would do well to discount all such "single-outcome" tests.

One can ask a deeper question about any commercial employing someone's subjective judgment about the quality of a product, whether the person in question is a celebrity, some ordinary person, or even an alleged expert (e.g., alleged experts on wines who tell viewers how good some "vin ordinaire" is or how much better one "vin ordinaire" is than another). We all depend on other persons for judgments about products we've not yet tried, but normally we rely only on the judgments of persons whose tastes we have some reason to respect. However, it is clear that many viewers respond favorably to commercials featuring the subjective judgment of someone whose tastes are in fact not known to them at all. I shall suggest an explanation for this irrational viewer behavior later.

In some cases advertisers undo their effort to present interviews that have the appearance of being candid by broadcasting virtually identical interviews employing different Consumers. For example, there are the recent Total cereal commercials in which we find an Interviewer who converses with a Consumer in front of a board comparing the nutritional merits of the Consumer's favorite cereal and Total cereal. The difficulty with these commercials is that the interviews differ very little from each other either in what the Interviewer and the Consumers say and do. Consider commercial (10).

(10)   Total cereal (ABC, 11/12/79, 6:22 p.m.)
          Type: Live action
          Setting: Studio
          Characters: Interviewer (man) and Consumer (woman)

          TEXT
          Interviewer: *We're showing Carol that one ounce of fortified Total has 100% of the recommended daily allowance of these nine important vitamins plus iron. Carol, what cereal did you have for breakfast?*
          Woman: *Mmm. I had corn flakes.*

Interviewer: *How do you think one ounce of cornflakes will compare with Total?*
Woman: *I don't know—Total looks hard to beat.*
Interviewer: *Let's compare.*
Woman: *Total is a lot higher.*
Interviewer: *If you want 100% of these nine vitamins and iron, get Total.*
Woman: *That's some difference.*
Interviewer: *That's the total difference.*

I have seen three different versions of this commercial, but each employs essentially the same language as the others (e.g., *Total looks tough to beat* versus *Total looks hard to beat* or *That's a big difference* instead of *That's some difference*). Moreover, some features of the acting are the same. As each of the three Consumers tries to recall what he or she ate for breakfast, he or she raises his or her right hand to his or her lips. Any viewer who notices the similarity between these commercials will surely recognize that they are scripted. I submit that such viewers will, or at least should, also find these commercials to be somewhat unconvincing.

There exists a special subtype of the Interview-type commercial that is like an Interview in that there is someone who represents the product who converses with a Consumer. However, in this type of commercial the Interviewer (henceforth, Product Representative) doesn't actually interview the Consumer. Instead the Product Representative, who may be a real person, an animated person like Mr. Clean, or even an animated animal, tries to persuade the Consumer that the product being promoted is right for him or her. In general, Consumers in this type of commercial play a supporting role. They may verbally reinforce what the Product Representative says, often by using what Jefferson (1972) calls "questioning repeats." They may pose questions or challenges that might be expected to occur to viewers. They may also endorse claims made on behalf of the product.

In the following commercial for Liv-a-Snaps, a product fed to dogs as treats, we find an animated dog—not the Consumer's pet—playing the role of Product Representative.

(11)   Liv-a-Snaps (WUAB, Cleveland, 2/24/78, @ 12:58 p.m.)
         Type: Live action with animated dog
         Setting: Kitchen
         Characters: Product Representative (animated dog) and Consumer
         (adult female)

         TEXT
         Woman: *Sit, Lucky. Sit.*
         Dog: *Hey! Don't forget to reward him.*

Woman: *Huh?*
Dog: *Don't forget his Liv-a-Snaps.*
Woman: *I don't like to give him too many treats.*
Dog: *He can eat lots of Liv-a-Snaps. They're nutritious treats you can give a dog any time.*
Woman: *Nutritious treat?*
Dog: *Sure. They're made with real liver and dogs love them.*
Woman: *So I can treat him to Liv-a-Snaps any time?*
Voice over (adult male): *Treat him to Liv-a-Snaps 'cause dogs love liver . . .*
Dog: *. . . any time.*

In this commercial, the Consumer challenges the Product Representative by raising an objection that might occur to viewers by saying, *I don't like to give him too many treats,* and questions the supposition that a treat could be nutritious. The latter challenge, a questioning repeat, reinforces for viewers what the Product Representative has said and invites him to defend his claim. The Consumer then evidences having drawn conclusions from what the Product Representative has said by saying, *So I can treat him to Liv-a-Snaps any time?* The word *so* signals that an inference has been drawn. In being worded as a question, the speaker invites the Product Representative to confirm the correctness of the inference. Interestingly, the Voice Over statement does not respond directly to what the Consumer has said. Compare (12) with (13).

(12)   Treat him to Liv-a-Snaps any time because they're nutritious.

(13)   *Treat him to Liv-a-Snaps 'cause dogs love liver any time.*

Sentence (12) would be responsive to what the Consumer has said, but (13) is not. Instead, it shifts the focus from the nutritiousness of Liv-a-Snaps to its taste.

In commercial (11), the Consumer plays a supporting conversational role. So also does the Consumer of (14).

(14)   **Ex-Lax** (ABC, 1/6/81, 6:13 p.m.)
         Type: Live action
         Setting: Home
         Characters: Consumer (adult female) and unseen adult male Product
         Representative

         TEXT
         Man: *Mrs. Clay, are you all right?*
         Woman: *Oh, fine. Sort of.*
         Man: *Little constipation?*

> **Woman:** *I wish I felt better about my laxative.*
> **Man:** *You'll feel good about this one. It's gentle. It's the overnight wonder.*
> **Woman:** *Ex Lax?*
> **Man:** *The overnight wonder. Give me your hand.*
> **Woman:** *Why it's a pill.*
> **Man:** *Right. Developed by Ex-Lax to gently restore your system's own natural rhythm.*
> **Woman:** *So it really is gentle.*
> **Man:** *You'll feel the difference in the morning. Try Ex-Lax pills, the overnight wonder.*

This commercial has several features of interest. Note, for instance, that the Product Representative, who appears to be a stranger to the Consumer of this commercial, would have to be a psychic to guess that the woman is suffering from constipation. What we have here is condensation, a device used to speed up the pace of the conversation.[6] The Consumer's question, *Ex-Lax?* is also of interest. She says this on being presented with a box of Ex-Lax. The fact that the Consumer uses a question requires the Product Representative to take another turn. The word *Ex-Lax* is pronounced with question (rising) intonation and can be interpreted in at least two ways. It could signal surprise, surprise that Ex-Lax is gentle or is the *overnight wonder* or both. A more likely interpretation is that the Consumer is signaling for confirmation that the so far unnamed product is in fact Ex-Lax.

Also somewhat difficult to interpret is the Consumer's statement (15).

(15)   *So, it* [Ex-Lax] *really is gentle.*

As I noted in connection with commercial (11), the sentence prefix *so* is sometimes used to signal the drawing of an inference. Viewers who construe it this way (and who are not paying especially close attention) might assume that evidence supporting the inference that Ex-Lax really is gentle has been presented. Such evidence has not, of course, been presented. Another possible interpretation is that the Consumer has heard that Ex-Lax is gentle and signals through her use of *so* that what the Product Representative has said has confirmed this belief. In either event, the Consumer's comment endorses what the Product Representative has said, as is characteristic of this type of commercial.

Much the most interesting feature of this commercial is its effort to persuade viewers that Ex-Lax is effective. The Consumer indicates a certain unhappiness with the laxative she has been using. This could be

---

[6]Condensed conversations are those that leave out "steps."

because it isn't gentle or isn't effective or some other reason. The Product Representative then claims that Ex-Lax is *the overnight wonder.* This phrase is quite vague. It is reminiscent of *overnight success* and I submit that this phrase will be interpreted by most viewers as signifying that Ex-Lax is effective. The Product Representative then goes on to say that it has been developed *to gently restore your system's own natural rhythm.* Interestingly this statement doesn't entail that Ex-Lax is effective. This claim simply says what Ex-Lax was developed to do, but it does not follow from this that it actually does what it was developed to do. However, most viewers can be counted on to draw the inference (a conversational implicature based on the Maxim of Relevance) that Ex-Lax does in fact do what it was developed to do.

The claim that Ex-Lax was developed to *restore* the *natural rhythm* of the woman's system entails that this woman's (and, by extension, everyone else's) system has a natural rhythm. This is a metaphorical use of the word *rhythm* and conjures up a view of bowel movements that some may wish to question. Even more interesting is the use of the word *restore.* To claim that Ex-Lax was developed to restore people's natural rhythm is to claim that it was developed to bring one's system back to its natural state, i.e., to cure constipation. To restore a painting is to bring it back to its natural state.[7]

The conversational role of the Consumers of Interviews depends on whether the Interviewer (Product Representative) solicits opinions from Consumers or lectures them. In the former case the Consumer makes the claims, and the Interviewer's function is to elicit these claims and sum them up in the form of a punch line or company slogan. The credibility of this type of commercial depends heavily on the authenticity of what the Consumer says and how he or she says it. An important factor bearing on the authenticity of what the Consumer says is its felicitousness in style and register. Advertisers do not seem fully aware of this.

In Interviews featuring a Product Representative who lectures a Consumer, the conversational role of the Consumer is much more highly restricted. In this type of commercial, the Product Representative makes the claims and the role of the Consumer is to facilitate the making of these claims and, then, to endorse them. He or she facilitates the making of claims primarily through the use of questioning repeats (which play the dual role of reinforcing for viewers what the Product Representative

---

[7]The advertiser of Ex-Lax is not alone in how it uses the word *restore.* A commercial for Primatine Mist (NBC, 1/8/81, 10:32 p.m.) claims that Primatine will *restore free breathing in as fast as 15 seconds.*

says and passing the conversation back to him) and through the use of challenges.

Minidramas

As I am using the term, *Minidramas* are "slice of life" commercials in which the characters appear in naturalistic settings. They come in three varieties: those in which a Celebrity interacts with a Consumer, those in which a Consumer interacts with another Consumer who is represented as being some sort of expert in the relevant commercial area, and those in which two or more ordinary Consumers interact. In all three types of commercials one of the characters plays the role of Consumer Authority. If a Celebrity appears, he or she is invariably the Consumer Authority. In cases in which only ordinary people appear, one of the Consumers is usually represented as more knowledgeable than the others and he or she plays the role of Consumer Authority. It is the latter type of commercial which is of greatest sociolinguistic interest.

I shall restrict my attention here to Minidramas containing explicitly didactic elements. I shall therefore exclude commercials such as the justifiably famous "Mean Joe Greene" commercial in the *Have a Coke and a Smile* campaign. I shall also exclude commercials like contemporary American Express Traveler's Cheque commercials in which the explicitly didactic elements are sharply separated from the Minidrama itself.

Celebrities routinely appear in monological advertisements and, less frequently, in commercials in which they interact with Consumers. In both types of commercials, they almost invariably appear as themselves. The reason that Celebrities so rarely appear as characters in Minidramas is, I believe, that their credibility as people is transferable to commercials only when they appear as themselves.[8] When they appear playing other roles, their credibility is largely determined by the credibility of the roles they play.

As I noted earlier, the Celebrities that appear in Minidramas serve as Consumer Authorities and the Consumers that appear play a supporting role. Consider the following Sanka commercial featuring Robert Young.

---

[8] I believe that the fact that celebrities virtually always appear as themselves may explain why so many viewers drew the inference from Polaroid One-Step commercials that James Garner and Mariette Hartley are married (which they are not). In these commercials Mr. Garner and Ms. Hartley appear in familial settings and their banter is characteristic of intimates. These two facts combined with the fact that celebrities normally play themselves in commercials suggests that they enjoy a familial relationship.

(16)   Sanka (ABC, 1/6/81, 6:08 p.m.)
         Type: Live action
         Setting: Office
         Characters: Robert Young and Consumer (adult female)

TEXT
Woman: *Still busy.*
Robert Young: *Hey, why's my favorite lawyer so tense?*
Woman: *Sorry, the doctor says caffeine makes me nervous.*
Robert Young: *Lois, you should drink Sanka Brand decaffeinated
     coffee.*
Woman: *But I only like real coffee.*
Robert Young: *Sanka Brand is real coffee. It tastes it, try it.*
Woman: *M-m, it is real coffee, delicious.*
     (time elapses)
Robert Young: *Lois, you look so relaxed.*
Woman: *Glad you noticed. Open and shut case for Sanka Brand.*
Robert Young: *Ha, ha, ha. Sanka Brand, enjoy your coffee, and enjoy
     yourself.*

The conversation of commercial (16) is a good deal more natural than typical Interviews, for the Consumer plays a substantive conversational role. As in the case of Interviews this woman raises a challenge concerning the product that must occur to some viewers: (*But I only like real coffee*), reinforces the message of the commercial (*It is real coffee, delicious*) and endorses the product (*Open and shut case for Sanka Brand*).

Although the conversation is more natural than that of Interviews, there are non-natural elements. The Consumer refers to her doctor as *the doctor* rather than *my doctor.*[9] Normally, we do not use *the* in definite descriptions unless the referent of the noun it occurs with has already been identified or the sentence itself establishes the referent. Moreover, no background for the reference to caffeine has been made, for normally one does not consume caffeine directly. A reference to the woman's having consumed something containing caffeine—a cola, tea, or coffee—is missing. What we have here is a small condensation of the conversation. Condensation also occurs in Robert Young's line, *Lois, you should drink Sanka Brand decaffeinated coffee,* for Mr. Young's remark is overspecific in referring to a specific brand. Compare (17) with (16).

[9]All Sanka commercials featuring Robert Young that I am familiar with use the phrase *the doctor,* as in (16). Clearly, the advertiser means for viewers to draw the inference that there is medical evidence supporting the contention that consuming caffeine can cause nervousness. One wonders why Sanka commercials don't boldly assert that there is medical evidence supporting this contention.

(17)   **Robert Young:** Lois, you should drink decaffeinated coffee.
        Woman: But I only like real coffee.
        Robert Young: Try Sanka. Sanka's real coffee. It tastes it.

Condensation (the overly early reference to Sanka) is employed here, I would imagine, to avoid promoting decaffeinated coffee generally. This sort of condensation is quite common in advertising. The reason for this is that the advertiser wants to promote use of his product, not use of just any product in the same class.

Compare (16) with (18).

(18)   Brim (NBC, 1/2/81, 10:11 a.m.)
        Type: Live action
        Setting: Art gallery
        Characters: Two Consumers (adult females)

        TEXT
        Woman 1: *Joan, I just think I sold the Well's sculpture.*
        Woman 2: *Wonderful, have some coffee.*
        Woman 1: *Whoa.*
        Woman 2: *Only half a cup? Don't you like my coffee?*
        Woman 1: *Mmmm. Love the rich taste. It's the caffeine I could do
        without.*
        Woman 2: *You happen to be drinking Brim decaffeinated coffee.*
        Woman 1: *This is Brim?*
        Woman 2: *This is freeze dried Brim, and it's decaffeinated. So you don't
        have to stop at half a cup.*
        Woman 1: *If it tastes this rich, I don't want to stop. Fill it to the rim . . .*
        Woman 2: *. . . with Brim.*
        Voice over (Male): *Fill your cup to the rim with rich tasting Brim. Ground
        or freeze dried.*

Observe that (18) employs condensation in much the same way (16) does. The earliest reference to decaffeinated coffee contains a reference to the specific product being promoted. Moreover, commercial (18) promotes precisely the same concepts that are promoted in (16).

The primary difference in ratiocinative content between (16) and (18) is that Sanka is said to be real coffee and to taste like real coffee while Brim is said to have a rich taste. Since the question whether or not Sanka is "real coffee" is purely definitional, this difference comes down to the distinction between a coffee that is said to taste like real coffee and one that is said to have a rich taste (not much of a difference). If commercial (16) is effective, I submit that this is primarily because Robert Young himself has credibility. The success of this commercial, if it is successful, could not, I think, derive from what is said about Sanka. On the other hand, since (18) employs no celebrity endorsement its success would have to depend on what is said and how what is said is said.

A common feature of Minidramas is an abrupt transition from a naturalistic setting to something like a laboratory setting in circumstances in which how products work is demonstrated. We noted this earlier in connection with the Liquid Plumr commercial. Consider the following commercial for Polident.

(19)   Polident (CBS, 1/15/81, 6:34 p.m.)
        Type: Live action
        Setting: Drug store
        Characters: Martha Raye and a Consumer (adult female)

        TEXT
        Woman 1: *Aren't you Martha Raye, the movie star?*
        Martha Raye: *That's me.*
        Woman 1: *You use Polident?*
        Martha Raye: *Oh, for years. Polident cleans even tough stains from my dentures. Look, these tough food stains are no problem for Polident.*

Photograph 6.4

Photograph 6.5

Polident's penetrating formula has five powerful ingredients. Helps clean tough stains even in between.
Woman 1: *You sold me on Polident.*
Martha Raye: *Now, you're talking. Take it from Martha Raye, the big mouth. Polident Green helps get tough stains clean.*

The setting of this commercial is a drug store (see Photograph 6.4). During Martha Raye's second turn, the scene shifts to a close-up shot of denture material (see Photograph 6.5) that is then dropped in a glass of liquid. Associated with this "magical" shift in scene is a shift in speech style, from a consultative style to a style more characteristic of a chemistry lecture than a conversation in a drug store. Especially unnatural is statement (20).

(20)   *Polident cleans even tough stains from my dentures.*

It is odd, in part, because it conventionally implicates (21), thanks to the use of *even*, although no conversational foundation has been laid for a concern with tough, as opposed to ordinary, stains.

(21)   One would not expect Polident to clean tough stains.

This is another example of the use of condensation in commercial conversations.

One indicator of formal speech is the use of sentences that are relatively dense semantically. Note in this connection the use of modifiers in *even tough stains, these tough food stains, Polident's penetrating formula,* and *five powerful ingredients.* In ordinary conversation, one would not find so many complex noun phrases in so short a message.

It is worth asking what effect the abrupt shift in scene and language has on viewers. One possibility is that viewers have been conditioned to expect such visual and verbal transitions in commercials and do not attach any particular significance to them. According to this view transitions such as the one we are considering are accepted in the same way as transitions of scene and language in television programs are accepted, as a consequence of the "willing suspension of disbelief" with which we approach fictional art. Certainly, a suspension of disbelief is required in order to accept the idea that Martha Raye and a Consumer would engage in a conversation about Polident in a drug store with a camera fortuitously present. Perhaps anyone who would accept this would accept anything else happening within the commercial.

We have hit upon what I think is the real strength of the use of Minidramas in advertising, namely that viewers will react to them in much the way they react to fictional programs, namely by accepting the premises of the commercial without question (unless these premises are wholly incredible). However, in my view, the unaesthetic transitions of scene and language in a commercial like (19) will not go unnoticed by attentive viewers and cannot help but weaken the force of the commercial. I shall return to this question later.

Minidramas in which only Consumers appear are much more common than are those featuring Celebrities. However, as in those commercials featuring Celebrities and in all Interview-type commercials, one of the Consumers is set up as a Consumer Authority. It is he or she who provides the didactic elements of such commercials.

In general, advertisers employ familiar stereotypes in order to set up the Consumer who serves as Consumer Authority in Minidramas as an expert. Clerks in drug stores, who might be taken as pharmacists, are represented as authorities on OTC drugs; plumbers are authorities on drain cleaners; service station attendants know about cars and car care; etc. We might call these "vocation specific" stereotypes. In other cases, Consumers with relevant consumer experience are set up as Consumer Authorities. Thus, women who have had children are represented as having more knowledge about child care than those who have not and wives are represented as having more knowledge about everything used in a household from dog food to OTC drugs than husbands. This latter conceit is especially interesting since men otherwise dominate advertising. Even in commercials that feature women, men are virtually always employed to read voice over messages.

Presumably, the effectiveness of a Minidrama is a function of what the characters say about the product being promoted and, unless the Minidrama is intentionally comedic in character, of the credibility of the characters. An important ingredient of character credibility is the felicitousness of what these characters say relative to the social context they are placed in and to the roles they play.

Commercials featuring Consumers who, by virtue of their vocation, serve as Consumer Authorities, and didactic Minidramas featuring Celebrities are like Interviews, in that such people normally present an explicitly didactic message. That such commercials are often explicitly didactic is quite natural, for the persons in question would be widely (if somewhat uncritically) accepted as consumer authorities.

As the commercials just cited show, advertisers normally use vocational stereotypes in order to set up one Consumer as a Consumer Authority. Advertisers rarely depart from this relatively safe advertising technique. A commercial that does is the following, refreshingly different commercial for Trac II blades.

(22)   Gillette Trac II blades (CBS, 6/2/78, @ 9:38 p.m.)
         Type: Live action
         Setting: Retail store
         Characters: Two Consumers (adult males) and adult male store clerk

         TEXT
         Customer 1: *Gillette Trac II, please.*
         Clerk: *Mm Mm. Sold out again. Say, you look like a double edge man to me. Daring, unafraid.*
         Customer 1: *No, no. The Gillette Trac II gives me a more comfortable shave.*
         Clerk: *Silly me. These other twin blades'll fit your Trac II handle.*
         Customer 1: *Yeah, but they're not Gillette Trac II's.*
         Clerk: *Yeah, but . . .*
         Customer 1: *Sorry.*
         Voice over (Male): *To guys who use the twin blade, Gillette Trac II, no other blade'll do.*
         Customer 2: *Uh, Gillette Trac II, please.*
         Clerk: *Muh.*

In this commercial, the clerk is represented as a rather silly man who will do anything for a sale. The first customer is represented as firm in his conviction that Trac II blades are best for him, a conviction that is supported by the "fact" that the clerk is sold out of Trac II blades. Of no small importance is that the product name is mentioned six times in the commercial.

I would like to turn now to consider Minidramas featuring only Consumers, none of whom has any vocational claim to consumer expertise. In these commercials, as in all others being considered in this chapter, one of the Consumers is set up as a Consumer Authority. Perhaps the most interesting of this class of commercial on my tapes is one for Pampers disposable diapers. It employs a stereotype—experienced mothers know more about child care than inexperienced ones—to set up one of the two women as the more knowledgeable one. However, in this case the language of the commercial plays an important role in establishing this woman as having superior status.

(23)   Pampers (CBS, 2/24/78, @ 12:34 p.m.)
         Type: Live action
         Setting: Rummage sale
         Characters: Two Consumers (adult females), who are visibly pregnant

         TEXT
         Woman 1: *Did you wanna buy this?* [a baby carriage]
         Woman 2: *No, we've already got one.*
         Woman 1: *This isn't your first baby?*
         Woman 2: *No.*
         Woman 1: *Could I ask you something?*
         Woman 2: *Sure.*
         Woman 1: *For instance, which diaper do you use?*
         Woman 2: *Nothing but Pampers.*
         Woman 1: *Isn't cloth drier?*
         Woman 2: *Uh, uh. Wet a cloth diaper and a Pampers. Pampers stay-dry lining stays drier to help keep your baby's skin stay a lot drier than cloth.*
         Woman 1: *Ya know, I think I'm getting the hang of this baby business.*
         Women 1 & 2: [laughter]
         Voice over (adult male): *Ask any mother about Pampers' dryness.*

This commercial uses language in a relatively subtle way to establish Woman 2 as being of superior status. In the first four turns, Woman 2 is established as an experienced mother. Her relatively higher status is further signaled by her relatively brief responses to Woman 1's attempts to engage her in conversation. The relatively inferior status of Woman 1 is also signaled by the fact that all of her turns but the last are questions. Although Woman 2's responses are pleasant sounding, her first two replies, *No, we've already got one,* and *no,* do not encourage further conversation.

The question *Could I ask you something?* constitutes a polite request for permission to ask a personal question. This is interesting, for Woman 2 grants permission without having any idea what sort of question might be asked. I would suspect few people would grant such an open-ended request to a stranger in real life. The question that follows is not a very personal one, in my view. This somewhat artificial step in the conversation was clearly scripted to effect a switch in the conversation to diapers. This illustrates the difficulty of embedding commercial messages in natural conversation.

As Woman 2 begins her last turn, there is a radical shift in scene from the rummage sale (Photograph 6.6) to something like a laboratory scene in which two babies magically appear (Photograph 6.7). What continuity exists is provided by the fact that we see two hands—one from each woman?—and the fact that Woman 2 continues speaking. However, there is a radical shift in speech style in Woman 2's last turn from a consultative to a formal style. Woman 2 abandons her short responses for semantically quite dense utterances more appropriate to a scientific demonstration than to a conversation at a rummage sale.

The clearest example of a style shift is the use of the Imperative-type sentence, *Wet a cloth diaper and a Pampers,* as an instruction of the type

Photograph 6.6

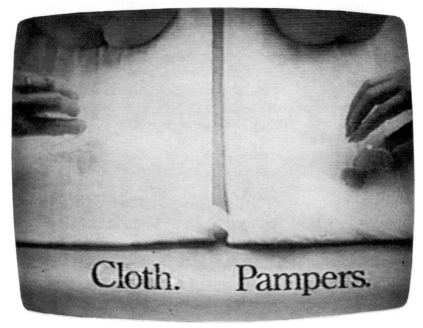

Photograph 6.7

found in recipes or instructions as to how to assemble something or perform a chemistry experiment, and the like. Such uses of language are quite impersonal. Note the striking difference between this line and the line that follows it and Woman 1's reply *Ya know, I think I'm getting the hang of this baby business,* which is highly colloquial in character.

As in the case of the Martha Raye commercial, it is worth asking whether or not the radical shift in scene and language in the Pampers commercial will militate against the effectiveness of the commercial. It is entirely possible that viewers have been conditioned to regard such transitions as acceptable in much the way a "flashback" in a movie is acceptable. On the other hand, it is possible that a commercial like (23) be successful in spite of such discontinuities in conversation.

The most strikingly unnatural conversation I recall ever having seen in a commercial occurs in a recent Amway commercial. In this commercial the setting is a class reunion. The woman in this commercial is the product spokesperson.

(24)   Amway (ABC, 1/16/81, 6:13 p.m.)
         Type: Live action
         Setting: Class reunion
         Characters: Two men and one woman

TEXT
Man: *Look. Norrie!*
Woman: *What's the most promising graduate doing these days?*
Man: *Oh, still . . .*[10] *And you?*
Woman: *I have my own Amway business.*
Man: *Amway?*
Woman: *Right. I'm building financial independence with an extra income as an Amway distributor part time.*
Man: *Great! Need a partner?*
Woman: *Sorry. Meet my husband, the other half of the business.*
Woman's husband: *Hi.*
Woman: *With your own Amway business, you can do it too.*
Voice over (Male): *Contact an Amway distributor and get the whole story.*

Everything the man of this commercial says is consistent with the nature of the conversation. The ellipsis of *Still . . . , and you?* (*I'm still . . . , and what are you doing these days?*) and *Need a partner?* (*Do you need a partner?*) are characteristic of casual speech (style) between people who know each other (register). On the other hand, what the woman says after the man's questioning repeat is wholly unnatural.

The woman's claim, *I'm building financial independence with an extra income as an Amway distributor part time,* is much too dense semantically to be a credible statement in any kind of normal conversation, much less a casual conversation of the sort that would be expected at a class reunion. This is the sort of sentence one might possibly write, but not the sort of thing one would ever say spontaneously. It stands in stark contrast to the highly elliptical sentences said by the man.

The speech register of the woman's third turn is incongruous as well. I can imagine an investment counselor using the phrase *build financial independence* in talking with a client, i.e., in a conversation between people whose relationship is a business relationship (hence a *business* register), but not in a conversation between two people who are renewing an old acquaintance.[11] Register shifts do occur in conversation, but nothing that has been said in this conversation warrants the shift from a social to a business register.

Amway's 1981 advertisements appear to have been constructed around claim (25).

(25)   *I'm building financial independence with an extra income as an Amway distributor part time.*

[10]This line is virtually unintelligible.

[11]The phrase *financial independence* has no precise meaning. Normally we use it to refer to a condition in which a person has sufficient wealth that they need not depend on others for sources of income. As a result, (25)–(27) constitute extraordinarily strong claims.

In another (also dialogical) television commercial (ABC, 1/6/81, 6:25 p.m.), line (26) occurs, and in a magazine advertisement in *Newsweek* (3/2/81), we find line (27) used in dialogue.

(26)   *We're building financial independence as Amway distributors part time.*

(27)   *As Amway distributors, part time, we're building financial independence.*

It is reasonably clear from this that the claim being made in (24)–(26) is central to the 1981 Amway campaign and I suspect that it was chosen without regard to how unnatural sentences like those in (24)–(26) would sound in conversation.

The woman's last contribution is wholly out of place conversationally. Although the man asks if the woman needs a partner, this (in my view) sounds more like he's making a joke or a pass than making a serious request that they join business forces. A sufficient conversational background for the woman's giving the man business advice has not been established. What we have here is considerable condensation in the conversation.

One of the more remarkable conceits of television advertising is that wives are represented as being more knowledgeable about most things than are husbands. With the exception of commercial (2) of this chapter, wherein the husband is a plumber and, hence, a genuine Product Authority, in every commercial on my tapes in which a husband and wife appear, the wife is treated as being the more knowledgeable person. Consider, for instance, commercial (28).

(28)   **Vicks 44D** (NBC, 1/8/81, 8:39 p.m.)
        Type: Live action
        Setting: Drug store
        Characters: Two Consumers (adult male and adult female)

        TEXT
        Man: [cough]
        Woman: [To unseen clerk]: *Vicks Formula 44D, please.*
        Man: *Helen, with this nasty cough, plus congestion, I need . . .*
        Woman: [To unseen clerk]: *Formula 44D.*
        Man: *But Helen, I need a decongestant, not just strong cough medicine.*
        Woman: *You'll need Formula 44D. It's strong like Formula 44, has the strongest non-narcotic cough suppressant you can buy, plus ingredients to help unstuff your nose and loosen upper chest congestion.*
        Man: *It's what I said.* [To unseen clerk]: *Formula 44D.* [To viewing audience]: *Strong for coughs plus congestion.*

The relative superiority of the wife to the husband is shown by the fact that it is the wife who places the order with an unseen and unheard clerk, by the fact that the wife, in her second turn, ignores what the husband is saying and talks over him, and by the fact that it is the wife who possesses useful knowledge in this area. The foolishness of the husband is shown by his childish attempt in his last turn to maintain that Vicks 44D is what he wanted all along.

The style of this commercial is quite unnatural. The husband's first line, were it to have been completed, would have involved a sentence-initial complex prepositional phrase (*With this nasty cough, plus congestion, I need [something that has a decongestant]*), something more characteristic of formal than casual speech. The phrase *with this nasty cough, plus congestion*, is especially unnatural. Phrases of the sort *such-and-such with* X *plus* Y, and variants thereof, are examples of a standard verbal formula of OTC drug advertising. Consider

(29)   *Introducing new Flintstone's with extra C—all the vitamins of a multivitamin plus all the vitamin C of a single C tablet.*   (NBC, 1/5/81, 8:46 a.m.)

(30)   *When your child has a stuffy nose, fever from a cold, it's time for St. Joseph's Cold Tablets for children. It helps with two kinds of relief, an effective nasal decongestant plus the same aspirin in St. Joseph's Aspirin for Children, the brand widely recommended by doctors.*   (WUAB, Cleveland, 2/24/78, @ 12:01 p.m.)

It is, of course, one thing to put phrases of this sort in the mouth of an Interviewer and quite another to put them in the mouths of the Consumers of advertising Minidramas. In (28) the wife's third turn also contains a variant of the *with* X *plus* Y type construction. This occurs in a compound sentence, itself more characteristic of formal than casual speech.

I suspect that the "wife knows best" advertising strategy is used primarily for those advertised products that are (or are believed to be) more commonly purchased by wives than husbands. It is also consistent with the longstanding practice in television situation comedies of portraying wives or women as being superior to husbands or men. In both cases, it seems that those who make television commercials and television shows are trying to cater to women especially.

There can be no doubt that shifts in scene and style and register shifts within "naturalistic" conversations result in commercials that are aesthetically defective. Whether such commercials are ineffective as a result is quite another matter. Such shifts are so common, it is tempting to suggest that consumers have become so inured to them that they have been linguistically desensitized to the styles and registers employed in television advertising. A second possibility is that those who write copy are themselves unaware of such sociolinguistic factors.

As we have seen, it is characteristic of commercials employing dialogue that there be someone (an Interviewer, Celebrity, or Consumer) who presents the advertiser's message and a Consumer who endorses it. I have argued that the authenticity of such commercials comes down, at least in part, to the felicitousness of the conversations that occur within them. As we have seen, such conversations sometimes employ unnatural speech styles and speech registers. Although no one appears to have done any research on the question, it is surely the case that viewers will be sensitive to these matters of style and register. The question arises as to the effect of infelicities of style and register on viewers.

In the case of monological advertisements, the credibility of the advertisement depends on the credibility of what is said and the quite intangible credibility of the person presenting the message. In the case of commercials employing conversation, viewers must be willing to accept the premises of the conversation. Viewers must be willing to believe that the Consumers of product tests such as the Dristan test [commercial (1), p. 132] or Blatz beer test [commercial (9), p. 142] actually took these tests and that the results of the tests are as represented. In such commercials, what is said is of great importance. I submit that how what is said is said is also important.

In cases of Interviews in which the Interviewer converses with a Consumer in a naturalistic setting, and Minidramas, which invariably employ naturalistic settings, and Minidramas, which invariably employ naturalistic settings, some sort of viewer suspension of disbelief analogous to that required for the appreciation of fictional art is required if the commercial is to be effective. Viewers must be willing to believe that what is said and seen is possible, at least in principle. I submit that how the conversants of such commercials talk to each other is crucial to sustaining the viewer's suspension of disbelief. The more natural appearing the Minidrama or Product Spokesman Interview, the more important it will be that conversation occurring within them be natural.

It is interesting that viewers appear to be willing to suspend disbelief in the case of television advertising. A genuinely skeptical consumer would hardly be willing to do so. That viewers are willing to suspend disbelief doubtless derives from the fact that those watching fictional television programs, which constitute the vast majority of programs, are already in this state. Anyone who wanted to know who "really" shot J.R. is surely disposed to believe that Robert Young "really" does go around promoting Sanka to everyone he sees who is tense or nervous from drinking too much undecaffeinated coffee.

Chapter 7
Children's Television Advertising

In this and the next two chapters, I turn to consider television advertising directed at children. In Chapter 8, I shall examine advertisements promoting fruit-flavored products, including gum, candy, cookies, and cold breakfast cereals. The issue to be addressed there is how children will interpret the ubiquitous verbal and visual references to fruit in such commercials. In Chapter 9, I shall examine the advertising of cold breakfast cereals. I shall focus there on the language of the nutrition statements contained in such commercials and on the impact on children of the constantly repeated message that the centerpiece of breakfast should be a sweet food. In this chapter, I address a variety of background questions, including, in particular, whether or not young children have sufficiently linguistic and cognitive competence and "real world" experience to evaluate television advertisements properly.

Although children get product information from a variety of sources (peers, parents, in-store displays, product packages, etc.), television is by far the most important communications medium used systematically to advertise to children (Ward, Wachman, & Wartella, 1977). It has been estimated that the average child saw some 20,000 television commercials a year in the mid-1970s (Adler, 1978). At 30 seconds per commercial, this amounts to about 167 hours of watching commercials, or the amount of time a grade school child spends in the classroom in a 6½-week period, which is itself slightly longer than one-sixth of the school year.[1] Obviously a great deal of teaching and learning is going on in front of the nation's television sets.

Not all of the commercials a child watches are directed at children. Indeed one of the several inadequacies of present efforts at industry

[1]I base this estimate on the amount of time (5 hours) my child spent in the classroom in the fourth grade each day.

163

self-regulation, according to critics of children's television advertising practices, is the fact that National Association of Broadcasters (NAB) Code Authority guidelines regulating children's advertising do not cover prime time television shows and (with some apparently rare exceptions) shows broadcast after school lets out each day. In a 1973 study, it was discovered that only 20% of children's favorite programs were covered by NAB guidelines (Adler, 1978). Nevertheless, children do see commercials targeted specifically at them during the Saturday morning cartoon shows, some Sunday morning shows (e.g., *Wonderama* and *Kids are People Too*), the weekday morning show *Captain Kangaroo*, during shows broadcast after school (e.g., *Brady Bunch* reruns), and during prime time (e.g., *Peanuts* cartoon shows).[2]

Children's television commercials promote products that are of special interest to children of course, and, as a result, relatively few different types of products are promoted. In a 1978 survey of children's commercials (Barcus & McLaughlin, 1978), it was discovered that toys (11.6%), cereals (34.4%), candies and sweets (29.6%), and eating places (14.8%) constituted 90.4% of the products advertised in broadcasts directed at children by network-affiliated stations. This particular survey was done in June of 1968. In the several months just before Christmas, the percentage of commercials for toys would go up significantly.

The practice of advertising on television to children has become quite controversial in recent years. Acting on petitions from Action for Children's Television and the Center for Science in the Public Interest, the FTC initiated its rule-making procedure in 1978, in an attempt to determine the merits of FTC staff proposals that (*a*) television advertising directed at young children (children under the age of 8) be banned; (*b*) advertising of heavily sweetened products be banned during times when significant numbers of older children (children under the age of 12) can be expected to be in the television audience; and (*c*) television advertising of sweetened foods not covered by (*b*) be balanced by health and nutrition disclosures. In late 1978, the FTC took written testimony from interested parties and in February and March of 1979, informal hearings were held in San Francisco and Washington, D.C., respectively. This FTC inquiry was terminated as a result of congressional action in 1980.

[2]I believe that it is generally possible to recognize which commercials shown after school or in prime time are directed at children from those that are directed at adults. If a food commercial promotes a product of interest to children, employs animation, features children rather than adults, is designed to entertain rather than inform, and (in the case of food advertisements) places greater emphasis on taste than nutrition, then the odds are very good that the commercial is targeted at children. Toy commercials directed at children differ from those directed at adults primarily in that children rather than adults are shown playing with the product being promoted.

The concern with the advertising of sweetened foods to children is not surprising in the light of the fact that advertisements for sweetened foods (candy, cookies, gum, presweetened cereals, etc.) dominate children's television advertising. Since I have no expertise in areas of health and nutrition, I do not propose to discuss the merits of preceding FTC proposals (b) and (c). However, I shall discuss the nature of the advertising of foods that are fruit flavored, all of which are sweet, and of cold breakfast cereals, most of which are presweetened, in Chapters 8 and 9.

I shall also not take a position on the merits of the proposal to ban television advertising to young children here. However, there is one question I shall discuss and this is whether or not children, especially young children, have the linguistic and cognitive competence and the "real world" experience to understand and evaluate television advertising properly. This question is not only of great social importance, but is central to an understanding of the impact on children of such advertisements as I focus on in the next two chapters.

The question of whether young children have the competence to understand and evaluate television advertising properly involves three factors: their linguistic competence, their cognitive competence, and their "real world" experience. These three factors are intimately related. It has been shown by a number of researchers (see Turner & Rommetviet, 1967, and Hayhurst, 1967, for example) that preschool children have difficulty with what are called "reversible" passive sentences and that how such passive sentences are interpreted depends on the child's knowledge of the world. Consider, for instance, the following pairs of active and passive sentences.

(1)   a. The dog chased the cat.
        b. The cat was chased by the dog.

(2)   a. The girl ate the spinach.
        b. The spinach was eaten by the girl.

Now, a reversible passive sentence is one that would make sense if interpreted as if it were an active sentence, i.e., if the surface subject [*the cat* in (1b)] and object of *by* [*the dog* in (1b)] of the passive sentence are interpreted as the logical subject and object, respectively, of the verb. Passive sentence (1b) is reversible, for (3) makes sense.

(3)   The cat chased the dog.

On the other hand, (2b) is not reversible, for (4) does not make sense.

(4)   *The spinach ate the girl.

What has been discovered is that preschool children tend to interpret a sentence like (2b) correctly, but not (1b). The child's knowledge that cats can chase dogs, but that spinach cannot eat girls determines how he or she will interpret passives like (1b) and (2b). Children who misunderstand sentences like (1b) clearly do not fully control the passive construction, for how they interpret passive sentences is determined, not just by their knowledge of the language, but also, in part, by their knowledge of the world.

It is clear from the preceding example that what children know about the world can influence how they interpret language. This fact has an important bearing on how children interpret the language of television advertising. As we shall see in Chapter 8, commercials for artificially fruit-flavored products abound with verbal and visual references to fruit. Children who do not know that fruit flavors can be chemically simulated must interpret some of these verbal and visual references to fruit as indicating that there is fruit in the product being promoted when there is not.

The child's cognitive abilities clearly have a bearing on how they will understand and evaluate television advertising. It is the child's cognitive abilities that are responsible for how the child relates language to the world, an ability that is central to the child's development of semantic competence. Moreover, the child's cognitive skills are crucial to how he or she will evaluate the claims made by advertisers. In this connection it is worth observing that young children do not have particularly well developed critical intellectual skills.

A general discussion of the cognitive competence of children would take us far afield from the focus of this study. However, a number of representatives of the advertising and broadcasting industries, including ABC, NBC, and the NAB, argued before the FTC that young children's linguistic development lags behind their cognitive development and that, therefore, verbal measures of children's cognitive abilities will underestimate these cognitive abilities. This line of argument was designed to discredit experimentation employing verbal means (in experimental instructions, questions, etc.) showing that children have difficulties of various sorts with television advertising. This line of argument, were it correct, would also somewhat mitigate the force of what I shall have to say about the language of children's television advertising. Therefore, since this argument was based on few papers, and since the whole of the directly relevant scholarly literature is quite manageable, I propose to devote a few pages to this issue here. First, I propose to examine children's linguistic competence.

The Language of Children's Television Advertising

The language of television advertising directed at children is normally colloquial in style. The use of colloquial style in television advertising serves several ends. It is a style all children are familiar with and most frequently use. It is more personal than formal styles, which tend to be used by speakers in public contexts. It is less complex syntactically, and thus, semantically. It also employs a less precise vocabulary than does formal English. In the case of children's television advertising, the need to use colloquial English is even greater than it is in advertising directed at adults, for few children use formal styles and, because of its richer vocabulary, most young children encounter difficulties in understanding formal English. This represents just one of the respects in which children are disadvantaged linguistically.

Fully consistent with the colloquial style of children's television advertising is the fact that language play is an extraordinarily common feature of such advertising. We find language play in the coining of product names. Note the alliteration of *Crazy Cow* (cereal), *Tic Tac* (candy), *Kit-Kat* (candy), or *Hot Wheels Criss-Cross Crash* (race set), the use of punning in *Bubble Yum* (bubble gum), *Elfwich* (cookie), or *Alphabits* (cereal), the unusual spelling of *Froot Loops* (cereal) or *Trix* (cereal), and the use of such ridiculous names as *Boo Berry* (cereal), *Count Chocula* (cereal), or *Bonkers* (toy). Interestingly, rhyme is not employed in any of the product names on my tapes, though partial rhymes (*Kit-Kat, Tic Tac, Froot Loops,* etc.) do occur.

Language play also occurs frequently in advertising copy. Rhyme and alliteration are very commonly used. In an advertisement for Crazy Cow cereal we find rhyme employed as well as a play on the word *how,* plays on the aphorism *Man's best friend is his doggy,* and the diction exercise *How now brown cow.* We also see the name *Crazy Cow* being used ambiguously to refer both to the cereal and to the animated cow of the commercial.

(5)   Crazy Cow cereal (ABC, 3/11/78, @ 8:02 a.m.), exerpt
       Boy (singing): *My best friend is a cow.*
       Crazy Cow (singing): *And how.*
       Voice over (adults, singing): *How now Crazy Cow.*
       Crazy Cow (singing): *That's me.*
       Voice over (adults, singing): *Makes chocolate milk—wow!*
       Girl: *Wow!*
       Voice over (adults, singing): *How now crazy cow.*

We find alliteration in a line from a Cocoa Puffs commercial, where

Sonny, an animated bird, says *I'm cuckoo for Cocoa Puffs, cuckoo for Cocoa Puffs* (ABC, 3/11/78, @ 8:16 a.m.). It appears that a cuckoo bird was chosen to be the animated spokesbird for Cocoa Puffs primarily in order to provide the opportunity for this alliterative line. In this commercial, we also find the phrase *munchy, crunchy, chocolately Cocoa Puffs,* which employs both rhyme and alliteration as well as onomatopoeia (see *munchy* and *crunchy*).

Plays on words are very frequent in children's television advertising. After a porcupine has struck a toucan (serving as the animated spokesbird for Froot Loops) with a quill, the following lines occur:

(6)   Froot Loops Cereal (CBS, 7/18/78, 8:16 a.m.), exerpt
        Porcupine: *Sorry. Gee. Getting somebody to have breakfast with is sticky business.*
        Toucan: *Cheer up, my porcupine pal. A fruitiful breakfast we'll share right now. Follow your nose. It always knows.*

In this commercial, we find plays on the word *sticky* and *nose/knows* as well as partial rhyme (*pal, now*) and a novel form *fruitiful* /frútif̣l/. Commercials for Captain Crunch cereal frequently employ the "food thief" motif (someone or something steals Captain Crunch cereal and is later caught because he is heard munching on the cereal) primarily, it seems, to provide an excuse for Captain Crunch to say, *You can't get away with the Crunch 'cause the crunch gives you away,* which includes a play on the adverb-cum-particle *away* and allows use of the onomatopoeic "buzz" word *crunch* twice. We also find a piece of language play in the following excerpt from a Sugar Smacks commercial.

(7)   Sugar Smacks (CBS, 7/18/78, 8:49 a.m.), exerpt
        Father: *What's that frog doing?*
        Frog: [In a bird bath] *Deep sea diving.*
        Father: *How deep is it?*
        Frog: *Knee deep.*

This line has nothing whatever to do with the rest of the commercial and is there apparently only to amuse children.[3]

Advertisers also play with English morphology. In a commercial for Cheerios, the "morpheme" *io* (*Cheer + io + s*) is reduplicated in the yodeled "word" *cheerioios* [čɪrióioz] and is combined with the morpheme *oat* in the lines *Cheerios, crunchy toasted oatios.* In another line, *oat* occurs

---

[3]A complete transcript of this commercial can be found in Chapter 9.

as an infix (in a play on the word *yodel*): *When you want the great taste of Cheerios, just Cheeriotel* [čɪióɒl].

I presume that the purpose of the use of language play in children's television advertising is to amuse children and thus keep their attention. This is presumably also the reason why so many children's commercials employ minidramas, virtually always animated, portraying some sort of adventure. It should be pointed out that such minidramas do not differ greatly from the programs they surround, and young children may not distinguish them from programs as a result.

Normally an advertiser will use language that the children he is interested in reaching will understand. In some cases, where the product is directed to relatively old children, the language employed can be somewhat sophisticated. I believe that the language of the following commercial would be beyond the capacity of the average preschool child:

(8)   Radarc Car (ABC, 12/15/79, 10:41 a.m.)
       Type: Live action
       Setting: Indoors
       Characters: Two boys

       TEXT
       Voice over (adult male): *It's Kenner's new Radarc. Flip the on/off switch
          and Radarc is on the move. Two 9-volt and two D batteries not included
          provide the power. Muscle electricity provides the direction control.*
       Boy 1: *How'd 'e do that?*
       Boy 2: *My muscle electricity triggers Radarc's signal transmitter. I flex my
          muscle . . . Radarc circles in reverse. Flex again . . . Radarc moves
          forward.*
       Voice over: *Some CB radio signals interfere with Radarc's direction
          control. Radarc, new from Kenner.*

In this commercial two disclaimers appear, namely (9) and (10).

(9)   *Two 9-volt and two D batteries not included provide the power.*

(10)   *Some CB radio signals interfere with Radarc's direction control.*

Both (9) and (10) are long and employ language beyond the capacities of preschool children. However, it could be argued that the toy is not intended for children that young and that the child who does not understand (9) and (10) will probably not understand the commercial as a whole.

It is in regard to the disclaimers that appear in children's television advertising that the question of the linguistic competence of children is most critical. Clearly, if a child cannot understand a disclaimer there is no point in presenting it to him. There is reason to believe that some disclaimers in children's television advertising will not be intelligible to young children.

Disclaimers

The following types of disclaimers regularly occur in children's advertising (X refers to a product):

(11)   *Partial assembly required.*

(12)   *X sold separately.*

(13)   *Batteries not included.*

(14)   *Artificially flavored.*

(15)   *At participating stores.*

(16)   *While supplies last.*

(17)   *In specially marked boxes.*

(18)   *You have to put it together.*

With the exception of (18), none of these disclaimers can be said to be colloquial in style, and, in my view, most of them will present problems for young children.

There is published research (Liebert *et al.*, 1977) showing that most second-grade children do not comprehend disclaimer (11) and that some even have trouble with the very much simpler disclaimer (18). Moreover, there is research (Gentner, 1975) showing that the verb *sell* [see (12)] presents problems to children of this age. And as noted earlier, there is research showing that young children have trouble with the passive construction [see (11)–(14) and (17)]. However, to my knowledge research has not been done relevant to the assessment of the remaining disclaimers. Nevertheless, I believe that a good case can be made in support of the view that (11)–(17) are beyond the linguistic capacity of most young children.

There exist a number of syntactic and semantic theories making very different claims about the relationship between syntax and semantics and about how syntactic and semantic phenomena should be described. I propose here to adopt a transformational (Chomsky, 1965) approach to the analysis of (11)–(18) primarily because it details the relative complexity of linguistic constructions in a particularly perspicuous way.

Disclaimers (11)–(17) are extraordinarily elliptical and, if they are to be understood, the child must "recover" the elliptical (deleted) material. Paraphrases (19)–(25) bring out some, but by no means all, of the elliptical material (X refers, as before, to a product).

(19)   Partial assembly of X is required.

(20)   X is sold separately.

(21)   Batteries are not included with X.

(22)   X is artificially flavored.

(23)   This offer is good at participating stores.

(24)   This offer is good while supplies last.

(25)   X can be found in specially marked boxes.

Disclaimers (11)–(14) appear to have undergone a transformational "rule" that deletes the verb *be*, as well as "rules" deleting the noun phrases that refer to products mentioned in the commercial. Reconstruction of the elliptical material in (15)–(17) is a more complicated process for me and presumably also for the children to which they are addressed.

Although English has a variety of deletion rules, sentence fragments (11)–(14) do not result from the application of any actual rules of English syntax.[4] There are similarities between (11)–(14) and the language of telegrams and newspaper headlines, but both of these language styles are beyond the linguistic experience of most young children. The question arises as to how children can be expected to know how to interpret these sentence fragments if the "rules" that effect the deletions are not actual rules of English.

Disclaimers (11)–(14) are agentless passives and in order to understand them fully, the child must recover the deleted agent phrase. Compare (19)–(22) with (26)–(29). (Y refers to the advertiser–manufacturer.)

(26)   Partial assembly of X is required by Y.

(27)   X is sold separately by Y.

---

[4]English has rules that delete the verb *be*—compare *A boy who is from Boston* and *A boy from Boston*. However, the verb *be* of a sentence like *A boy is being given a present* cannot be deleted unless the sentence functions as a noun phrase in another sentence. We can say *I saw a boy being given a present*, but cannot say **A boy being given a present* as a sentence in isolation.

(28)   Batteries are not included with X by Y.

(29)   X is artificially flavored by Y.

In order to understand (11)–(14), children must not only recover the elliptical agent phrases [the *by*-phrases of (26)–(29)], they must recognize that Y is the logical subject of each of the sentences (26)–(29). From the transformational perspective, this is tantamount to recognizing that (26)–(29) are derived from (30)–(33), and therefore have the same meaning as (30)–(33).

(30)   Y requires partial assembly of X.

(31)   Y sells X separately.

(32)   Y does not include batteries with X.

(33)   Y artificially flavors X.

The claim that (11–14) are passives is to say that the surface subjects of these sentence fragments are not their logical subjects. It is this fact about passive sentences that presents problems for preschool children. In a study of the acquisition of passive sentences, Turner and Rommetviet (1967) showed pictures of events to children between the ages of 4 and 9 and asked them which of two active sentences or which of two passive sentences was the better "name" for the picture. The sentences in each pair differed only in their grammatical relations, i.e., as (34a) differs from (34b) or (35a) differs from (35b).

(34)   a. The dog chased the cat.
         b. The cat chased the dog.

(35)   a. The dog was chased by the cat.
         b. The cat was chased by the dog.

Turner and Rommetviet found that while nursery school children gave correct responses in 75% or more of the cases in which pairs of active sentences [see (34)] were tested, they were correct in less than 40% of the trials with pairs of passive sentences [see (35)]. As noted earlier, reversible passives like (35b) presented special problems to such children. The success rate for such passives in the case of nursery school children was below 40%. Children in the first and second grades continued to have problems with reversible passives, with a success rate of about 55% in the case of first graders and about 75% in the case of second graders.

The Turner and Rommetviet study and the Hayhurst study (cited earlier) establish that young children do not fully control the passive construction. This fact alone makes problematic the use of the passive voice in stating disclaimers in advertising directed at young children. There are no studies of the effect of the "rule" of *be*-deletion and the "rules" that delete the various noun phrases of (26)–(29) that do not show up in (11)–(14), if only because these are not actual English syntactic rules. However, although these ellipsis operations simplify disclaimers in the sense of making them shorter, they make the disclaimers much less transparent semantically and therefore perceptually. As a result it is difficult to see how young children can be expected to understand (11)–(14) without instruction.

There is solid empirical evidence that children have difficulty with *partial assembly required*. No research has been done on disclaimers (12)–(14) though there is evidence that young children have problems with the verb *sell*. I would like to turn now to consider each of (11)–(14) individually in an attempt to assess just how lingusitically complex each is.

In addition to *partial assembly required* the disclaimer *some assembly required* also occurs on my tapes. Both are phenomenally complex syntactically and semantically. As we have seen, (36a) is an elliptical variant of (37a); the same reasoning supports the view that (36b) is an elliptical variant of (37b).

(36)　　a. *Partial assembly required.*
　　　　b. *Some assembly required.*

(37)　　a. *Y* requires partial assembly of *X*.
　　　　b. *Y* requires some assembly of *X*.

Even (37a) and (37b) are elliptical. In order to understand them properly, children must recognize that they (or their agents) must do the assembling in question. Compare (37a) and (37b) with (38a) and (38b), respectively.

(38)　　a. *Y* requires you to assemble *X* partially.
　　　　b. *Y* requires you to assemble *X* to some degree.

Sentences (38a) and (38b) make explicit that the children in the viewing audience (or their agents) must do the assembling.

From a transformational perspective there would have to be said to be a syntactic relationship between (36) and (38). Other analyses are possible, of course. Nevertheless, it can be maintained that children hearing (36a) or (36b) must, if they are to understand them, assign semantic interpretations that are essentially the same as those that are assigned to (38a) and (38b).

Within a standard transformational approach, (38a) and (38b) would be said to be derived from underlying structures consisting of two clauses. We can represent these structures schematically as in (39).

(39)   a. *Y* requires (you assemble *X* partially)
         b. *Y* requires (you assemble *X* to some degree)

In order to derive the disclaimers of (36), the subordinate clauses of (39) must first undergo a rather complex nominalization process that ultimately results in the noun phrases *partial assembly* and *some assembly*. One of the more interesting features of this process is that the adverbials *partially* and *to some degree* become adjectives (*partial*) or determiners (*some*).

The use of degree expressions like *some* or *partial* as determiners or adjectives is not restricted to the disclaimers being discussed, as shown in (40a)–(40c).

(40)   a. A partial reconstruction of his mouth was required.
         b. Some recognition from his boss would be appreciated.
         c. Full restitution of the stolen funds is expected.

To my knowledge, no one has studied the acquisition of derived nominals, to say nothing of constructions like (40) where the derived nouns are accompanied by a degree word as determiner or adjective. However, it is clear that this is the sort of construction that will be acquired relatively late in language acquisition. Moreover, the word *assembly,* according to the interpretation it has in the disclaimers being discussed, must be rare in anybody's speech, to say nothing of children's speech. Things like *Some assembly of this toy will be required* just aren't the sort of things adults say to children.

Liebert *et al.* (1977) have shown that young children do have problems with the specific disclaimer *Partial assembly required.* The Liebert group made three videotapes of each of two television commercials for toys and erased the disclaimers appearing on them. On one of the copies, no disclaimer was used; on the second, the disclaimer *partial assembly required* was recorded; on the third, the disclaimer *you have to put it together* was recorded. Two groups of children were tested for comprehension of these disclaimers, one consisting of kindergarten children and the other of second grade children. On being shown the commercials with no disclaimer, less than 20% of the younger group realized the need for assembly of the toy while around 30% of the older group came to this conclusion. These correct judgments presumably were based on seeing the toys in the commercials and on their experience with such toys. Interestingly the younger group shown the commercial with the disclaimer *partial assembly required* had slightly better results (a little less than 30% correct) than did the control group whereas second graders shown this commercial showed no improvement over the control group. Thus, something like 70% of both kindergarteners and second graders did not understand the disclaimer *partial assembly required*. Even the linguistically simpler disclaimer *you have to put it together* presented problems for the younger children. Only about half of the younger group understood this disclaimer. A little over 30% of the older group failed to understand this disclaimer. As the Liebert group's study demonstrates, it is no small problem to construct language that young children can understand.

The disclaimer *you have to put it together* is now being used in some children's television commercials. However, in one commercial (which I saw just once and do not have recorded) it occurred embedded as a nonrestrictive relative clause modifying the product name (which I did not catch). The result was something like (41).

(41)   Giggle Gaggle, which you have to put together, is a great toy.

The problem with this ploy is that sentences containing relative clauses are more difficult to understand than simple declarative sentences, and relative clauses are perceptually less salient than are simple declarative sentences. It is clear that disclaimers should take the form of simple declarative sentences in children's advertising.

In another commercial (which I do have on tape), for the toy *Don't Upset Me,* the disclaimer is pronounced with the intonation contour of (42).

(42)   ''you   have   to   put   it   to''gether

Unfortunately, with this intonation contour, the child's (or parent's) need to put the toy together is made to appear to be a product advantage, rather than a product disadvantage. One variant of this disclaimer that I have heard (but do not have on tape) is *you put it together,* in which the verb of obligation *have* is suppressed. A quite natural interpretation of this disclaimer, in my view, is as a description of a product advantage.

It would be useful to know exactly why *partial assembly required* presented such problems to children. The following factors are relevant: the fact that it is in the passive voice, the fact that it is quite elliptical, the fact that it employs a derived nominal, and the fact that the derived nominal in question, *assembly,* rarely occurs in colloquial speech. Since the last factor could alone account for the problems children have with this disclaimer, no general conclusions that are applicable to (12)–(14) can legitimately be drawn.

Disclaimers of the form X *sold separately* are used in commercials in which several different toys are shown in a commercial. In one type of commercial, a doll might appear in a commercial that promotes doll accessories. The sort of disclaimer used in this type of commercial is (43).

(43)   *Action figure sold separately.*

In a second type of commercial, several different toys are promoted equally. The disclaimer used in this context is (44).

(44)   *Each sold separately.*

As noted earlier, disclaimers like (43) and (44) are agentless passives, which have undergone the rule of Agent Deletion and the noncolloquial rule of *be*-deletion. Thus, (43) and (44) are variants of (45) and (46), respectively.

(45) Y sells the action figure separately.

(46) Y sells each (toy) separately.

Expressions (45) and (46) are themselves elliptical, as can be seen by comparing them with (47) and (48).

(47) Y sells the action figure separately from X.

(48) Y sells each (toy) separately from the others.

In the case of (47), X refers to the toys that are being promoted along with the action figure.

The phrase *action figure* has no conventional meaning in colloquial English. To my knowledge, it occurs only in toy advertising and on toy packages. In some cases, its meaning would be reasonably clear to adults. In the case of a commercial for doll accessories in which the doll also appears, it would be clear to most adults, I think, that the doll is the action figure. I have less confidence that young children would draw this inference. However, the phrase *action figure* can be used quite arbitrarily. I was once shown a package on which was depicted a person on a horse. The phrase *action figure not included* appeared on the box. The adult who showed me this had decided that the horse was the action figure, but as it turned out, it was the person that was the action figure.

No one appears to have done a study of how well children understand *action figure sold separately* and *each sold separately.* However, Gentner (1975) has shown that the verb *sell*, which appears in these disclaimers, presents problems for children. Gentner did a study of the acquisition of the verbs *have, give* and *take, sell* and *buy*, and *spend.* She argued that *give* and *take* are semantically more complex than *have*, for *give* and *take* both involve a change of possession. Thus, for (49) to be true, X must have Y

at some time T_1 and Z must have Y at some time T_2, where T_1 is earlier than T_2.

(49) X gave Y to Z.

Now consider (50), where W is an amount of money.

(50) X sold Y to Z for W.

For (50) to be true, X must have Y at T_1, and Z must have Y at T_2, where T_1 is earlier than T_2, and Z must have W at T_3 and X must have W at T_4, where T_3 is earlier than T_4. In a sense *sell* (or *buy*) describes twice as complex a situation as does *give* (or *take*). Not surprisingly, Gentner found that children have a good deal more trouble with *sell* and *buy* than with *give* and *take*.

Gentner created an experimental situation in which each of two dolls, the Muppets, Bert and Ernie of *Sesame Street* fame, were placed at small tables on which there were both small objects and money. The children, who ranged in age from 3½ to 8½ years old, were given instructions like *Make Bert give a truck to Ernie*, or *Make Ernie sell a truck to Bert*. Children from 3½ to 4½ years old showed a good understanding of *give* (almost 100% correct) and *take* (a little over 80% correct), but showed virtually no understanding of *buy* and *sell*. Children between 4½ and 5½ scored a little over 30% correct for *sell* and a little below 25% for *buy*. This was the only group for which *sell* was easier than *buy*. Children of ages from 5½ to 6½ understood *buy* correctly about 45% of the time but understood *sell* correctly a little over 30% of the time. Children between 6½ and 7½ years old performed correctly about 70% of the time for *buy*, but only about 45% of the time in the case of *sell*. The oldest group of children, those between 7½ and 8½ years old showed virtually complete mastery of *buy* (95% correct responses) but continued to have problems with *sell* (about 65% correct).

It is clear from the Gentner study that a disclaimer such as *action figure sold separately* is going to present problems to children for it employs a verb (*sell*) children have trouble with, employs a conceptually different adverb (*separately*), is a passive sentence, and employs a non-English rule in its generation (*be*-deletion). Although no one has done a study of the comprehensibility of any specific versions of this disclaimer, I don't think it can be seriously doubted that young children will have difficulty with it.

In the case of *some/partial assembly required*, a simpler (though not unproblematic) alternative was available. A simpler version of *action figure sold separately* or the even more difficult disclaimer *each sold separately* (more difficult because it employs the quantifier *each*) would be

difficult to construct. *Action figure sold separately* might be replaced with
X *does not come with* Y, where Y is the product being promoted and X is
the product not included with Y. *Each sold separately,* said when several
different toys are promoted together, is even more difficult to "paraphrase." In my view, the real problem here is the nature of the commercials themselves. Showing the "action figure" during a commercial promoting accessories for the "action figure" or promoting several toys
together cannot help but confuse children about what exactly is being
offered.

The disclaimer *batteries not included,* like the others, is a passive. It is a
reversible passive, for *batteries* can be a logical subject of the verb *include,*
as in (51).

(51)   This battery does not include battery acid.

As a result, young children may have some difficulties with it. I know of
no studies of the acquisition of *include,* but my intuition is that it is less
colloquial than *contain.* Compare (52) and (53).

(52)   X does not include Y.

(53)   X does not contain Y.

A simpler disclaimer would not be difficult to construct, for example
(54).

(54)   You must buy the batteries.

A commercial for a Kenner *Radarc* toy uses the *batteries not included*
disclaimer in a way that is particularly strange linguistically, as I noted
earlier. Recall line (53) from this commercial.

(55)   *It's Kenner's new Radarc. Flip the on/off switch and Radarc is on the*
        move. **Two 9-volt and two D batteries not included provide the power.**
        Muscle electricity provides the direction control [emphasis added].

This disclaimer consists of a main clause (*Two 9-volt and two D batteries*
provide the power) and the residue of a nonrestrictive relative clause (*not*
included) that modifies the subject. The problem with this disclaimer is
that it is ungrammatical, and only marginally intelligible.[5] The phrase
two 9-volt and two D batteries can be modified by a nonrestrictive relative
clause, as the grammaticality of (56) shows.

(56)   Two 9-volt and two D batteries, which are not included, provide
        the power.

---

[5] Were *not included* set off by "comma" intonation, the sentence would be grammatical.
Unfortunately it is not.

The syntactic problem with the disclaimer is that Whiz Deletion, a rule that deletes sequences consisting of a relative pronoun and some form of the verb *be* from relative clauses, cannot apply when the main constituent of the relative clause is an adjective unless Adjective Shift, a rule that moves adjectives from the right of a noun to the left of the noun also applies. Thus, as Chomsky (1965) has noted, (57) can be mapped into (58) and (58) can be mapped into (59).

(57)   The Chinese, who are industrious, will never go hungry.

(58)   *The Chinese, industrious, will never go hungry.   (Whiz Deletion).

(59)   The industrious Chinese will never go hungry.   (by Adjective Shift)

As the ungrammaticality of (58) shows, Adjective Shift must apply to truncated relative clauses consisting of an adjective. In the disclaimer we are discussing, Adjective Shift has not applied (and, for that matter cannot apply), resulting in an ungrammatical sentence.

There are three points worth making about this disclaimer. First, expressing a disclaimer as a subordinate clause deemphasizes it. Second, the practice of employing a complex construction to express a disclaimer in an advertisement broadcast to young children is problematic at best. Third, the ungrammaticality of the sentence containing this disclaimer may lead some children to suppress *not included* in order to assign an interpretation to the sentence as a whole.

The disclaimer *artificially flavored* is not often used in children's advertising largely because advertisements for artificially flavored foods require no disclaimer of this sort. However, this disclaimer does appear in an advertisement for Starburst candy as we shall see. Like the disclaimers we have been discussing, *artificially flavored* is an agentless passive which has undergone some ellipsis transformations.

The disclaimer *artificially flavored* contrasts with *naturally flavored*. These two notions have to do with whether or not the flavor is somehow derived from the natural substance that has this flavor. In the next chapter I shall argue that there is a basic distinction more relevant to children and this is whether or not a product that is said to have a particular flavor actually contains the substance that has this flavor. Within the terms of this distinction, the appropriate disclaimer would be X *(product name) has no Y* (natural substance) *in it* (e.g., *Starburst has no fruit in it*). This latter disclaimer is simpler linguistically and conceptually than is *artificially flavored*.

Let us now turn to consider the adverbial disclaimers (15)–(17), repeated as (60)–(62).

(60)   *At participating stores.*

(61)   *While supplies last.*

(62)   *In specially marked boxes.*

Disclaimer (60) appears in advertisements for fast-food outlets when some premium (small gift) or special offer is being made. It is a bit peculiar because it comes down to saying that the offer is good where it's good. All (60) communicates is that the offer is not good everywhere. I believe it can be argued that (60) entails (63), for if the offer is good at any given store it is, by definition, a participating store.

(63)   Only at participating stores.

Disclaimer (62) is employed in advertisements for cold breakfast cereals and is used to indicate that some premium is contained in boxes marked as containing that premium. Such offers are made in about 30% of the breakfast cereal commercials on my tapes. Now, although (60) entails (63), (62) clearly does not entail (64).

(64)   Only in specially marked boxes.

I say this because (65), which cancels inference (64), is not self-contradictory.

(65)   *X* is contained in specially marked boxes, and in some that are
            not specially marked as well.

Instead, (62) only conversationally implicates (64) (via the Maxim of Relevance).

Disclaimer (61) is normally used in retail operations such as fast-food chains by way of indicating that the offer is a limited one. This disclaimer entails (66).

(66)   Only while supplies last.

Disclaimer (61) comes down to saying that the offer is good as long as the offer is good.

As we have seen, two of (60)–(62) entail corresponding disclaimers containing *only* and the third conversationally implicates such a disclaimer. The question arises as to why advertisers do not say (63), (64), and (66), for they are all true and are more explicit about what the offer is. In general, the practice of relying on children to draw out the entailments and implicatures of some phrase or sentence, seems to me to be a problematic one. Moreover, I question the use of such words as *participating* and *specially* (and perhaps *supplies*) in a children's disclaimer. These are not the sorts of words that would normally be in a young child's repertoire. Finally, as comparison of (15)–(17) with (23)–(25) shows, these disclaimers are highly elliptical.

All of the disclaimers we have been discussing are elliptical. The question I would raise is whether they are too elliptical to be comprehensible to young children. In general, concrete term expressions (e.g., product names) and concrete predicates (e.g., color words and other words referring to physical properties and action verbs) are easier for children to learn than abstract nouns [*assembly* in (11)], or abstract predicates [*separately* in (12) or *participating* in (15)]. Yet the disclaimers frequently consist of just such relatively abstract nouns and predicates. In some cases, as in the case of *separately*, important term expressions (e.g., separately from what?) are suppressed which cannot help but confound the child's interpretation of the disclaimer.

A good deal of thought and testing should go into the construction of children's television disclaimers. In some cases (e.g., *you have to put it together* for *some assembly required*), superior alternatives are clearly possible. In others, the disclaimer in question describes so complex a situation that straightforward alternatives are difficult to construct. This is true of *each sold separately* and *action figure sold separately*. Perhaps the problem is with the nature of the commercials themselves. Showing a doll in a commercial promoting doll accessories must give rise to the view that they come as a package.

As I noted earlier, there are three important factors governing how well children understand and evaluate advertising, namely, their linguistic competence, their cognitive competence, and their knowledge of the world. In this section, I have discussed language problems involving passives and the acquisition of the verb *sell*. There are hosts of other linguistic constructions that children as old as 7, 8, and 9 years have problems with. Clark and Garnica (1974), for instance, report that children as old as 8 years have significant problems in using the verbs *go* (versus *come*) and *take* (versus *bring*). And C. Chomsky (1969) showed that 8 year olds have problems with the distinction between *easy to see* and *hard to see*, with the *ask–tell* distinction, and with the verb *promise*. Such language disabilities have two possible consequences. Children may fail to understand certain messages, as is the case with some disclaimers, or they may misunderstand and, therefore, be misled by other messages. Let us now turn to the cognitive competence of children.

Children's Cognitive Competence

Much of the scholarly literature concerning how well children evaluate television advertising is devoted to the child's ability to recognize the intent of television advertising. It is believed that children who do not recognize the selling intent of television commercials will necessarily be deceived by them, for they will confuse them with program content and public service announcements including the increasingly frequent nutrition and health messages that occur in children's television. Indeed, if children are to evaluate television advertising properly, it is imperative that they distinguish, for example, a commercial promoting the eating of some cold breakfast cereal from one promoting good eating habits, for the former is self-serving and commercially motivated, while the latter is not. This can be quite difficult as we shall see, for on occasion advertisers run self-serving advertisements that look very much like spots promoting good nutrition.[6]

Much of the research done on the question of the young child's ability to understand the purposes of advertising has been concerned only with the child's ability to distinguish commercials from program content. To facilitate the child's recognition of this distinction, the television networks now use a variety of devices (e.g., the "Stop" and "Go" signs on *Captain Kangaroo*) that separate off-program content from commercials. This is a good practice, but the capacity to distinguish commercials from program content is at most a necessary condition for recognition of the selling intent behind commercials. Moreover, the ability to distinguish commercials from program content does not entail an ability to distinguish commercials from public service messages, both of which occur during commercial breaks.

In the most comprehensive study of the child's understanding of the nature of commercials, Ward, Wachman, and Wartella (1977) (henceforth, WWW) found that as many as 96% of kindergartners, 74% of third graders, and 59% of sixth graders do not fully understand the purpose of television commercials, that is, do not have what WWW call "high awareness" of the persuasive intent of commercials. The WWW study consisted of in-depth interviews with about 600 children of the three age groups just mentioned in which, among other things, the children were asked questions about the nature and purpose of television commercials. They graded the children's responses as follows:

"Low degree of awareness" responses are simple perceptual descriptions of commercials (e.g., "they show kids playing with dune buggies") or affective responses ("They're funny"). "Medium-awareness" responses reflect some knowledge of the concept of advertising but no understanding of advertising's persuasive intent. "High awareness" responses show understanding of the intent of advertising, and some notions of sponsorship and/or technique [p. 59].

[6]See the Kellogg's "better breakfast" commercial of Chapter 9.

The figures cited earlier are the percentages of children who show "low" or "medium," but not "high" awareness of the purpose of television advertising.

In WWW and their testimony before the FTC (Ward, Wachman, & Wartella, 1979), these researchers do not sharply distinguish responses in which a child evidences recognition of the persuasive intent of commercials from responses indicating an awareness of their selling intent. This is important, for it is one thing for a child to recognize that commercials try to get them to "use," "get," or "try" a product (words that children employed in answers to the interview questions) and quite another for a child to recognize that commercials try to get them to "buy" a product. Health and nutrition announcements are normally persuasive in intent, but they are not intended to sell anything. As a result, the figures cited in the preceding paragraph may overestimate children's degree of awareness of the selling intent, as opposed to the persuasive intent, of commercials.

The Gentner (1975) study cited earlier, which was concerned in part with the acquisition of the verbs *buy* and *sell,* sheds some light on the results obtained by WWW and others. Consider (67) and (68).

(67)   John sold a book to Mary.

(68)   Mary bought a book from John.

Sentences (67) and (68) both describe the same commercial transaction. They differ syntactically and semantically in the perspective they take on this transaction. In (67), *John* is the agent and in (68) *Mary* is the agent. As I noted earlier, children had less trouble in general with instructions containing *buy* than with those containing *sell.*

Gentner (1975) was unsure "whether the poorer performance on 'sell' reflects some added conceptual complexity over 'buy' . . . or whether 'sell' is acquired later simply because the act of selling and the term 'to sell' are relatively infrequent in a child's experience [p. 240]." Certainly, children have little experience of selling, and, though Gentner gave no evidence supporting the view that *sell* may be used less frequently than *buy* around children, I see no reason to doubt this. On the other hand, I am inclined to doubt that *sell* is conceptually more complex than *buy* if what one means is semantic or logical complexity for they are mirror-image predicates semantically. However, I would suggest that one can account for the relative difficulty of *sell* in cognitive terms.

Children of the ages studied are widely recognized as having an essentially egocentric orientation toward events. As a result, they should have more difficulty with *sell* than with *buy* because sentences with *sell* (provided they are not passive sentences) are used to describe commercial transactions from the perspective of the seller. And since children are rarely sellers, these sentences would normally involve taking an essentially exocentric perspective toward such transactions. Sentences containing the verb *buy*, on the other hand, describe commercial transactions from the perspective of the buyer, i.e., from the perspective of the child or the child's agents (parents).

If children simply don't encounter the word *sell*, then, of course, they will not learn it. On the other hand, it is not clear why the fact that children have little or no experience as sellers should inhibit learning *sell*. Children learn all sorts of verbs describing actions they have not performed and have little direct experience with (e.g., *steal* or *kill*). Gentner's view that children have little experience of selling will therefore not account for the greater difficulty of *sell* over *buy*, for *buy* and *sell* are mirror-image predicates (*A bought B from C* is true if and only if *C sold B to A*, which reflects the fact that every buying event is a selling event, and conversely). As a result, where the child's lack of understanding of *sell* does not reflect the fact that he or she has not encountered it, I believe we must look to some deeper cognitive explanation such as the previously mentioned "egocentric orientation" explanation. Certainly, the major (perhaps the only) linguistic difference between (69) and (70), for example, is a difference of orientation or of point of view.

(69)   Someone sold me a candy bar.

(70)   I bought a candy bar from someone.

If children have difficulty with the verb *sell*, it should come as no surprise that they have problems recognizing the selling intent of commercials. The retail clerk who sells a child a candy bar is a visible element of the selling–buying experience. The sponsor of a children's television commercial is invisible. Moreover, in virtually no commercial is there any evidence at all bearing on the motive behind the broadcast of the commercial, nor is there a direct statement to the effect that the commercial is an advertisement. Compare this situation with the practice of publishers of newspapers and magazines of flagging advertisements that have the physical appearance of news stories with the word *advertisement*. Cartoon commercials differ little from some program segments and there is no explicit flag in or around commercially motivated advertisements (as opposed to public service announcements) that indicates that they are advertisements.

Some will object to my use of linguistic evidence to support conclusions about the cognitive capacity of children. Indeed, ABC, NBC, and the NAB and others argued before the FTC that children's linguistic skills lag behind their cognitive skills and therefore verbal measures of children's cognitive abilities may underestimate these abilities. According to this line of argument, a child who does not understand the verb *sell* may fully understand the phenomenon of selling. Indeed, the fact that there are children who control *buy* but not *sell* would appear to support this view, because their understanding of *buy* presupposes some understanding of the nature of commercial transactions.

There is some truth to the claim that children's linguistic development is independent of and lags behind their cognitive development. As Lenneberg (1967) noted, deaf children exhibit some cognitive development in the absence of language development (including sign language). And, children are able to manipulate objects long before they are able to describe what they are doing. Thus, a child may learn that a round peg can be pushed through a round hole long before he learns to use spatial terms like *through* or *round*.

The argument by ABC and the others that children's linguistic competence lags behind their cognitive competence and that verbal measures of cognitive abilities may underestimate children's cognitive abilities is based on just a few scholarly papers concerning just one linguistic phenomenon, namely, the acquisition of comparative pairs like *more–less, taller–shorter, longer–shorter*, etc. Interest in this linguistic phenomenon derives in part from the work of Piaget and Inhelder (1962) and others showing that children between the ages of 4 and 7 do not understand the principle of conservation of matter. It has been shown, for instance, that if identical amounts of water are put into identical glasses, G_1 and G_2, and if, in full view of children of these ages, the water in one of the glasses G_2 (say) is poured into a taller, thinner glass, G_3, the children will normally judge that the taller, thinner glass has a different amount of or more water in it than there is in the original glass G_1 because the water level is higher in this taller, thinner glass, G_3. Acquisition of comparative pairs like more–less, taller–shorter, etc., are quite relevant to the administration of conservation experiments because normally such experiments involve use of words like these in the questions children are asked. This is particularly true of the comparatives *more* and *less* and *same* and *different*. Thus the children of such experiments will be asked whether the glasses have the same amount of water or a different amount or whether one glass has more or less water in it than does another.

In this connection, ABC and the others approvingly cite a study by Seigel (1978) in which it is argued that children of the ages of interest understand the concepts "same" and "different" and "more" and "less", but not the corresponding words, and thus children's failures in conservation experiments may derive not from some cognitive limitation, but from a purely linguistic one. Seigel (1978) takes this sort of result to show that language development and cognitive development are independent and that "attainment of concepts can in no way be inferred from verbal responses [p. 64]." ABC (1978) employs this line of argument not just to discredit "experiments designed to classify a child within a particular Piagetian stage [p. 81]" but also the work of WWW and others showing that children do not understand the selling intent of commercials, for these experiments and studies employ language in instructions given to children and questions asked of them.

It is clear that young children do have problems with comparatives. Siegel cites two articles, one by Donaldson and Balfour (1968) and one by Lawson, Baron, and Seigel (1974) that show, to borrow a phrase from ABC, that children "confuse the meaning" of pairs like *more–less*, *longer–shorter*, etc. In these studies and others, including Donaldson and Wales (1970), it is shown that young children tend to give the same answer to such different questions as "Does this tree have more apples on it than that tree?" and "Does this tree have less apples on it than that tree?" Since children tend to answer questions employing *more* correctly and questions employing *less* incorrectly, the scholars doing these studies have assumed that children understand the meaning of *more* and that children think that *less* has the same meaning as *more*.

The linguistic limitation involving comparatives is well established. But what of the corresponding cognitive abilities? Siegel (and ABC) cites papers by LaPointe and O'Donnell (1974), Stern and Bryson (1970), and Estes (1976) that show that children of the ages of interest understand the concepts "more," "same," and "less." It would appear then that children's linguistic limitations are greater than their cognitive limitations, as Siegel and ABC wish to maintain.

Responding to Donaldson and Wales' (1970) paper, H. H. Clark (1970) notes that there is another hypothesis that will account for the observation that children "confuse the meaning" of pairs like *more* and *less*, namely, that children treat both as meaning "some," rather than treating *less* as meaning "more." He further suggests that the earlier mastery of *more*, *tall*, *long*, etc., over *less*, *short*, *short*, etc. reflects an underlying **cognitive** preference for the adjectives that refer to having extent along some dimension (e.g., *tall*) rather than to their privative counterparts (e.g., *short*). This conjecture was confirmed in an experiment by Klatzky, Clark, and Machen (1973), showing that young children learn nonsense words corresponding to the positive comparatives more quickly than they learn nonsense words corresponding to their privative counterparts. Thus, developmental studies of comparatives do not confirm that "attainment of concepts can in no way be inferred from verbal responses," as Siegel has claimed, for, as the Klatzky, Clark, and

Machen study shows, the linguistic preference for positive over privative comparatives directly reflects a cognitive preference for positive over privative concepts. Thus, far from being inadequate to measure the child's understanding of concepts, verbal measures of cognitive ability provide important prima facie evidence about children's cognitive abilities. Moreover, the problem ABC finds with research into children's cognitive abilities that employ language in one way or another, is a pseudoproblem. If words like *more* and *less* or *same* and *different* are to be employed to determine some specific cognitive ability, one can always determine with respect to other cognitive tasks whether or not children understand these words.

ABC and its colleagues do not say exactly what the bearing of the linguistic and cognitive development of comparative words and concepts has for determining whether or not children understand the selling intent behind television commercials. In fact there is none whatever. The concept "selling intent" presupposes the existence of a language within which it can be defined, as does any other concept that is arbitrary and abstract in nature. In science, the law, commerce, and in many other domains there exist concepts that can neither be defined nor learned in the absence of language. Contemplate how one might teach or test an understanding of such concepts as "manslaughter" or "inertia" or "inorganic compound" totally nonlinguistically. It cannot be done, of course. Similarly, I can see no way to teach or test the concept "selling intent of a commercial" nonlinguistically. That is, verbal measures of the attainment of this concept are not just the best measures, but the only measures. And, as WWW have shown, young children have a good deal of trouble with this concept.

There is an irony to the position taken by ABC, NBC, the NAB, and others to the view that children's verbal skills are too limited to measure their cognitive abilities. If, as ABC notes, children "confuse the meaning" of words referring to such basic concepts as "more," "less," "same," and "different," then it is not clear how the practice of directing television commercials to children that employ language can be justified. The linguistic limitations cited earlier in this chapter and cited by ABC and others demonstrate that young children are significantly limited linguistically. ABC puts its finger on the key point, and this is that children will not only fail to understand some of the things that experimenters (and, presumably also, advertisers) might say to them, they may also **misunderstand** what experimenters (and, presumably, advertisers) say to them. How ABC and other elements of the broadcasting industry might justify the practice of using language to advertise to young children, given their views on the linguistic limitations of young children, is anything but clear.

Chapter 8
The Advertising of Fruit-Flavored Products to Children

In this chapter, we shall consider the advertising to children of fruit-flavored products—candy, gum, cookies, and breakfast cereals. Such commercials are particularly interesting linguistically because they commonly make visual and verbal reference to fruit whether or not the products being promoted contain fruit or are naturally flavored. In none of the commercials we shall be examining is it directly asserted that a product contains fruit or is made from fruit when this is not the case. However, in some commercials, language is used that entails or implies that fruit is present in products that contain no fruit, and in others, the verbal and visual references to fruit cannot help but encourage such a belief.

As I noted in the preceding chapter, how a child interprets and evaluates a given commercial will be a function of the child's linguistic and cognitive abilities and of his or her knowledge of the world. In the case of advertisements for fruit-flavored products what the child knows and doesn't know about the manufacture of such products will be of decisive importance in determining what inferences he or she draws from commercials promoting such products. I take it that there are basically three ways in which a product can come to have a particular flavor. It may contain the substance that has the flavor in question, as in the case of homemade lemonade. It may contain an extract of that substance, as in vanilla ice cream. Or it may contain some other substance that has a flavor that is like the flavor in question. In the first two cases the food can be said to be naturally flavored. In the third case, it would be said to be artificially flavored. Interestingly, packages containing artificially flavored foods must state that the product is artificially flavored, but commercials for such products need not state this.

This distinction between naturally and artificially flavored products is a relatively sophisticated one. Another possible distinction is between products that contain fruit (e.g., juices and/or pulp) and those that do not. Given this distinction, cereal products like Raisin Bran or Apple Jacks, both of which contain fruit, would be classified differently from Froot Loops, which is naturally flavored but contains no fruit. In my opinion, based on much informal discussion with children, the distinction between products that contain fruit and those that do not is not only simpler to grasp than the natural flavor versus artificial flavor distinction, but is also the distinction that most matters to children. Children are concerned with the quality of flavors and appear to believe (with some reason) that products containing fruit taste better than those that do not.

I presume that all children know that fruits are themselves fruit flavored and that most will have eaten fruit-flavored foods that contain detectable pieces of the fruits. Some will have seen fruit-flavored foods being prepared from fruit at home. As a result, it is only natural that children believe that if a food is fruit flavored this is because it contains fruit. It is perhaps worth noting that the regulations requiring that packages of artificially flavored products state that these products are artificially flavored are designed to protect, not children, but adults from this very natural inference.

The most important item of knowledge relevant to the interpretation and evaluation of any advertisement for a fruit-flavored food is, of course, that fruit flavors can be simulated. A reasonably sophisticated consumer who sees an advertisement for a fruit-flavored product that does not assert that the product contains fruit or is naturally flavored might infer (a conversational implicature based on the Maxim of Strength) that the product is artificially flavored on the grounds that advertisers normally make the strongest claims they can. But the consumer who does not know that fruit flavors can be simulated cannot do otherwise than assume that foods that are advertised as having fruit flavors contain fruit or are made from fruit unless the advertisement makes clear that the advertised product has no actual relationship to fruit. As we shall see, not only do children's advertisements for artificially fruit-flavored foods normally not say that they are artificially flavored, many such children's commercials stress a wholly imaginary connection between fruit and the product being promoted.

The names of fruit-flavored products commonly suggest the presence of fruit. Froot Loops cereal consists of loops (i.e., doughnut-shaped cereal) and is naturally flavored but contains no fruit. Fruit Stripe gum has colored stripes on sticks of gum but is artificially flavored. Fruit Roll consists of rolled-up sheets of dried fruit. Thus, the child who encounters names of fruit-flavored products can be misled if he or she assumes that the descriptive terms contained in them have their normal referents. The practice of employing product names like Froot Loops, Fruit Stripe, and Fruit Roll cannot help but present problems to children until they learn that that descriptive terms in product names are not semantically compositional.[1] I have no idea when children can be expected to learn this, but I think we can be sure that they will not do so until they have learned a good deal about American commerce.

Advertisers sometimes use singular fruit names in linguistic contexts in which there is no solid linguistic basis for determining how these words are to be interpreted. Consider the following example, which is extracted from a Starburst candy commercial:

(1)   [Starburst Fruit Chews] *taste like mouth-watering orange. . . .*[2]   (ABC, 12/15/79, 10:40 a.m.)

Claim (1) is anything but clear in meaning. Were *orange* plural, its meaning would be quite clear, as can be seen by examining (2).

(2)   Starburst Fruit Chews taste like mouth-watering oranges.

The only alternative to this interpretation is one in which *orange* is construed as referring to orange flavor. Compare (1) with (3).

(3)   Starburst Fruit Chews taste like mouth-watering orange flavor.

The problem with (3) is that things are usually said to taste like other things, not like flavors of things. Thus (3) is itself rather peculiar. The practice of employing language in nonstandard ways in advertising claims directed at young children is rather questionable. Young children have trouble enough with linguistically straightforward claims. How they can be expected to cope with sentences like (1) is beyond my understanding.

I submit that children, especially young children whose knowledge of what is and is not well formed linguistically is limited, will normally assign interpretations to semantically deviant sentences and that the interpretation assigned to any particular semantically deviant sentence will be one that is also assigned to the sentence that differs least from it lexically and syntactically. According to this principle, (1) will be assigned the same interpretation as (2), for the only other alternative, namely (3), is itself odd. The linguistic and nonlinguistic context can, of course, have

[1]See my discussion of the use of descriptive terms in brand names in Chapter 5.

[2]The Starburst commercial in question is discussed later in this chapter [see commercial (17)].

an important bearing on how a deviant sentence is interpreted. Were oranges to be visually in evidence as (1) is said, interpretation (2) would even be more strongly favored.

We might begin our examination of children's commercials for fruit-flavored products by considering the following commercial for Tic Tac candy:

(4)   Tic Tac candy (ABC, 3/11/78, @ 8:20 a.m.)
        Type: animated
        Setting: The planet Orange, the Land of Wild Fruit, Earth. In the first two
            scenes, candy is seen marching into Tic Tac packages, which simulate
            space ships. These packages fly into space and land on the planet
            Earth.
        Characters: Orange soda pop and wild berries and cherries

        TEXT
        Voice over (adult male): *On the Planet Orange, the last of the orange Tic
            Tacs are boarding their milk white capsule for the flight to Earth. And an
            orange soda pop cries out.*
        Orange Soda Pop (male voice): *They're gonna love you.*
        Voice over (adult male): *At the same moment, from the Land of Wild Fruit,
            berry and cherry Tic Tacs take off in their double white pack.*

Photograph 8.1

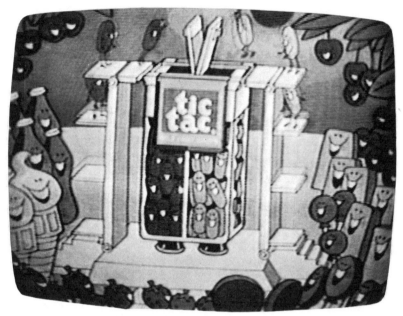

Photograph 8.2

Cherries and Berries (male voice): *Remember the wack!* [We then hear "wack, wack."]

Voice over (adult male): *Together, these terrific fruit flavors fly onto Earth, where you'll find them in the Tic Tac tree.* [We then hear the noise "wack, wack."]

The Tic Tac commercial is of interest for two reasons. First, there is a verbal association between fruit and Tic Tac candy, especially in the second voice over statement. Second, this commercial illustrates the fine visual detail so characteristic of animated children's commercials. During the first voice over message, we see a scene (see Photograph 8.1) that abounds with sweet things. In this photograph, we see bottles of soft drinks, ice cream, suckers, etc. Of particular interest is the fact that the sun looks like a cross section of an orange and there are orange trees in the background.

The second voice over message is accompanied by a scene similar to the first, as Photograph 8.2 demonstrates. Again, the sun (moon?) looks like a fruit, perhaps a plum. As the cherry and berry Tic Tacs say *Remember the wack!* we see a close-up of these fruits (see Photograph 8.3). Fruit is, then, much in evidence in the Tic Tac commercial despite the fact that Tic Tac has no actual relationship to fruit.

Photograph 8.3

The language of this particular commercial is relatively unextravagant for a children's commercial. The phrase *orange Tic Tacs* is a noun compound consisting of the noun *orange* and the proper noun *Tic Tacs*. The phrase *orange Tic Tacs* can be interpreted along the lines of 'Tic Tacs with the flavor of oranges' or along the lines of 'Tic Tacs made from oranges.' To the child who does not know that orange flavor can be simulated this is of course a distinction without a difference.

A good deal more problematic is line (5).

(5)   *At the same moment, from the land of wild fruit, berry and cherry Tic Tacs take off in their double white pack.*

Claim (5) makes an explicit reference to wild fruit that provides a context favoring an interpretation of *berry and cherry Tic Tacs* along the lines of 'Tic Tacs made from berries and cherries.' This interpretation is further encouraged by the appearance of the talking cherries and berries of Photograph 8.3.

I do not know what the impact of the fine visual detail of this commercial will be on children. As far as I am aware, no research appears to have been done that would have a direct bearing on this issue. However, it is widely agreed that we absorb a good deal more visually than we are conscious of. The impact of the verbal and visual references to fruit in this commercial is a good deal clearer, for the child who does not know that fruit flavors can be simulated or who does not have a substantive understanding of what it means for a product to be artificially flavored must, I think, take these verbal and visual reference to fruit as indicating that Tic Tacs are made from fruit.

The television advertising of Froot Loops cereal, a naturally flavored product that contains no fruit, uses language alone to make the connection between Froot Loops and fruit. Consider, first, commercial (6).

(6)   Froot Loops cereal (CBS, 7/18/78, @ 8:16 a.m.)
        Type: Animated
        Setting: Jungle
        Characters: Lion, porcupine, and a toucan (the spokesbird for Froot
          Loops cereal)

TEXT
Lion: *Ouch. Oh* [after being struck by a porcupine quill].
Porcupine: *Sorry.*
Toucan: *Ouch* [after being stuck by a porcupine quill].
Porcupine: *Gee. Getting somebody to have breakfast with is sticky business.*
Toucan: *Cheer up, my porcupine pal, a fruitiful breakfast we'll share right now. Follow your nose. It always knows.*
Porcupine: *I smell it. Kellogg's Froot Loops cereal.*
Toucan: *Oranges, lemons, cherries, and other natural flavors. Start with a balanced breakfast, including Kellogg's Froot Loops. Follow your nose.*
Porcupine: *Froot Loops are good. How can I thank you?*

In every Froot Loops commercial I am familiar with the novel word *fruitiful* is used. This word appears to have been coined on analogy with the word *beautiful*.[3] Although some might choose to disagree, I believe the suffix *-ful* is not being used productively in *beautiful*, that is to say that *beautiful* does not mean 'full of *beauty*'. Those who coined the word *fruitiful* might argue that they do not mean *-ful* to be interpreted productively in *fruitiful* either. The problem with this line of reasoning is that nonproductivity is a property only of suffixes used in **existing** words. To coin a new word using a given affix is necessarily to use that affix productively. Thus, claim (7) **must** be interpreted as having the same meaning as (8).[4]

---

[3]See commercial (12), p. 197.

[4]The coiners of *fruitiful* might argue that it is created from *fruity*, not *fruit*. However, *fruitiful*, if composed of *fruity* and *-full*, would have to mean 'full of fruity', which is meaningless. Thus, it is inconceivable that children read it this way.

(7)   *Cheer up, my porcupine pal, a fruitiful breakfast we'll share right now.*

(8)   Cheer up, my porcupine pal, a breakfast full of fruit we'll share right now.

Claim (7) is false according to this interpretation, for Froot Loops contains no fruit.

This Froot Loops commercial contains the wholly ungrammatical line (9).

(9)   *Oranges, lemons, cherries, and other natural flavors.*

Line (9) may have resulted from an error made by the actor reading the Toucan's lines. I say this because in other commercials, we hear (10), instead of (9).

(10)   *Orange, lemon, cherry, and other natural flavors.*

However, the oddness of (9) is so striking that it is inconceivable that the makers of this commercial did not notice it.

The plural fruit names of (9) refer to fruit, not to fruit flavors.[5] As a result, it is entirely possible that children will interpret this line as claiming that Froot Loops contains fruit or counts as fruit, etc. Such an interpretation is, of course, consistent with the earlier line (7), which employs the word *fruitiful.* Consider now, commercial (11), which was provided to me by Rhonda Ross, who used it in an interesting study of children's perceptions of commercials for fruit-flavored commercials.[6]

(11)   Froot Loops
        Type: Animated
        Setting: Jungle
        Characters: Mole and toucan

        TEXT
        Mole: *Where am I?*
        Toucan: *The Jungle.*
        Mole: *The jungle! And me without grub. I'll starve.*
        Toucan: *Mr. Mole, don't despair, a fruitiful breakfast is in the air. Follow your nose.*
        Mole: *Yahoo.*
        Toucan: *It always knows the flavor of fruit.*
        Mole: *I smell oranges, and lemons, and cherries.*

[5] No fruit is in evidence as line (10) is said.
[6] The research just mentioned (Ross, Campbell, Heislon-Stein, & Wright, 1981) was published too late for it to be included in this study. It appears to support my contention that children are misled by commercials for fruit-flavored products.

> Toucan: *Kellogg's Froot Loops cereal. Real natural flavors. Start with a good breakfast, including Kellogg's Froot Loops. Follow your nose.*
> Mole: *These Froot Loops are good! But, you're a funny looking chicken.*

As in commercial (6), commercial (11) employs the word *fruitiful.* The sequence of lines beginning with the one containing the word *fruitiful* is especially interesting. Children are told by the Toucan that a breakfast full of fruit is in the air and that the Mole's nose knows the flavor of fruit and are then told that the Mole can smell oranges, lemons, and cherries. It would hardly be surprising if young children were not to assume from this that Froot Loops contains fruit. The advertiser may see the reference to fruit flavor (*the flavor of fruit* and *real natural flavors*) as mitigating the force of the references to fruit, but, of course, these references to fruit flavors are in no way inconsistent with Froot Loop's containing fruit. Indeed, if the Mole smells oranges, lemons, and cherries, the most natural assumption is that this is because there are oranges, lemons, and cherries in evidence.

The advertising campaign in which (6) and (11) figure continues to run. Consider the following 1981 commercial for Froot Loops.

(12)   Froot Loops (ABC, 1/18/81, @ 10:23 a.m.)
        Type: Animated
        Setting: Jungle
        Characters: Gooney bird and toucan

        TEXT
        Bird: *Look out below.*
        Toucan: *A gooney bird?*
        Bird: *Yeh, searching for fruit but I'm coming up empty.*
        Toucan: *To end your search, my crashing friend. Follow my nose to a fruitiful land. Follow my nose.*
        Bird: *Fruitiful, beautiful.*
        Toucan: *It always knows.*
        Bird: *Fruit flavors. I know they're here somewhere.*
        Toucan: *Kellogg's Froot Loops cereal. Orange, lemon, and cherry and other natural flavors. Fortified to be part of this nutritious breakfast.*
        Bird: *Mmm. Froot Loops. What fun!*
        Toucan: *I guess he really fell for 'em.*

In this commercial, the Froot Loops toucan tells the gooney bird that his search for fruit will be ended at a land full of fruit, where there is Froot Loops cereal. How young children can do otherwise than draw the inference from this that Froot Loops contains fruit or counts as fruit is difficult to see.

As I have pointed out, singular fruit names can be used to refer to fruits or to fruit flavors. In this light, consider the following commercials for Starburst candy.

(13)   **Starburst candy** (NBC, 7/29/78, 9:37 a.m.).
         Type: Live action
         Setting: Three boys at a movie theater, a boy and a girl in a convertible automobile
         Characters: No on-screen characters speak

         TEXT
         Voice over (adult male): *The Starburst blast off. It happens every time you eat a Starburst.* [Sound of rocket.] *Because Starburst gives you a burst of flavor from the very first chew.* [Sound of a rocket.] *A burst of strawberry, lime, orange, and lemon. Starburst fruit chews.* [Sound of a rocket.] *You get a burst of fruit flavor from the very first chew.*

On the visual side, we see several different scenes (three boys at a movie theater, a boy and a girl in a convertible automobile, etc.). One of the persons in each scene bites down on a piece of Starburst. We then hear the sound of a rocket blast off; the person rises like a rocket and is followed up the screen by a variety of fruits simulating a rocket's exhaust, as Photograph 8.4 illustrates.

The line containing singular fruit names is (14).

(14)   *A burst of strawberry, lime, orange, and lemon.*

Since (14) is sandwiched between two lines referring to fruit flavor, one of which contains a noun phrase identical to (14) in form [see (15)], the most natural interpretation of (14) is one in which the singular fruit names are construed as names of flavors.

(15)   *Because Starburst gives you **a burst of fruit flavor** from the very first chew* [emphasis added].

According to this view, (14) would have the same interpretation as (16).

(16)   A burst of strawberry, lime, orange, and lemon flavor.

However, there is nothing in the oral language text of this commercial that precludes a child's drawing the inference that this product contains fruit, an inference that is supported by the fact that before or after each oral reference to fruit flavor or to fruit, pieces of fruit appear on screen simulating the levitating person's exhaust. I may be stretching a point, but it does seem possible that some children will construe line (14) as referring to bursts of fruit, for the streams of fruit that appear on screen could be taken as the bursts in question.

Photograph 8.4

This commercial is somewhat unusual in that, at the beginning of the commercial, the printed disclaimer *artificially flavored* occurs. This will avail little in the case of children who can't read, do not understand this phrase, or don't notice it. Nevertheless, it could have the effect of forestalling the inference that Starburst contains fruit in the case of older children. A printed disclaimer is better than nothing, but disclaimers in children's television advertising should, of course, be oral.

As I noted, the oral text of (13) in no way precludes the inference that Starburst contains fruit. In another Starburst commercial the oral text is much less problematic, for a disclaimer, *naturally and artificially flavored,* is both printed (at the beginning of the commercial) and spoken (at the end). However, the visual references to fruit in this commercial are a good deal more extravagant than in the other Starburst commercial:

(17)   Starburst candy (ABC, 12/15/79, 10:40 a.m.)
        Type: Live action
        Scene: Outdoors and studio shots of fruit
        Characters: No on-screen characters speak

        TEXT
        Voice over (adult female, singing): *Starburst fruit chews . . . a burst of refreshing fruit flavor for you. Tastes like . . . mouth-watering*

orange . . . lip-smacking lime . . . luscious strawberry and tangy
lemon. You get a burst the very first time . . . you bite into a Starburst.
It's true, a burst of refreshing fruit flavor for you.
Voice over (adult female, talking): *Naturally and artificially flavored.*

This commercial makes an explicit reference to fruit flavor at the
beginning and end of this commercial. Sandwiched between is line (18).

(18)   *Tastes like mouth-watering orange, lip-smacking lime, luscious*
          strawberry, and tangy lemon.

As I noted earlier, (18) is anything but clear in meaning. It is furthermore, ungrammatical. Were the fruit names of (18) plural, however,
this claim would be grammatical and quite clear in meaning. In such a
case, these fruit names would refer to fruits. The only other possibility is
that these fruit names refer to fruit flavors. The difficulty with this is
that a line like (19) is very odd.

(19)   Starburst tastes like orange flavor.

Things can taste like other things. They cannot taste like the flavor of
other things. In light of this, I believe children must interpret the fruit
names of (18) as referring to fruits. Such an interpretation is encouraged
by the fact that as the child hears the phrases *mouth-watering orange,*
lip-smacking lime, luscious strawberry, and *tangy lemon,* the camera pans
over arrays of the fruits in question.

This particular commercial contains the disclaimer *artificially flavored*
twice, printed at the beginning of the commercial and spoken at the end.
Thus, few of any adults would be likely to be misled by the curious line
(18) or the visual references to fruit. But children who do not understand the meaning of the phrase *artificially flavored* or do not have a
substantive understanding of what it means for something to have an
artificial flavor, may be misled despite these disclaimers. In any event,
the practice of employing linguistically deviant constructions in television advertising directed at young children is questionable on linguistic
grounds.

I would like to turn now to consider a commercial for Fruit Stripe
gum, a wholly artificially flavored product. Because it will be relevant
later, I offer a photograph of a package of this gum (see Photograph
8.5). Let us now examine the text of a commercial for Fruit Stripe.

(20)   **Fruit Stripe gum** (ABC, 3/11/78 a.m.)
          Type: Animated
          Scene: Outdoors
          Characters: Several zebras and young children

Photograph 8.5

TEXT

Head Zebra (singing): *Hey kids. There's a whole herd of flavors in my Fruit Stripe gum.*

Zebras (singing): *Four great flavors for more chewin' fun.*

Zebras (talking): *And now our fruit stripes are bigger. And there's even more fruit flavor.*

Individual Zebras (singing): *There's more orange. More lemon. More cherry. More lime.*

Zebras (singing): *And more fruit flavor makes your mouth taste fine. There's a whole herd of flavors in Fruit Stripe gum.*

Child: *With more fruit flavor for more chewin' fun.*

Head Zebra (on package, talking): *Delicious.*

There are two features of the language of this commercial worth noting. Consider, first, lines (21a) and (21b).

(21)   a. *And now our fruit stripes are bigger.*

        b. *And here's even more fruit flavor.*

Line (21a) does not overtly assert that Fruit Stripe consists of fruit; however, the phrase *fruit stripes* entails that there are stripes of fruit in this product. There is simply no other way this phrase can be interpreted. However, there is no fruit in Fruit Stripe gum whatever—it is wholly artificially flavored. Sentence (21a) is therefore quite false. The stripes in question are merely printed on the surface of the gum. The advertiser appears to want children to believe otherwise. Note that these stripes are portrayed as being solid in Photograph 8.6. Photograph 8.6 provides a referent for the phrase *fruit stripes*. Since these stripes are represented as solid, the phrase *fruit stripes* may be taken by some children as referring to solid stripes of fruit.

Lines (21a) and (21b) jointly implicate (Maxim of Relevance) that the larger stripes of Fruit Stripe gum are responsible for the increase in flavor. The fact that each conjunct contains a comparison involving fruit—bigger fruit stripes and more fruit flavor—will surely lead many children to draw the inference that the larger stripes are responsible for the increase in flavor, an inference that is made all the more credible by the fact that the stripes are said to be stripes of fruit. However, as far as I

Photograph 8.6

can determine, not only are there no fruit stripes in this gum, the stripes printed on Fruit Stripe gum have nothing whatever to do with the flavor of the gum.

Next consider line (22), in which singular fruit names are used.

(22)   *There's more orange. More lemon. More cherry. More lime.*

As each of these comparatives is uttered, we see an individual stick of gum and a zebra. A piece of the fruit referred to enters the picture and attaches itself to the zebra's nose (see Photograph 8.6.). There are two ways in which each of the comparatives of (22) can be read. *There's more orange,* for instance, can have the same meaning as (23a) or (23b).

(23)   a. There's more orange in it.
         b. There's more orange flavor in it.

The advertiser might argue that since (22) is sandwiched between two sentences speaking of fruit flavor, these comparatives will or should be interpreted along the lines of (23b). However, there are three reasons for believing that children may interpret (22) along the lines of (23a). First, the commercial has said that Fruit Stripe contains stripes of fruit. Second, the fact that line (22) is sandwiched between two sentences referring to fruit flavor does not in fact force reading (23b), for the role

(22) plays in this discourse is to explain why there's come to be an increase in fruit flavor. As a result, we do not have a construction particularly favoring an ellipsis reading. Note that sentence (24), which makes explicit the explanatory character of (22), favors a reading like (23a).

(24)   There's even more fruit flavor because there's more orange, more lemon, more cherry, and more lime.

The third fact supporting my view that the fruit names of (22) will be interpreted as names of fruit is that as each comparative is uttered by the zebra on screen, a piece of fruit appears that becomes attached to the zebra's nose, as we noted in connection with Photograph 8.6. The presence of a piece of fruit having the same color as the stripes on the stick of gum favors interpretation (23a), in which the fruit names that occur in these comparatives are interpreted as referring to fruit.

The Fruit Stripe commercial, unlike the Starburst commercials, does not indicate that this product is artificially flavored. Interestingly, in several different scenes in which packages of Fruit Stripes are shown on screen, the statement *artificially flavored lemon, lime, orange, and cherry,* which occurs on real packages (see Photograph 8.5), does not occur, as Photograph 8.7 shows. The omission of this disclaimer was clearly deliberate, as is every decision made in an animated commercial.

Photograph 8.7

    I would like to conclude my examination of the children's commercials for fruit-flavored products appearing on my tapes with an advertisement for Keebler Fruit Creme cookies.

(25)   **Keebler Fruit Creme cookies** (ABC, 3/11/78, a.m.)
        Type: Animated
        Scene: Rural
        Characters: Fruit Peddler and Keebler Elf

        TEXT
        Peddler: *Oranges, lemons, coconuts. Get your real fruit here.* (To elf):
          Good morning. Do you elves need any fruit today?
        Elf: *Funny you should ask. We're baking new Keebler Fruit Cremes.*
          Creamy fruit-flavored fillings sandwiched between crisp cookies.
          Orange, lemon, and coconut flavors. An irresistible taste combination.
        Peddler: *Mmm. Keep an eye on my stuff, Keebler. I've got Keebler Fruit*
          Cremes.
        Voice over (adult male): *New Keebler Fruit Cremes. An irresistible taste*
          combination.

Although there is a linguistic blunder in this commercial—the *taste combination* of the elf's first speech incorrectly suggests that orange, lemon,

Photograph 8.8

Photograph 8.9

and coconut flavors are combined in individual cookies—the commercial is otherwise cleverly crafted linguistically.

It is not uncommon for commercials for fruit-flavored products to make fruit, not the product being promoted, the initial topic of the commercial [see commercial (12), p. 197, for instance]. This is also true of the Keebler commercial. Indeed, in using the odd phrase *real fruit* in the Peddler's first speech (ersatz fruit does not exist), the Keebler company is making quite sure that the commercial gets children's minds set firmly on fruit. Moreover, the cart the peddler is pushing reads *FRUIT* on its front and fruit is visible on the cart (see Photograph 8.8). The change of topic of this commercial is effected by the elf when he says *funny you should ask,* a phrase that is used only to indicate a coincidence. Let us note in passing that the elf, in saying this, is rejecting the offer of fruit. The elf does not tell children what the nature of the coincidence is between fruit and his cookies. A possible interpretation of the remark, *funny you should ask,* is that the elf's fruit-flavored cookies contain fruit or are as good as fruit, etc. As it turns out, Coconut Fruit Cremes have some coconut in them. "Coconut" is listed seventh immediately after flour, sugar, shortening, cornstarch, dextrose, and corn syrup and before leavening, salt, lecithin, and artificial flavoring. We may

Photograph 8.10

conclude from this, however, that there is very little coconut in these coconut-flavored cookies. "Orange" and "lemon" are not specified in the list of ingredients for the orange and lemon cookies. Instead, in the case of orange and lemon Fruit Cremes, the list includes natural flavor (tenth) and artificial flavor (thirteenth and last). Thus, it would appear that these two types of cookies contain no fruit.

After the elf concludes his speech, we note that the peddler has replaced the fruit that was on his cart with Keebler cookies (see Photograph 8.9). Moreover, what the peddler once called *real fruit* he now calls *stuff*. This verbal put down of fruit combined with the peddler's replacement of his fruit with cookies is clearly designed to lead children to believe that Keebler Fruit Creme cookies are preferable to fruit.

Is this advertisement deceptive? I believe that it is, for the coincidence suggested by the elf between fruit and the Keebler cookies will probably be interpreted by children as a substantial one, that is, that there is fruit in all three types of cookies. But, as I have already noted, there appears to be no actual fruit in orange- and lemon-flavored cookies. It is worth noting that the commercial at several points places pieces of actual fruit together with cookies in still photographs. In one, fruit, cookie packages, and cookies are so arranged as to suggest that the packages are little factories, with fruit going in at one end and cookies coming out at the other (consider Photograph 8.10).

It is in its use of written language that the Keebler commercial is most interesting. After cookies have replaced fruit on the peddler's cart the cart continues to read *FRUIT* on the front, as can be seen in Photograph 8.9. This constitutes false labeling, for there is no fruit on the cart at this time. The most fascinating part of this commercial, however, concerns the small signs on the cart. While fruit is on the cart, these signs are either blank or have intentionally illegible squiggles on them, as in Photograph 8.8. After the cookies have been placed on the cart, these signs, from front to rear, read *orange, lemon,* and *coconuts* (consider Photographs 8.9 and 8.11). Coconut Fruit Creme cookies have coconut in them, as I noted earlier, but orange and lemon flavor Fruit Cremes appear to have no fruit in them. Could this explain why *coconuts,* which unambiguously refers to coconuts, is plural, but *lemon* and *orange,* which must, I think, be interpreted as names of flavors in this context, are singular? I refuse to believe that this pattern of singular and plural words is an accident, for the odds against this particular pattern of singular and plural words occurring, if one allows for the possibility of

Photograph 8.11

blank signs, is 27 : 1. The odds are 8 : 1 against this particular combination if blank signs are not included as possibilities. The singular names *orange* and *lemon* hedge on the relationship between fruit and the cookies; the plural name *coconuts* doesn't hedge—it falsely labels what is on the cart.[7]

These small signs will surely have no influence on children who cannot read. In the case of reading children, and any adults who might see this commercial, the small signs are not likely to be consciously noticed. I noticed them only on examining still slides taken of my television screen. But to the degree that these small signs are unlikely to be noticed consciously, they constitute a kind of subliminal advertising. This sort of fine visual detail abounds in animated children's advertising, as I have already noted. Perhaps it has no effect, but it seems to me that the advertiser must think it does. Why else would it go to the trouble to make these small signs legible only after cookies have replaced the fruit?

As we have seen, the practice of making verbal and visual reference to fruit in the advertising of fruit-flavored products to children is a pervasive one. I believe that this practice is a deceptive one—certainly in the case of artificially flavored products and possibly also in the case of naturally flavored products that contain no fruit (i.e., juices and/or pulp). In my view, the distinction between products that contain fruit and those that don't is more meaningful to children than the distinction between natural and artificial flavoring. It is, after all, the pulp and juices of fruits that children have direct experience with.

The practice of making verbal and visual reference to fruit in the advertising of artificially flavored products is especially problematic, for such products enjoy no relationship to fruit beyond an alleged similarity of flavor. The reader might consider how he or she would react to a commercial for ersatz fireplace logs that makes verbal and visual reference to hickory wood fires. Yet ersatz fireplace logs enjoy a much closer relationship to real hickory logs—they burn and give off heat—than artificially fruit-flavored products do to fruit.

The most puzzling feature of the deceptive practices identified in this chapter is that they are quite unnecessary. Children are sitting ducks for television advertising and it is hardly necessary to deceive them about the content of a product that is sweet tasting in order to stimulate an interest in the product. However, so long as any one advertiser exaggerates the relationship between his product and fruit, it is likely the rest will feel it necessary to do so too in order to be competitive. This is a situation ideally suited for action by the NAB.

[7]Use of singular fruit names on signs such as these is rather peculiar. It would be more natural, I think, to use plural names.

Chapter 9
The Television Definition of Breakfast

No type of product is more heavily promoted to children on television than cold breakfast cereals.[1] In the Barcus and McLaughlin (1978) study cited earlier, it was found, for instance, that cold breakfast cereal commercials constitute a little more than a third of all children's commercials. There are basically two reasons for this: Children seem to like cold breakfast cereals (they come presweetened or are sweetened by the consumer) and they offer parents the ultimate in convenience. The only other breakfast food that is promoted to children in commercials on my tapes is frozen waffles, and this type of product is normally eaten with syrup, jam, or some other sweetener and is also easy to prepare.

Although children surely receive a certain amount of nutrition training at home and at school, I don't believe it can be doubted that the most systematic and most frequent training children receive in breakfast nutrition is provided by Saturday morning television commercials. These commercials present the invariant message that the centerpiece of a nutritious breakfast should be a sweet food, preferably a presweetened cereal. Commercials for breakfast cereals uniformly push a breakfast of juice, toast, cereal, and milk. Commercials for frozen waffles push a juice, milk, and waffle breakfast. In each type, the main course is a presweetened food or a food that will have some sort of sweetener added. The extraordinary uniformity of the conception of breakfast

[1]This is a revised version of a study I did at the request of Administrative Law Judge Morton Needelman, Presiding Officer of the Federal Trade Commission hearings on children's television advertising. The original study was based on 36 commercials taped in 1978. The present study is based on these and on 14 additional commercials taped in December 1979.

Photograph 9.1

promoted in children's television commercials has resulted, at least in part, from requirements of the NAB.

In every cold breakfast cereal commercial directed at children, one will find a visual depiction of a sample breakfast that always includes juice, toast, cereal, and milk. This visual sample breakfast is invariably accompanied by some oral comment that expresses the advertiser's view of the nutritional soundness of this sample breakfast. Both the visual and oral messages are required by the Code Authority of the NAB. The relevant guidelines are:[2]

(1)   Advertisements for edibles shall . . . seek to establish the proper role of the advertised product within the framework of a balanced regimen.

(2)   Each commercial for breakfast-type products shall include at least one audio reference to and one video depiction of the role of the product within a balanced regimen.

The sample breakfasts that are shown on screen in the 50 commercials I have on my tapes always show cereal, milk, juice, and toast. Photo-

[2]Adler (1978, p. 196) is my source for these NAB guidelines.

graph 9.1 illustrates this practice. In some cases, as is shown by Photograph 9.2, a bowl of fruit is also depicted. The great majority of nutrition statements are like (3), (4), or (5) in form (emphasis added).

(3)   *Cookie Crisp cereal is **part of a complete breakfast**.*   (ABC, 3/11/78, 8:16–8:30 a.m.)

(4)   *Cap'n Crunch, **a good part of any good breakfast**.*   (ABC, 7/29/78, 8:45 a.m.)

(5)   *Enjoy **a complete breakfast with Frankenberry**.*   (CBS, 7/15/78, 8:18 a.m.)

Many of the nutrition statements that occur in the commercials on my tapes are linguistically problematic. Statement (4), for instance, employs the ambiguous adjective *good*. On one reading, *good* can be construed as meaning 'good for you.' On the other, it means 'good tasting.' Thus, according to one interpretation, (4) is equivalent in meaning to (6).

(6)   Cap'n Crunch, a good tasting part of any good tasting breakfast.

According to this interpretation, (4) does not indicate the "role of the product within a balanced regimen." Moreover, whether construed as a statement about how good Cap'n Crunch tastes or as a statement about

Photograph 9.2

the nutritional soundness of this product, claim (4) is extraordinarily strong. It entails that if Cap'n Crunch is not in a breakfast, the breakfast cannot be good. This is patently false however we interpret the word *good*. Moreover, it is clearly inconsistent with guidelines (1) and (2), for guideline (1) requires that nutrition statements indicate the *proper* role of the product in a balanced regimen, and it is obviously not true that Cap'n Crunch must be part of a breakfast if that breakfast is to be a good one.

In this chapter, I shall examine cold breakfast cereal commercials with the focus being on the language of the nutrition statements that appear in them. As we shall see, many of the nutrition statements occurring in breakfast cereal commercials do not satisfy the language of NAB Code guidelines. The inescapable conclusion of this fact is that the NAB does not take its guidelines seriously or does not take seriously the language of the nutrition statements contained in children's television advertisements for breakfast cereals.

Some Themes of Cereal Commercials

Children's commercials for breakfast cereals are unquestionably the most imaginative and entertaining of children's commercials. Most are wholly animated or contain some animation and many consist of a minidrama involving an adventure of some sort. These minidramas frequently highlight some property of the cereal being promoted. Thus, Alphabits commercials consist of adventures in which a child is threatened by something, the name for which has been spelled out by letter-shaped bits of cereal, highlighting the fact that the cereal is letter-shaped. In Cap'n Crunch commercials, someone or something steals some cereal and is caught as a result of the crunching sounds that are made as the thief eats the cereal. Hence, the line, *You can't get away from the Crunch, 'cause the crunch always gives you away* (CBS, 7/15/78, 9:12 a.m.). This "food-thief" motif is very common in children's television advertising and can be found in some adult commercials. Honeycomb commercials often involve an encounter by children with animated giants of some sort ("Big Stone People" or "Big 6-arms") and an argument ensues as to whether chunks of the children's cereal (Honeycombs) or of the giants' cereal are bigger. The children always win.

The food-thief motif is used in 8 of the 50 commercials I have on tape. Commercial (7) illustrates use of the food-thief motif.

(7)   Cap'n Crunch (CBS, 7/15/78, 9:12 a.m.)
        Type: Animated

Setting: Boat
Characters: Four children, Captain Crunch, Goo Goo bird

TEXT
Voice over (adult male): *This strange creature is the invisible Goo Goo.*
Goo Goo bird: *Goo goo, goo goo.*
Voice over (adult male): *He takes things that don't belong to him.*
Goo Goo bird: *Hey!*
Voice over (adult male): *And when chased, he simply disappears.* [The Goo Goo Bird becomes invisible.]
Girl: *Captain Crunch, he took our cereal.*
Captain Crunch: *Not to worry. You can't get away from the Crunch, 'cause the crunch always gives you away.*
Goo Goo bird (eating): *Crunch, crunch, crunch.*
Captain Crunch: *See!* [Captain Crunch catches the invisible Goo Goo bird with a net.]
Goo Goo bird: *Goo goo.*
Boy: *Where is he?*
Captain Crunch: *I donno. But I think I got 'im. Captain Crunch cereal, a yummy part of a good breakfast. Right?*
Goo Goo bird: *Goo goo.*

In this commercial, the Goo Goo bird is caught but not punished. This is characteristic of food-thief commercials. Clearly children are supposed to learn from this that the cereal in question is worth stealing and perhaps also that being deprived of the cereal is punishment enough for the thief. It can also be argued that the food-thief theme is designed to suggest to children that they sneak a handful of cereal from time to time. In a commercial for Cocoa Pebbles and Fruity Pebbles, the Flintstone character Barney employs the rather macabre device of pretending to have died and to have come back as an angel in order to con Fred Flintstone out of his cereal.

(8)   Cocoa Pebbles and Fruity Pebbles (CBS, 7/15/78, 9:20 a.m.)
       Type: Animated
       Setting: Outdoors, and Fred Flintstone's kitchen
       Characters: Fred Flintstone, Barney, Barney's wife

TEXT
Barney: *Watch me fool Fred into givin' me his Cocoa Pebbles. Hello, Fred.* [In an angel's outfit.]
Fred: *Barney, ya looked so alive yesterday. How can I make it up to you for the times I didn't treat ya right.*
Barney (ghostly voice): *Cocoa Pebbles.*
Fred: *Here Barn, you always loved Cocoa Pebbles.*

Barney (ghostly voice): *Mmm. Heavenly flavor.*
Barney's wife: *Barney, we're going to be late to the costume party.*
Fred: *Costume party? You're no angel.*
Barney: *You said it, Fred.* [laughter]
Voice over (adult male): *Post Cocoa and Fruity Pebbles cereals, a great tasting part of a balanced breakfast.*

We note again that the food thief is caught, but not punished.

A Frosted Flakes commercial (CBS, 7/18/78, 8:17 a.m.) employs a variation on the food-thief theme. In this commercial, the "secret formula" for the sugar frosting is kept in a vault under guard. Here, much the same point is made as in the food-thief commercials: The product promoted is so desirable that the formula for making it is worth stealing. In another commercial for Frosted Flakes (ABC, 12/29/79, 10:45 a.m.), someone dressed as Tony the Tiger, the animated spokesanimal for Frosted Flakes, falsely takes credit for inventing this "secret formula."

Closely related to the food-thief theme is the "search" theme, where the cereal or someone who has the cereal, or some ingredient of the cereal is sought by children or other figures in the commercial. The Froot Loops commercials cited in Chapter 8 are of this type. Such commercials suggest the desirability of the sought-for item. In the case of the Froot Loops commercials, the aroma of Froot Loops leads a toucan that serves as the Froot Loops' spokesbird and some other animal to the Froot Loops.

Part of the appeal of the food-thief motif derives from the fact that people ordinarily don't steal things unless they are desirable. The idea that a cereal might be so desirable as to cause someone or something to do something he or it might not otherwise do appears also in a Cocoa Puffs commercial (ABC, 3/11/78, 8:02–8:16 a.m.), where Sonny the Cuckoo bird goes berserk out of desire for this cereal: *I'm cuckoo for Cocoa Puffs.* Two Sugar Corn Pops commercials (ABC, 12/29/79, 9:14 a.m.; ABC, 12/29/79, 10:10 a.m.) involve a large yellow cowboy called "Big Yellow" who is willing to trade anything (always something yellow of course) for a bowl of this cereal.

In all of these themes, it is some aspect of the behavior of one or more characters of the commercial that "demonstrates" the desirability of the product being promoted. Since all such commercials are scripted and few employ real people, these "demonstrations" are totally contrived. However, I should be very surprised if many young children were to recognize this, for young children find it extraordinarily difficult to distinguish what they see on television from reality.

Ratiocinative Aspects of Cereal Commercials

Adult commercials for breakfast cereals, if my tapes are any guide, focus primarily on nutrition. I do not recall ever seeing an adult commercial for presweetened cereals, but there are commercials for unsweetened cereals that extol the fact that they have no added sugar. Consider, for instance, the following adult commercial for Shredded Wheat.

(9)   Shredded Wheat (NBC, 2/25/78, evening)
        Type: Live action
        Setting: Kitchen
        Characters: Man

        TEXT
        Voice over (adult male): *Hey, trying to cut down on sugar? Maybe you should start with your breakfast cereal . . .*
        Man: *Sugar?*
        Voice over: *. . . because most cold cereals add sugar.*
        Man: *Sugar. Again?*
        Voice Over: *5% there, 16% there, 40% there*
        Man: *Sugar.*
        Voice over: *But spoon sized Shredded Wheat adds no sugar.*
        Man: *Hey, no sugar!*
        Voice over: *100% natural whole wheat crunchiness in every bite, but no added sugar. Spoonsize Shredded Wheat—100% whole wheat, 0% added sugar.*

It is worth asking, I think, why advertisers do not promote sweetened cereals to adults on the grounds of their sweetness. This cannot be because adults don't like sweet foods. I believe the answer is that most adults are aware that the consumption of sweet foods carries with it certain health consequences, and that adults are therefore better able to defend against commercials for sweet foods. Children, on the other hand, do not appear to care very much about nutrition.

Commercials for breakfast cereals directed to children virtually always focus on taste rather than nutrition, which is not surprising since children seem to be more interested in taste than nutrition. Sweetness is touted in the presweetened cereals, of course. Flavor is highlighted in most commercials. Some are chocolate flavored. A number are fruit flavored and one even contains *bits of real apple* (as if there were synthetic apples) (Apple Jacks, ABC, 3/11/78, 9:01 a.m.). In one case the flavor of a nonexistent berry is promoted. A Crunch Berry commercial (ABC,

3/11/78, 9:15–9:26 a.m.) begins with a reference to a *crunch strawberry flavor* (whatever that is) and then states, *There's nothing like the taste of a crunchberry in season.* I suspect some children will be persuaded that there is such a thing as a crunchberry. Certainly, there are berries with stranger names than this. Flavor is the primary focus of the Cookie Crisp commercials I have on tape: *It looks and tastes like cookies, see?* (ABC, 3/11/78, 8:16 a.m.–8:30 a.m.).

Texture is the third taste related feature of cereals that cereal commercials focus on. Two words recur in these commercials: *crisp* and *crunch* (and morphologically related forms). These words also occur in candy advertisements directed at children. It appears that advertisers believe most children don't like soggy foods and, since cereals normally have milk poured over them, sogginess is an inevitable problem. There is a paraphonological reason why *crunch* occurs so frequently: it is onomatopoeic. One might also argue that words that begin with *cr* ([kr—]) are sound symbolic. Note that *crack, crackle, (Snap, Crackle, and Pop), crash, crisp, crunch, crush,* and *crust* all involve a sharp sound or a brittle (hence crisp) object. In any event, *crisp* and *crunch* are "buzz" words in children's advertising.

Only three of the commercials on my tape focus on nutrition, which is the usual focus of adult cereal commercials: a Kellogg's "better breakfast" commercial that I shall have much to say about later, and two commercials for the new product Body Buddies that were taped in 1979. I do not know whether this cereal was introduced because the advertiser believes that children are not wholly unconcerned with nutrition or because they hope to win over parents, or both.

One last ratiocinative element in cereal commercials worth mentioning is the use of premium offers (i.e., small toys like Star Wars stickers, metallic state coins, a mold for making popsicles, a "scary" door knocker, etc.) in commercials. They occur in 14 (or 28%) of the 50 commercials I have on tape. Such offers are not unique to cereal commercials (Burger King routinely employs them) or to children's advertising (adult commercials for detergents sometimes employ premium offers). The use of premiums in the marketing of cereals has a long history, of course. Their function is to provide a basis (albeit an artificial one) for product differentiation.

The Nature of the Products

If we may believe Cookie Jarvis, the animated magician featured in Cookie Crisp commercials, Cookie Crisp cereals consist of cookies. Consider the following commercial for Cookie Crisp cereal.

(10)   Cookie Crisp (ABC, 3/11/78, 8:16–8:30 a.m.)
         Type: Live action, with animated magician
         Setting: Breakfast
         Characters: Girl, boy, magician (Cookie Jarvis)

         TEXT
         Girl: *Where's Cookie Jarvis?*
         Boy: *There. He dropped his magic wand again.*
         Girl: *Here.*
         Cookie Jarvis: *Kanoodle, kazam. Oh, ho, ho. Thanks a lot. Cookie Crisp
             cereal hits the spot. It looks and tastes like cookies, see? But even in
             milk, it stays crisp as can be. Cookie Crisp cereal is part of a complete
             breakfast, you know. Bye, now. Gotta go. Oops!* [drops wand.]
         Girl: *Here.*
         Cookie Jarvis: *Heh, heh. Oh. Thanks for the favor, in chocolate chip or
             vanilla wafer flavor . . .* [drops wand] *. . . Oh, oh .*

The terms *chocolate chip* and *vanilla wafer* are names of types of cookies,
of course. In another commercial, a new flavor, "oatmeal cookie" flavor,
is introduced. Consider commercial (11).

(11)   Cookie Crisp (ABC, 7/29/78, 8:11 a.m.)
         Type: Live action, with animated magician
         Setting: Bedroom, kitchen
         Characters: Two boys, magician (Cookie Jarvis)

         TEXT
         Cookie Jarvis: *Good morning!*
         Boys: *It's Cookie Jarvis.*
         Cookie Jarvis: *Please follow me. I've got new oatmeal cookie flavor
             Cookie Crisp cereal, see? It's a brand new flavor, oatmeal cookie, I
             think you'll favor.*
         Boy: *I bet it tastes like oatmeal cookies.*
         Cookie Jarvis: *But it's different from cookies as you can see, 'cause it's
             crispy in milk as a cereal should be.*
         Boys: *Wow! Three Cookie Crisp cereals.*
         Cookie Jarvis: *Each one is part of a complete breakfast.*
         Boys: *How'd he do that?*
         Cookie Jarvis: *Do what?*

In this commercial, Cookie Jarvis differentiates his cereal from cookies
when he says line (12).

(12)   *But it's different from cookies as you can see, 'cause it's crispy in milk as
         a cereal should be.*

The claim that Cookie Crisp differs from cookies in that they stay crisp in milk conversationally implicates (Maxim of Strength) that Cookie Crisp is in all other respects like cookies. The product name *Cookie Crisp* says the same thing, of course. In commercial (13), Cookie Jarvis makes quite clear that Cookie Crisp consists of cookies.

(13)   **Cookie Crisp** (ABC, 3/18/78, 8:10 a.m.)
        Type: Live action, with animated magician
        Setting: Breakfast table, set outdoors
        Characters: Two boys, magician (Cookie Jarvis)

        TEXT
        Younger boy: *Hey, it's Cookie Jarvis.*
        Cookie Jarvis: *That's me, your Cookie Crisp cereal magician. I've come
            from afar to change your dish into a cookie jar. Heh, heh, spilunk,
            spilar.*
        Older boy: *Cookies for breakfast?*
        Cookie Jarvis: *Oh, heavens no, unless they're my cereal, you know.*
        Younger boy: *Crisp in milk.*
        Cookie Jarvis: *Part of a complete breakfast. I hope you'll favor chocolate
            chip and vanilla wafer flavor. Heh, heh. Cookie Crisp cereal for you.*

The older boy (of the two featured in this commercial) comes out squarely against the idea that cookies should be eaten for breakfast, for his question *Cookies for breakfast?* presumes the truth of (14).

(14)   Cookies are not for breakfast.

Cookie Jarvis endorses this sentiment when he says *Oh, heavens no.* However, his utterance, *unless they're my cereal, you know,* given the linguistic context, comes down to his saying (15).

(15)   *Cookies are not for breakfast unless they are my cereal.

Sentence (15) is odd on semantic grounds, for the *unless*-clause presupposes the truth of proposition (16).

(16)   *The cookies are my cereal.

However, (15) would be quite well formed semantically if the phrase *my cereal* is construed as referring to cookies, as in (17).

(17)   Cookies are not for breakfast unless they are my cookies.

It is clear that the makers of this commercial intend to convey (17) to children. The claim that Cookie Jarvis has come to change the children's dishes into cookie jars further supports the view that Cookie Crisp consists of cookies. Note the visual transformation in Photographs 9.3 and 9.4.

Photograph 9.3

Photograph 9.4

Commercial (13) implies that Cookie Crisp has some special property that makes it acceptable for breakfast. However the commercial does not actually say what this property is. I presume it is the vitamin and mineral fortification permitted in cereals but not cookies. Is Cookie Jarvis correct in saying (albeit obliquely) that Cookie Crisp consists of cookies? Comparison of lists of ingredients of Cookie Crisp vanilla wafer flavor cereal and Keebler vanilla wafer cookies supports this claim. Compare (18) and (19).

(18)   Cookie Crisp: Sugar, yellow corn meal, rice flour, wheat flour, oat flour, coconut oil, salt, artificial flavor, sodium ascorbate (vitamin C), reduced iron, niacin-amide, yellow no. 5, artificial color, vitamin A palmitate, BHT (a preservative), pyridoxine hydrochoride (vitamin B6), riboflavin (vitamin B2), thiamine mononitrate, vitamin D2 and vitamin B12.

(19)   Keebler Vanilla Wafer cookies: Enriched flour (wheat flour, niacin, iron, thiamine mononitrite, and riboflavin), sugar, beef fat, whey, corn syrup, salt, leavening (sodium bicarbonate and monocalcium phosphate), butter, lecithin, artificial flavoring, and vanilla.

As these two lists show, there is a fundamental similarity in ingredients between Cookie Crisp cereal and the Keebler cookies, for the primary ingredients of both are sugar, flour, and fat. Nutritional information was not given for the Keebler cookies, so I cannot provide a comparison of the relative degree of vitamin and mineral fortification of the two products. Nor do I know which of the two contains the most sugar, but Cookie Crisp is sweeter to my taste than the cookies.

In general, sugared breakfast cereals differ from cookies in the process of manufacture, in the vitamin fortification permitted in cereals, but not cookies (except in the flour used), in the use of leavening, and sometimes in the type of flour used. It would be interesting to know how parents would react to the idea, advanced by Cookie Jarvis and supported by comparisons of lists of ingredients, that when they are feeding their children sugared cereals, they may be feeding them vitamin fortified cookies.

Nutrition Statements in Cereal Commercials

NAB guidelines (1) and (2) are anything but models of clarity. The requirement that commercials for breakfast foods include a video depiction of the **role** of the food in a balanced regimen cannot be taken very seriously. Advertisers have construed it to mean that they must include a photograph or drawing of a sample breakfast containing the advertised product. However, these sample breakfasts consisting of juice, toast, cereal, and milk do not depict the **role** of the cereal being advertised in a balanced regimen any more than an artist's still life of a bowl of fruit depicts the **role** of fruit in a balanced diet. Advertisers could quite reasonably argue that this requirement simply cannot be satisfied if taken literally. The video depictions of sample breakfasts convey nutritional information only in conjunction with the verbal nutrition statements that accompany them. The requirement that an advertiser of a breakfast food "include at least one audio reference to . . . the role of the product in a balanced regimen" is somewhat vague, however. In my view, an audio reference to the proper role of a food in a balanced diet should consist of a statement of what the food contributes to human nutrition. This statement might also contain information of a negative sort as well. In the case of eggs, the advertiser might include not only a statement to the effect that eggs contribute essential proteins to the human diet but also that eggs contain cholesterol and should perhaps not be eaten too frequently by persons whose bodies contain high levels of cholesterol. Advertisers of breakfast cereals have interpreted this requirement to mean that they should simply provide some comment (sometimes modest, but sometimes extraordinarily strong) about the nutritiousness of a breakfast that includes cereal. As I interpret the language of NAB guideline (2), such comments are at best in minimal compliance with this guideline.

Almost all of the nutrition statements on my tapes are like (3), (4), and (5) in form. These statements instantiate noun phrase schemas (20)–(22), respectively, where "Quant" is a cover symbol for quantifiers like *a, the, any,* etc., and "Adj" is a cover symbol for such adjectives as *delicious, yummy, nutritious, balanced.*

(20)   Part of Quant Adj breakfast. (*Cookie Crisp cereal is part of a complete breakfast.*)

(21)   Quant Adj part of Quant Adj breakfast. (*Cap'n Crunch, a good part of any good breakfast.*)

(22)   Quant Adj breakfast with X (where X refers to the cereal being promoted). (*Enjoy a complete breakfast with Frankenberry.*)

Noun phrases like (20) and (21) normally occur as predicates [as in (3)] or as nonrestrictive appositives [as in (4)]. These are, for all practical purposes, equivalent uses. Noun phrases like (22) in form occur as parts of larger sentences [as in (5), for example].

Construed literally claims like (20)–(22) are quite empty, for a food that contributes no nutrients at all could be said to be part of a nutritious breakfast if the breakfast would be nutritious without it. However, claims like (20)-(22) conversationally implicate that the cereal makes a nutritional contribution to the breakfast. The Maxim of Relevance is responsible for this implicature. What this nutritional contribution is is normally not made clear, and children may assume that the cereal is nutritionally the most important part of the breakfast.[3]

The adjectives that occur in the construction Quant Adj *breakfast* are *nutritious, balanced, complete,* and *good,* as well as the adjective phrase *roarin' good.* When used in phrases of the form Quant Adj *breakfast,* these adjectives are set-theoretic predicates, for they ascribe properties to sets of foods. As such, the concepts expressed by these adjectives are relatively complex. Although I have no experimental evidence to back me up, I suspect that if the words *nutritious, balanced,* and *complete* mean anything to young children, they mean no more than 'good for you'.

The adjective *good* is ambiguous, meaning either 'good for you' or 'good tasting'. It occurs in 15 of the 50 commercials I have on tape. In addition, the adjective phrase *roarin' good* is used in one commercial (Frosted Rice, CBS, 7/15/78, 8:27 a.m.) and *smackin' good* in another (Sugar Smacks, CBS, 7/18/78, 8:49 a.m.). In each of the 15 commercials in which *good* is used, the overall emphasis is on taste rather than nutrition and, as a result, children may tend to interpret *good* as 'good tasting'.[4] Such an interpretation is particularly favored in nutrition statements like (23) or (24) that focus on taste.

(23)   *Cap'n Crunch cereal, a yummy part of a good breakfast.*   (CBS.
        7/15/78, 9:12 a.m.)

(24)   *Toasted wheat for a smackin' good breakfast.*   (Sugar Smacks,
        CBS, 7/18/78, 8:49 a.m.)

Similarly, it is difficult to see how *good* could be interpreted otherwise than as 'good tastin'' in (25).

(25)   *Remember Kellogg's Frosted Rice cereal is part of a roarin' good
        breakfast.*   (CBS, 7/15/78, 8:27 a.m.)

People generally do not "roar" about a meal because of its nutritional goodness. Since nutrition statements employing the phrase *good breakfast* can be interpreted as comments on how good the breakfast tastes, such statements would appear not to be in compliance with the NAB Code. Statements (24) and (25) are clearly in violation of this code.

---

[3]See the February 1981 issue of *Consumer Reports* for a study of the nutritional value of cold breakfast cereals.

[4]Words that are associated with taste greatly outnumber words that are associated with nutrition in breakfast cereal commercials.

Although *nutritious, balanced,* and *complete* are all used in nutrition statements, they do not have the same meaning. A nutritious breakfast is presumably a breakfast that consists of nutritious foods. A balanced breakfast is one that consists of nutritious foods that contribute some of each kind of nutrient the body requires. Thus, a breakfast can be nutritious without being balanced. The concept of a complete breakfast is rather curious. I presume it refers to balanced breakfasts in which a third of the body's required nutrients are provided. A breakfast that is "good for you" is presumably just a nutritious breakfast.

How do children go about learning these nutrition predicates? There are just two ways. They can learn what these predicates refer to by being shown examples. This is a reasonably efficient way of learning words that refer to concrete objects, but not abstract words (e.g., the nutrition adjectives being discussed). One can also acquire a predicate by learning its meaning. We can think of the meaning of a predicate as being the "rule" we employ to identify the referent of the predicate. Were we to say that a balanced breakfast is one that contains foods from each of the four food groups (vegetables and grains, meat, dairy products, and fruit), then anyone who has learned this "rule" would be said to know the meaning of *balanced breakfast.* Television commercials for breakfast cereals provide an invariant referent for the phrases *good breakfast, nutritious breakfast, balanced breakfast,* and *complete breakfast* via the sample breakfasts shown on screen, namely, breakfasts consisting of juice, toast, cereal, and milk. The inevitable effect of these breakfast cereal commercials on children is a relatively impoverished understanding of these phrases and a highly distorted perception of what breakfasts should consist of.

The strength of the nutrition claims that appear in cereal commercials depends primarily on the quantifiers that occur in them. Let us first consider those that occur in *part of* Quant Adj *breakfast* nutrition statements, including cases in which this construction occurs as part of the larger Quant Adj *part of* Quant Adj *breakfast* construction. The following examples occur on my tapes:

(26) a. *Part of this complete breakfast.* (3 commercials)
      b. *Part of a complete breakfast.* (4 commercials)
      c. *Part of a balanced breakfast.* (6 commercials)
      d. *Part of your good breakfast.* (7 commercials)
      e. *Part of a good breakfast.* (3 commercials)
      f. *Part of any good breakfast.* (2 commercials)
      g. *Part of a roarin' good breakfast.* (1 commercial)
      h. *Part of your complete breakfast.* (1 commercial)

i. *Part of this nutritious breakfast.*   (2 commercials)
j. *Part of a nutritious breakfast.*   (4 commercials)
k. *Part of your nutritious breakfast.*   (1 commercial)

Of the quantifiers that appear in (26), the most modest is *this*. The quantifier *this* is deictic, that is, it refers to something in the context of utterance. In these nutrition statements, *this breakfast* refers to the visual sample breakfast that appears on screen. The strength of a claim like (26a) depends on what is in this sample breakfast. If the breakfast were to consist of a glass of milk and a small "variety pack" box of cereal, the claim *part of this complete breakfast* would make a relatively strong claim on behalf of the cereal. If the breakfast were to consist of a steak, two eggs, milk, home fries, toast, a grilled tomato, orange juice, and cereal, this claim would be relatively empty.

At the other extreme are nutrition statements like (26f) that employ the universal quantifier *any*. The two cases in which *any* occurs are (27) and (28).

(27)   *Cap'n Crunch, a tasty part of any good breakfast.*   (CBS, 7/15/78, 8:24 a.m.)

(28)   *Cap'n Crunch, a good part of any good breakfast.*   (ABC, 7/29/78, 8:45 a.m.)

Nutrition statements (27) and (28) entail (not just conversationally implicate) that if Cap'n Crunch is not part of a breakfast, the breakfast cannot be good. This observation is supported by the fact that (29), which attempts to cancel this inference, is a contradiction.

(29)   *Cap'n Crunch, a good part of any, but not all breakfasts.

These Cap'n Crunch nutrition statements thus make an extraordinary claim on behalf of this cereal. Just as extraordinary is the fact that the NAB and the three television networks appear to regard nutrition statements (27) and (28) as consistent with code guidelines (1) and (2). These statements obviously are not.

The quantifier *a*, when it occurs in a sentence like (30), would normally be said to mean 'some' and conversationally implicate 'one.'

(30)   Joe was served a breakfast of sausage, eggs, toast, and orange juice.

The quantifier *a* is said to mean 'some' rather than 'one' because a sentence like (30) is consistent with Joe's having been served two such breakfasts. Sentence (30) does implicate that only one such breakfast was served. The Maxim of Strength is responsible for this implicature.

It is clear that *a* does not mean 'some' and does not implicate 'one' in nutrition statements (26b), (26c), (26e), (26g), and (26j). Consider (31)–(33).

(31)   Cookie Crisp is part of some complete breakfasts, but not all complete breakfasts.

(32)   *Cookie Crisp is part of a complete breakfast, but not of all complete breakfasts.

(33)   *Cookie Crisp is part of any complete breakfast, but not of all complete breakfasts.

Sentence (31) is well formed semantically. However, (32) and (33) are rather odd. In light of this, we might want to say that *a* has universal quantifier force in (32) and in the nutrition statements that contain it.

In his study of generic constructions, Carlson (1977) notes that noun phrases that employ *a* generically differ semantically from those that employ *any*. Thus (34) would be falsified by the existence of a dog that has three legs, but (35) would not.

(34)   Any dog has four legs.

(35)   A dog has four legs.

In light of this, (34) would appear to be stronger than (35). On the other hand, (35) is vastly stronger than (36).

(36)   Some dogs have four legs.

Sentence (36) would be true if there were only one dog with four legs, but in this circumstance, (35) would be false (according to the intended interpretation).

Sentence (35) has essentially the same meaning as (37).

(37)   Any normal dog has four legs.

We might say then that *a dog* in (35) refers to any normal dog.[5] According to this view *a* is a restricted universal quantifier in (35). This is consistent with one's intuition that a claim like (35) is stronger than (36), but weaker than (34).

In light of the preceding argument, I believe we must say that (38) is weaker than (39), but stronger than (40).

(38)   Cookie Crisp is part of a complete breakfast.

---

[5] Jespersen (1929) claims that "with *a*, the subject refers to all members (or any member) of the class or species it denotes but only as a representative of the members."

(39)   Cookie Crisp is part of every complete breakfast.

(40)   Cookie Crisp is part of some complete breakfasts.

What we seem to want to say is that (38) makes essentially the same claim as (41).

(41)   Cookie Crisp is part of any normal, representative, complete breakfast.

It should be clear that nutrition statements like (26b), (26c), (26e), (26g), and (26j), which employ *a* generically, are extraordinarily complex and extraordinarily strong. I have no idea how young children interpret them. Nonetheless, since these nutrition statements are false, they are inconsistent with NAB guidelines. The fact that the television networks and the NAB permit such statements suggests that they do not understand these statements or that they do not take the NAB guidelines seriously.

Nutrition claims like (42) appear to be used in two different ways in the commercials on my tapes.

(42) X is part of your Adj breakfast.

In a commercial for Rice Krispies (CBS, 7/18/78, 8:54 a.m.), nutrition statement (43) occurs and in this case *your complete breakfast* appears to refer to the on-screen breakfast of the character Bob.

(43)   *You know Kellogg's Rice Krispies cereal is a delicious part of your complete breakfast.*

According to this interpretation *your complete breakfast* seems to have exactly the same interpretation as *this complete breakfast of yours.* Statement (43) is therefore quite modest.

In another commercial, the nutrition statement (44) occurs and appears to be addressed to the television-viewing audience.

(44)   *Apple Jacks cereal from Kellogg's, part of your good breakfast.*   (ABC, 3/11/78, 9:01 a.m.)

In my view, there is something a bit odd about this use of the phrase *part of your good breakfast.* I also have the same feeling about (45).

(45)   Your good breakfast should consist of foods from the four food groups.

In (45), the phrase *your good breakfast* seems to refer to a kind of meal rather than to an individual meal. The problem with this is that no one can eat a kind of meal per se. One can only eat individual meals. Moreover, *good breakfast* strikes me as naming a peculiar kind of meal. A good deal less odd are such kinds of meals as high protein breakfasts and low carbohydrate breakfasts.

As I noted earlier, *your complete breakfast* in (43) refers to the on-screen breakfast of one of the characters in the commercial. It therefore has the same meaning as (46).

(46)   You know Kellogg's Rice Krispies cereal is a delicious part of this complete breakfast of yours.

Claim (44), which is directed at the viewing audience, must be interpreted quite differently, for (44) and (47) do not have the same meaning.

(47)   Apple Jacks cereal from Kellogg's, part of this good breakfast of yours.

In my view, (44) has essentially the same meaning as (48).

(48)   Apple Jacks cereal of Kellogg's, part of any good breakfast of yours.

In support of this conjecture, note how strange (49) sounds:

(49)   *Apple Jacks cereal is part of your good breakfast but not of every good breakfast of yours.

In any event, (44) is only marginally intelligible. The NAB Code does not require fully intelligible nutrition messages, but considering the nature of the audience, such a policy does seem desirable.

Naturally, a strong nutrition claim can be weakened by other elements of the sentence it occurs in. Consider (50).

(50)   *It* [Alphabits] *can be part of your nutritious breakfast.*   (ABC, 12/29/79, 10:10 a.m.)

The modal *can* weakens the force of *part of your nutritious breakfast*. However, none of the very strong nutrition messages (e.g., *part of any good breakfast*) is weakened in this or any other way in the commercials I have on tape.

Some of the nutrition claims of the form *part of* Quant Adj *breakfast* occur as part of a larger construction of the form Quant Adj *part of* Quant Adj *breakfast*. The ones I have on tape are

(51)   a.   *Crunchberry cereal, a dandy part of a good breakfast.*   (ABC, 3/11/78, 9:15–9:26 a.m.)

          b.   *Cap'n Crunch, a tasty part of any good breakfast.*   (CBS, 7/15/78, 8:24 a.m.)

c. *Cap'n Crunch cereal, a yummy part of a good breakfast.*   (CBS, 7/15/78, 9:12 a.m.)

d. *Post Cocoa and Fruity Pebbles cereals, a great tasting part of a balanced breakfast.*   (CBS, 7/15/78, 9:20 a.m.)

e. *It* [frosting formula] *makes Kellogg's Sugar Frosted Flakes a delicious part of your good breakfast.*   (CBS, 7/18/78, 8:17 a.m.)

f. *You know Kellogg's Rice Krispies cereal is a delicious part of your complete breakfast.*   (CBS, 7/18/78, 8:54 a.m.)

g. *Cap'n Crunch, a good part of any good breakfast.*   (ABC, 7/29/78, 8:45 a.m.)

h. *It's* [Post Super Sugar Crisp] *a tasty part of a good breakfast.*   (ABC, 7/29/78, 9:13 a.m.)

i. *Post Fruity and Cocoa Pebbles cereal, the delicious part of a nutritious breakfast.*   (ABC, 12/16/79, 11:22 a.m.)

j. *Rice Krispies will be a lively part of your good breakfast.*   (ABC, 12/15/79, 10:52 a.m.)

What was said previously of the *part of* Quant Adj *breakfast* construc-tions holds for the nutrition statements of (51). However, the Quant Adj prefixes of the latter nutrition statements very much alter their effect, because, with one exception (51g), the focus of these statements is on taste, not nutrition. The focus on taste could have the effect that children will interpret the ambiguous adjective *good* in (51a), (51b), (51c), (51e), (51h), and (51j) as meaning 'good tasting.' If so, none of these nutrition statements would be in compliance with the NAB Code.

Nutrition statement (51i) deserves special mention for it makes a stupendously strong claim on behalf of Post Fruity Pebbles and Cocoa Pebbles cereals. This nutrition claim entails that one or the other of these cereals must be part of a breakfast if it is to count as a nutritious break-fast (which is false) and that each is the only part of every representative nutritious breakfast that is delicious (which is also false). The fact that the three networks and the NAB permit Post to say this sort of thing suggests that these organizations do not monitor or simply do not care what advertisers say.[6]

---

[6]Judge Needelman of the FTC drew my attention to the phrase *the good part of any good breakfast.* This nutrition statement is ambiguous in four ways, for *good* can mean 'good for you' or 'good tasting' in each occurrence. It moreover entails that the cereal in question is the only good part of every good breakfast, which would be spectacularly false if said of any food.

In addition to nutrition claims employing the *part of* Quant Adj *break-fast* construction, one other type of construction occurs on my tapes. Consider the following:

(52)   a. *To keep me from going cuckoo for a complete breakfast with munchy, crunchy, chocolately Cocoa Puffs, you gotta get a gorilla to sit on me.*   (ABC, 3/11/78, 8:02–8:16 a.m.)

        b. *Kids, we're filming this complete breakfast with Trix.*   (ABC, 3/11/78, 8:30 a.m.)

        c. *Time for a complete breakfast with my Count Chocula.*   (ABC, 3/11/78, 9:27–9:41 a.m.)

        d. *Enjoy a complete breakfast with Frankenberry.*   (CBS, 7/15/79, 8:18 a.m.)

        e. *Start with a balanced breakfast, including Kellogg's Froot Loops.*   (CBS, 7/18/78, 8:16 a.m.)

        f. *A Nutritious breakfast with my Count Chocula is a bigger hit.*   (ABC, 7/29/78, 8:58 a.m.)

        g. *Halloween is the perfect time to scare up a nutritious breakfast with my delicious strawberry-flavored Frankenberry.*   *(ABC, 10/28/78, 10:13 a.m.)*

The nutrition claims of (52) make no very strong claims on behalf of the cereals being promoted, for the quantifier *a* that occurs in these statements is a genuine existential quantifier. Thus (52c), for example, is no stronger than (53).

(53)   Time for **some** complete breakfast with my Count Chocula.

The statements of (52) thus appear to be in compliance with the NAB Code.

In addition to the nutrition claims already discussed, the following statements also occur on my tapes:

(54)   *Juice, toast, milk, and delicious fruit-flavored Trix. The right disguise will get me some.*   (CBS, 7/15/78, 8:17 a.m.)

(55)   *Cheerios, crunchy toasted oatios. The tasty way to round out this complete breakfast.*   (CBS, 7/15/78, 8:31 a.m.)

(56)   *Toasted wheat for a smackin' good breakfast. Kellogg's Sugar Smacks.*   (CBS, 7/18/78, 8:49 a.m.)

(57)   *A nutritious breakfast of Post Honeycomb gives you a big bite.*   (ABC, 12/15/79, 10:40 a.m.)

(58)   *This Body Buddies breakfast, with juice, toast, and milk, helps give your muscles energy, with vitamins like B1, B2, and Niacin.*   (ABC, 12/16/79, 9:58 a.m.)

(59)   *Kellogg's Sugar Corn Pops cereal plus toast, juice, and milk and spread is a smart start to your day.*   (ABC, 12/29/79, 9:58 a.m.)

(60)   *And I* [Tony the Tiger] *made them* [Kellogg's Sugar Frosted Flakes] *a smart start and a good breakfast.*   (ABC, 12/29/79, 10:45 a.m.)

The noun phrase of (54) makes no nutrition claim at all, for it simply lists the elements of the breakfast shown on screen. It, therefore, is not in compliance with the NAB Code. Claim (55) is interesting. It is relatively weak, for in using the deictic quantifier *this,* the claim applies only to the on-screen breakfast. The verb *round out* suggests that Cheerios makes a contribution to the "completeness" of the on-screen breakfast. However, the focus of (55) is on taste, not nutrition and thus does not specify the role of Cheerios in a balanced regimen (unless one argues that the correct role of Cheerios is primarily to contribute to the taste, not the nutritional soundness of breakfasts).

Claim (56) is not a nutrition claim at all. The phrase *smackin' good* refers unambiguously to taste, not nutrition. It evokes the phrase *lip smackin'.* I believe that the commercial containing (56) is a thinly disguised promotion of Sugar Smacks as a snack food. Consider the following commercial.

(61)   Sugar Smacks (CBS, 7/18/81, 8:49 a.m.)
        Type: Live action, with animated frog
        Setting: Patio and garden
        Characters: Boy, girl, father, mother, frog

        TEXT
        Voice over (adults, singing): *Put your two hands out for a dig'em smack.*
            [Smacking sound]
        Frog: *Dig 'em.*
        Voice over (adults, singing): *Watch a bowl appear like that. Kellogg's Sugar Smacks.*
        Frog: *Dig 'em.*
        Voice over (adults, singing): *Toasted wheat for a smackin' good breakfast. Kellogg's Sugar Smacks.*
        Frog: *Dig 'em.*
        Children: *Hi, dad.*
        Father: *Mornin'. Hey. What's that Frog doin'?*
        Frog: [In bird bath] *Deep sea diving.*
        Father: *How deep is it?*
        Frog: *Knee deep.*
        Voice over (adults, singing): *Kellogg's Sugar Smacks . . .*

Frog: *Dig 'em.*
Voice over (adults, singing): *... make a part of your good breakfast Kellogg's Sugar Smacks.*
Father: *That's a dig 'em smack.*

Consider line (62)

(62)   *Put your two hands out for a dig 'em smack.*

At one level of interpretation, (62) reminds one of the palm slaps athletes use in congratulating someone on a good play. At another level, (62) reminds one of the expression *close your eyes and put out your hands,* which is said to a child when one wishes to give him or her a treat (e.g., a snack food). In this connection it is worth noting that *smack* rhymes with *snack.*

The question whether commercial (61) promotes Sugar Smacks as a snack food is of some importance, for elements of the cereal industry argued during the FTC hearings that sugared cereals are infrequently eaten as snacks. This is of interest because sugared cereals present a greater dental care problem when eaten as snacks than when eaten with milk, for they are more likely to stick to the teeth if eaten dry. Even if the reader disagrees with my interpretation of commercial (61), it must be agreed, I think, that line (56) fails to satisfy NAB Code guidelines (1) and (2).

Lines (57) and (60) both suggest that Post Honeycomb and Kellogg's Sugar Frosted Flakes are all that need be eaten for a nutritious (57) or good (60) breakfast. The phrase *a breakfast of* X, Y, *and* Z conversationally implicates that only X, Y, and Z are in the breakfast. Thus (57) implies that a breakfast consisting only of Post Honeycomb is nutritious. This may be true, but it is inconsistent with the NAB guidelines. Sentence (60), entails that Sugar Frosted Flakes is by itself a good breakfast. The on-screen juice, toast, cereal, and milk breakfasts might cause children not to draw this inference, however.

Line (58) occurs in a commercial for a relatively new product, Body Buddies. It, like the commercial itself, offers a serious alternative to ordinary cereal commercials. Consider

(63)   Body Buddies (ABC, 12/16/79, 11:14 a.m.)
        Type: Animated
        Setting: Outdoors
        Characters: Four children and one man

        TEXT
        Man: *Let's ask kids what they want for breakfast.*
        Child 1: *Something that tastes good!*

Child 2: *That's good for me!*
Child 3: *With vitamins!*
Child 4: *And minerals!*
Man: *We gave them what they asked for—new Body Buddies. This Body Buddies breakfast, with juice, toast, and milk, helps give your muscles energy, with vitamins like B1, B2, and Niacin. Body Buddies is the cereal with 16 vitamins and minerals.*
Child 2: *Wow, 16!*
Child 3: *But does Body Buddies taste good?*
Man: *Corn pops with brown sugar and honey?*
Child 1: *Oh, boy!*
Man: *Also in natural fruit flavor.*

Although the focus of this commercial is as much on nutrition as on taste, it should be noted that this commercial is like all the others in touting the juice, toast, cereal, and milk breakfast.

Although children receive a certain amount of nutrition training at school and perhaps also at home, I should be very much surprised if the most systematic and most frequent training children receive in breakfast nutrition is not acquired sitting in front of their television sets. And, although the competition among cereal manufacturers does seem to be quite considerable, they are allied in their determination to push just one conception of breakfast to children. The inevitable effect of this will be to very badly distort children's ideas about the nature of breakfast nutrition.

Although American adults eat a wide range of foods for breakfast, including bacon, ham, steak, lox, eggs, cheese, grits, potatoes, etc., purveyors of these foods do not promote them to children as possible breakfast foods. Indeed, the only breakfast-type food promoted to children on my tapes besides cold cereals is frozen waffles. I have only two such commercials on tape, the text of one of which is as follows:

(64)   Aunt Jemima Waffles (ABC, 12/29/79, @ 9:57 a.m.)
        Type: Live action
        Setting: Circus
        Characters: Various circus persons

        TEXT
        Characters 1 and 2 (singing): *I'm a I'm a Aunt Jemima Jumbo Waffle eater.*
        Character 3 (singing): *Breakfast time is so much fun I'm always up to greet her.*
        Character 4 (singing): *In the morning, piping hot, those jumbo waffles hit the spot.*

Character 5 (singing): *Yeah, I'm a I'm a Aunt Jemima Jumbo Waffles eater.*
Voice over (adult male): *Aunt Jemima Jumbo Waffles, crispy outside, tender inside, full of flavor. Milk, juice, and jumbo waffles make a great breakfast.*
Everyone (singing): *I'm a I'm Aunt Jemima Jumbo Waffles eater.*

It is worth noting that waffles, like cereals, are normally eaten with some sweetener (syrup, honey, jam, etc.) and that the conception of breakfast as something that contains a sweet dish as its central element is also promoted in commercial (64).

As we have seen, some cereal commercials assert that a cereal breakfast is superior to other possible breakfasts, namely those that employ nutrition claims *part of any* Adj *breakfast,* and (in some cases) *part of a* Adj *breakfast,* and *part of your* Adj *breakfast.* One of the commercials I have on tape, directly argues for the superiority of the juice, toast, cereal, and milk breakfast.

Consider the following commercial presented by Kellogg's:

(65)   Kellogg's (ABC, 3/18/78, 8:28 a.m.)
        Type: Live action
        Setting: Large room (warehouse?)
        Characters: Seven children (both sexes, three races). All children
           speak.

        TEXT
        Child: *Hey, give us a hand. We're building a better breakfast.*
        Child: *What's that?*
        Child: *That's a breakfast with foods from at least three of the four food
           groups.*
        Child: *Look out for orange juice, in the fruit and vegetable group.*
        Child: *Here comes milk from the milk group.*
        Child: *Make room for corn flakes and toast.*
        Child: *From the bread and cereal group.*
        Child: *Now that's a well built breakfast.*
        Child: *Yep. It has the energy you need for a better start each day.*
        Children: *Build a better breakfast tomorrow.*
        Voice over (adult male): *This better breakfast message is from
           Kellogg's.*

In this commercial, a group of children is shown in front of a number of large blocks, on the surfaces of each of which is pictured some food ranging from cereal to fish (see Photograph 9.5). The children proceed to build a "better breakfast," consisting of juice, toast, cereal, and milk (see Photograph 9.6). Commercial (65) gives the appearance of being a public-

Photograph 9.5

Photograph 9.6

Photograph 9.7

service-type commercial promoting good nutrition. In fact, it is a thinly disguised promotion of the juice, toast, cereal, and milk breakfast. This commercial employs the phrase *better breakfast* which is, of course, an elliptical comparative that invites the response *better than what?* The commercial provides the answer in two ways. First, juice, toast, cereal, and milk are selected from a wide range of foods that, by implication, are inferior to those selected. Second, at the conclusion of this commercial, we see a four-quadrant split-screen visual representation of four breakfasts, one of which is Kellogg's "better breakfast" (see Photograph 9.7). This visual thus provides the direct answer to the question *better than what?* The juice, toast, cereal, and milk breakfast is superior to breakfasts consisting of such things as eggs, bacon, sausage, pancakes, and waffles.

I believe the effect of the cereal commercials on my tapes including, in particular, commercial (65), must badly distort children's perceptions of what breakfast should consist of. It is surely not in the best interests of children or of the society as a whole that children be taught that the centerpiece of breakfast should be a sweet food. Yet this is the force of the commercials on my tapes.

In recent years, network public service spots have begun to promote foods other than cereal for breakfast. Just how effective these (by contrast infrequent) spots will be is difficult to say. I fear that they will be ineffective thanks largely to most children's single-minded interest in putting sweet things in their mouths. The fact that purveyors of breakfast foods other than frozen waffles and cereals do not often (if ever) advertise to children suggests to me that they recognize that such advertising will be ineffective.

Chapter 10
Conclusion

Although television is primarily viewed as being a visual communications medium, there can be no doubt that what is said in television advertising is of decisive importance to its effectiveness. The reason for this is simply that there are very few products that have sufficient visual appeal to be sold on that ground alone. The attractiveness of an automobile can better be shown than described, and some aspects of its performance are better shown than described. But it would be very difficult to establish that some car is "more car for less money" nonverbally.

Automobiles have been sold on the basis of how they look for years. In certain other cases, though a product has little or no intrinsic visual appeal, it can be promoted visually through a live action or animated visual product demonstration. In most such cases, however, the demonstration would be meaningless were a verbal interpretation of what is going on on screen not provided. Moreover, the lesson to be learned from a product demonstration is normally better stated than shown.

The majority of products promoted on television have too little intrinsic visual appeal to be promoted on this basis, cannot be demonstrated visually, or differ too little from competing products at a visual level to be promoted visually. In such cases what is said during a commercial is of great importance to the effectiveness of the commercial and this is true whether or not claims are being made about a product, a consumer's opinion about a product is being solicited by an interviewer, or people are shown using and enjoying, and, in the process, talking about a product.

Television advertising occurs in real time and employs both the auditory and visual communications channels. This fact coupled with a perceptual uncertainty principle (namely, that although we can absorb information simultaneously on both the visual and auditory channels, we cannot consciously focus on both channels simultaneously) presents something of a problem to television viewers. Advertisers have exploited this in several ways:

- by presenting long, small print disclaimers in competition with the auditory message as well as other visual material;
- by presenting differing printed and oral verbal messages, one relatively weak and one quite strong;
- by presenting conflicting oral claims, e.g., a relatively weak claim early on in a commercial and a quite strong claim toward the end;
- by using misleading discourse nonsequiturs, i.e., claims that presuppose the prior establishment of the truth of some proposition which, in fact, has not been established as true;
- by saying things that sound good but that in fact don't say anything at all; and
- by implying, rather than overtly asserting, claims.

Given that television occurs in real time and thus cannot be studied carefully, and that it uses both the auditory and visual communications channels, it would be surprising if viewers were very often able to see through such techniques. The fact that viewers tend not to examine television advertising carefully renders this even less likely.

The fact that advertisers very commonly imply rather than overtly assert claims raises the question of what advertisers should be held responsible for. Clearly advertisers like everyone else should be held responsible for what they assert and for what their assertions entail and conventionally implicate. According to what I have called the "literalist" theory of truth in advertising this is all advertisers should be held responsible for. However, according to what I have called the "pragmatist" theory, advertisers should also be held responsible for conversational implicatures of what they say.

What an advertisement asserts, entails, or conventionally implicates follows directly from the meanings of the sentences that make up the advertisement. On the other hand, what an advertisement conversationally implicates, though dependent in part on the meaning of what is said, depends crucially on consumer reasoning. Moreover, different viewers can and sometimes will draw different conversational implicatures from the same advertisement. A literalist might argue that advertisers should not be held responsible for the results of consumer reasoning for they have no control over this reasoning. It might also be argued that the procedure for "calculating" conversational implicatures is too indeterminate to give incontrovertible results.

The central difficulty with the literalist theory of truth in advertising is that it presumes a cognitive-cum-semantic ability that logically un-tutored speakers do not have, namely the ability to distinguish valid from invalid inferences. To a logically untutored speaker, the distinction between an entailment or conventional implicature and an invalid, but compelling, conversational implicature is a distinction without a difference.

A realistic theory of truth in advertising must, I think, be based on actual, rather than ideal, human cognitive-cum-semantic abilities, that is, on how people will actually interpret the language of an advertisement rather than on how a logician might say they should interpret this lan-guage. If this principle is accepted then advertisers should be held re-sponsible for what their advertisements conversationally implicate, which is the thesis of the pragmatist position.

That differing people can draw different conversational implicatures from the same advertisement is, in my view, a pseudoproblem. Generally this happens whenever the Maxim of Strength and the Maxim of Rele-vance are opposed. We noted that a claim like (1) will implicate (2) to anyone who uses the Maxim of Relevance and (3) to anyone who uses the Maxim of Strength.

(1)   Wartsoff contains vivaline and vivaline removes warts instantly.

(2)   Wartsoff removes warts instantly.

(3)   Wartsoff probably does not remove warts instantly.

Sentence (1) is relevant to the consumer who has warts if and only if Wartsoff does what vivaline does. To a reflective and critical consumer, the fact that the advertiser does not actually assert (2), but merely implies it, would implicate, given the Maxim of Strength, that (2) either isn't true (Maxim of Truth) or can't be defended (Maxim of Evidence), and, thus, that (3) is true. In my view, when a conflict like this exists, any but the most critical of consumers will opt for inferences based on the Maxim of Relevance, which is to say that the Maxim of Relevance is perceptually more salient than the Maxim of Strength in such a case.

A use of the Maxim of Strength in a case like (1) depends crucially on recall of precisely what was said, but the fact that television advertising occurs in real time makes such recall rather difficult. Moreover, it has been established experimentally that people tend to recall pragmatic inferences of sentences with as much or more frequency than they recall what was directly asserted. It would be surprising if television viewers were not to do the same in the case of what is asserted and what is implied in television advertisements.

The claim that the method for calculating conversational implicatures is too indeterminate to give incontrovertible results presents a problem for the pragmatist theory of truth in advertising. Surely advertisers should be held responsible for conversational implicatures so long as there is uncertainty about what a given advertisement does or does not conversationally implicate. Consider, for instance, the Ramada Inn advertising claim (4), discussed in Chapter 2.

(4)   *We're building a reputation, not resting on one.*

To some this will implicate (5) and to others (6).

(5)   Some highly regarded hotel/motel chain is resting on its
        reputation.

(6)   Someone has asserted or believes Ramada Inn is resting on its
        reputation.

Both (5) and (6) are credible implicatures of (4). Which inference a given consumer will draw depends on what he or she believes to be true. A consumer who does not think much of Ramada Inn would probably go with (6). Anyone who has no particular views on the subject would probably go with (5). Thus, there is a certain indeterminacy as to what (4) implicates. However, the crucial point is that both (5) and (6) are credible implicatures.

In my view, as a practical matter, there will rarely be genuine uncertainty as to what is and what is not a credible conversational implicature of a given advertisement. Where there is uncertainty, this usually arises because of differing items of background knowledge that can be brought to bear on the interpretation of what is said. As a result, one can argue that an advertiser should be held responsible for any conversational implicature that hinges on credible and widely held pieces of background knowledge.

In order to understand how advertisers use language it is necessary to recognize two facts: that advertisers want to make the strongest cases they can on behalf of the products they are trying to sell and that advertisers can be and sometimes are required to defend the claims they make. The first of these facts leads advertisers to make the strongest claims they can. The second leads advertisers to adopt several courses of action designed to protect them from having to defend strong claims. Advertisers, who cannot defend strong claims, may imply that some proposition is true rather than assert it or employ strong sounding but logically weak language or employ language that is too vague to have determinate empirical consequences.

I have already dealt with the first strategy, namely, implying rather than asserting claims. I argued that advertisers (like all other speakers) should be held responsible not only for what their advertisements assert, entail, or conventionally implicate, but also for those conversational implicatures that do not derive from idiosyncratic consumer reasoning or beliefs.

Perhaps the most interesting linguistic advertising technique is the use of strong sounding but logically weak or empirically indeterminate language. In Chapter 3, I noted that there are a variety of linguistic elements that are quite weak from a logical point of view that occur frequently in advertising. Modal elements like *may, might, can,* or *could* or the quasimodal verb *helps* appear to weaken the claims in which they occur. Thus, (8) is vastly weaker logically than (7).

(7)   Wartsoff will remove your warts.

(8)   Wartsoff may remove your warts.

Sentence (7) is true if and only if Wartsoff will in fact remove anyone's warts if he or she uses it. On the other hand, (8) could be true even if Wartsoff had never successfully removed anyone's warts so long as it is at all possible that it might.

The problem posed by the use of these "force weakeners" is that claims employing them appear to be successful despite their weakness. How could so weak a claim as (8) possibly be effective, one wants to ask? We might try a line of reasoning that points to some incapacity of consumers. We might argue that some significant proportion of consumers are ignorant in some respect that is crucial to the evaluation of a claim like (8). However, I cannot myself believe that any speaker of English could reasonably be said not to know the meaning of *may*. What we might say is that people who know the meaning of *may* may not know its logical properties. In Chapters 2 and 3, I make a case for the view that how we ordinarily use language does not normally reflect what logicians might say about the logical properties of what we say, i.e., that there can be and sometimes is a systematic difference between the linguistic meaning and the logic of language. The consumer ignorance at issue, then, is an ignorance of logic, not language. I submit that advertisers should be held responsible not for how their claims might be interpreted by a logician but for how logically untutored (but nevertheless intelligent) consumers will interpret them.

In Chapter 3, I argued that a claim like (8) will be interpreted relative to other claims that a speaker might have made but didn't. The claims with which (8) would be compared are (7), (9), and (10).

(9)   Wartsoff may not remove warts.

(10)   Wartsoff will not remove warts.

d a metric for evaluating claims such as (7)–(10) that shows that
g a claim like (8), consumers untutored in logic will understand
it to claim that there is a better than even chance that Wartsoff will
remove their warts. However, upon hearing (9), a consumer would, I
think, conclude that there is something less than an even chance that
Wartsoff will remove his or her warts. In my view, advertisers should be
held responsible for how an intelligent but logically untutored speaker
will normally interpret a claim like (8), not for how a logician would
interpret it when doing a classical logical analysis.

As noted earlier, advertisers who cannot justify strong claims can
resort to the tactic of making claims that sound good but are so empirically indeterminate that they cannot actually be tested on objective
grounds. The claim that some margarine has a buttery flavor does not
mean that the margarine tastes like butter in all respects but only that it
tastes like butter in some respect. Such a claim cannot seriously be tested
but it does sound good. This is characteristic of all adjectivalization processes affecting nouns: There is a shift in reference from the thing the
noun refers to (*butter* refers to butter) to properties of the thing (something is buttery if it has some property that butter has).

There are several ways in which advertisers can increase empirical
indeterminacy. As noted, one can use a noun (*butter*) as an adjective
(buttery); one can use a count noun (*car*) as a mass noun (*a lot more car for
a lot less money*); one can use a noun (*orange*) in a noun compound
(*orange flavor*): or one can use an explicit simile (*this paint rolls like cream
and lasts like iron*). In all of these cases, there is a shift of reference from a
thing to a property of a thing. The result is inevitably a claim that is
fundamentally subjective in character. We can agree on what is or is not
butter, but may very well disagree on what is or is not buttery. The same
is true of what is *more car* or has an *orange flavor*, etc. Although claims
like these, all of which come down to similes, are empirically indeterminate, it is difficult to imagine an adult being in any way fooled by them.
This is not so clear in the case of children, especially young children (say,
under 8 years old).

It is clear that the real time character of television advertising and the
fact that television advertising uses the auditory and visual communications channels presents serious problems to adults. Obviously these facts
will present at least as much of a problem—surely much more of a
problem—to young children (children below the age of 8) than to adults.
This coupled with the fact that young children are significantly under-
developed linguistically and cognitively and are relatively inexperienced
as consumers, renders young children phenomenally vulnerable to television advertising.

Young children do not fully control language and are not fully developed cognitively, and, as a result, will fail to understand some things advertisers say and will misunderstand others. Misunderstanding will be exacerbated by young children who have limited knowledge of the world.

It is in the area of disclaimers, which are very common in toy advertising but also occur in food advertising, that failures of understanding are most likely. To their credit, toy advertisers virtually always present oral disclaimers in children's television commercials. The necessity of this is clear: Young children normally either can't read or can't read well enough to understand disclaimers. The problem is that the disclaimers that are used are commonly in the passive voice, are highly elliptical, and employ semantically complex words. Disclaimers like (11) have been proved to be unintelligible to young children.

(11)   *Partial assembly required.*

This is hardly surprising for it is linguistically unnatural in that it is not well formed syntactically, and employs two semantically complex words, *partial* and *assembly*, neither of which is very likely to be in the young child's repertoire. Much of the same is true of disclaimer (12).

(12)   *Each sold separately.*

A feeling for the complexity of (12) can be gained by trying to paraphrase it in words a young child would understand.

One of the peculiarities of television advertising is that while various types of disclaimers are required, no one requires that they be intelligible. Yet an unintelligible disclaimer is tantamount to no disclaimer. Clearly the disclaimers of children's advertising should be tested for intelligibility by young children. In cases like (12), where simpler disclaimers don't seem to be possible, the problem may be that it is the advertisement itself which is the problem. An advertisement showing two or more toys at once, each of which must be purchased separately, must lead young children to assume they come together. Such commercials may be inherently deceptive to young children.

Advertisements for cold breakfast cereals are required to present a visual depiction of and an oral statement of the role of the cereal in a balanced diet. Such advertisements uniformly show a cereal, juice, toast, and milk breakfast, a few adding a piece or bowl of fruit. The accompanying verbal statements range from very weak claims like (13) to extraordinarily strong claims like (14).

(13)   Sugar Cubes is part of this complete breakfast.

(14)   Sugar Cubes is the good part of any good breakfast.

Claim (14) entails that Sugar Cubes must be in a breakfast for it to be a good breakfast and that Sugar Cubes is the only good part of such breakfasts.

The monotonously uniform visual breakfast of cereal advertising coupled with the various very strong nutrition statements discussed in Chapter 9 and the virtual absence of advertisements for other foods that might be eaten for breakfast must have an extraordinary impact on children's perception of what should be eaten for breakfast. Certainly, the television advertising of cereals constitutes the most frequent and most systematic nutrition training most children receive.

What is the lesson of these commercials? Most of the cereals promoted to children are presweetened. Those that are not are likely to have sugar added to them. Combined with the occasional waffle advertisement—waffles are normally sweetened too—children's cereal advertisements promote the lesson that the centerpiece of breakfast should be a sweet food. How this sort of nutrition training serves the interests of children or the society they live in is beyond understanding.

It is clear that those responsible for monitoring children's television advertising—the NAB and the television networks—do not monitor the language advertisers use with any great care or do not care what advertisers say to children. Many of the nutrition statements in cereal commercials, statements that are required by the NAB, are in clear violation of the NAB Code. But it is in the advertising of fruit-flavored products that a lack of concern for the language of children's television advertising is most clear.

The television advertising of fruit-flavored products commonly uses language that entails or implies that these products contain fruit whether or not they actually do and whether or not the product is naturally or artificially flavored. In general, these commercials cannot help but deceive children.

The disregard of the NAB and the ABC, NBC, and CBS television networks for the language of advertising broadcast to young children is rather puzzling, for some of the claims that pass their scrutiny are transparently false. It is difficult to escape the conclusion that responsible elements of these organizations simply don't care what advertisers say to children. If this is correct then I suspect that this is because the adults who monitor television advertisements for compliance with governmental and industry guidelines and rules are no more competent to cope with the fact that television advertising occurs in real time and uses both the visual and auditory communications channels than are television viewers.

References

ABC. 1978. Written testimony submitted to the Federal Trade Commission concerning children's television advertising. (Reference number LL-44)

Adler, R. P. 1978. *Research on the effects of television advertising on children.* Washington: U.S. Government Printing Office.

Akmajian, A., Demers, R. A., & Harnish, R. M. 1979. *Linguistics: An introduction to language and communication.* Cambridge, Mass.: MIT Press.

Baker, S. S. 1968. *The permissible lie.* Cleveland: World Publishing Co.

Barcus, F. E., & McLaughlin, L. 1978. *Food advertising on children's television: An analysis of appeals and nutritional content.* Newtonville, Mass.: Action on Children's Television.

Böer, S. E., & Lycan, W. G. 1975. The myth of semantic presupposition. In A. M. Zwicky (Ed.), *Working Papers in Linguistics, 21,* 2-144. Columbus, Ohio: Department of Linguistics, The Ohio State University.

Bolinger, D. 1973. Truth is a linguistic question. *Language, 49,* 539-550.

Bolinger, D. 1980. *Language: The loaded weapon.* New York: Longman.

Carlson, G. N. 1977. *Reference to kinds in English.* Unpublished doctoral dissertation, University of California, Irvine.

Chisholm, R. M., & Feehan, T. D. 1977. The intent to deceive. *Journal of Philosophy, 74,* 143-159.

Chomsky, C. 1969. *The acquisition of syntax in children from 5 to 10.* Cambridge, Mass.: MIT Press.

Chomsky, N. 1965. *Aspects of the theory of syntax.* Cambridge, Mass.: MIT Press.

Clark, B. 1943. *The advertising smoke screen.* New York: Harper.

Clark, E., & Garnica, O. 1974. Is he coming or going? On the acquisition of deictic verbs. *Journal of Verbal Learning and Verbal Behavior, 13,* 559-572.

Clark, H. H. 1970. The primitive nature of children's relational concepts: A discussion of Donaldson and Wales. In J. R. Hayes (Ed.), *Cognition and the development of language.* New York: Academic Press, 269-278.

Cresswell, M. J. 1974. Adverbs and events. *Synthese, 28,* 255-481.

Donaldson, M., & Balfour, G. 1968. Less is more: A study of language comprehension in children. *British Journal of Psychology, 59,* 461-472.

Donaldson, M., & Wales, R. J. 1970. On the acquisition of some relational terms. In J. R. Hayes (Ed.), *Cognition and the development of languages.* New York: Academic Press, pp. 235-268.

Edmund Publications Corporation. 1977. *Edmund's 1977 car prices buying guide.* West Hempstead, N.Y.

Edmund Publications Corporation. 1978. *Edmund's 1978 new car prices.* West Hempstead, N.Y.

Edmund Publications Corporation. 1979. *Edmund's 1979 new car prices.* West Hempstead, N.Y.

Estes, K. W. 1976. Nonverbal discrimination of more and fewer elements by children. *Journal of Experimental and Child Development, 21,* 293–405.

FTC. 1978. *Federal Trade Commission staff report on television advertising to children.* Washington, D.C.: U.S. Government Printing Office.

FTC. 1979. *Federal Trade Commission staff report on advertising for over-the-counter drugs.* Washington, D.C.: U.S. Government Printing Office.

Gentner, D. 1975. Evidence for the psychological reality of semantic components: The verbs of possession. In D. Norman & D. Rumelhart (Eds.), *Explorations in cognition.* San Francisco: W. H. Freeman, pp. 211–246.

Grice, H. P. 1975. Logic and conversation. In P. Cole & J. L. Morgan (Eds.), *Syntax and semantics III: Speech acts.* New York: Academic Press, pp. 41–58.

Grice, H. P. 1978. Further notes on logic and conversation. In P. Cole (Ed.), *Syntax and semantics IX: Pragmatics.* New York: Academic Press, pp. 123–127.

Harris, R. J., & Monaco, G. E. 1978. Psychology of pragmatic implication: Information processing between the lines. *Journal of Experimental Psychology: General, 107,* 1–22.

Hayhurst, H. 1967. Some errors of young children in producing passive sentences. *Journal of Verbal Learning and Verbal Behavior, 6,* 654–660.

Jefferson, G. 1972. Side sequences. In D. Sudnow (Ed.), *Studies in social interaction.* New York: The Free Press, pp. 294–338.

Jespersen, O. 1929. *A modern English grammar.* Heidelberg: Carl Winter's Universitätsbachhandlung.

Joos, M. 1967. *The five clocks.* New York: Harcourt.

Klatzky, R. L. 1975. *Human memory.* San Francisco: W. H. Freeman.

Klatzky, R. L., Clark, E. V., & Machen, M. 1973. Asymmetries in the acquisition of polar adjectives: Linguistic or conceptual? *Journal of Experimental Child Psychology, 16,* 32–46.

LaPointe, K., & O'Donnell, J. P. 1974. Number conservation in children below age six: Its relationship to age, perceptual dimension, and language comprehension. *Developmental Psychology, 10,* 422–428.

Lawson, G., Baron, J. R., & Siegel, L. S. 1974. The role of number and length cues in children's quantitative judgments. *Child Development, 45,* 731–736.

Leech, G. N. 1966. *English in advertising: A linguistic study of advertising in Great Britain.* London: Longmans.

Lenneberg, E. H. 1967. *Biological foundations of language.* New York: Wiley.

Liebert, D., Sprafkin, J., Liebert, R., & Rubenstein, E. 1977. Effects of television commercial disclaimers on the product expectations of children. *Journal of Communication, 27,* 118–124.

McGuire, W. J. 1969. The nature of attitudes and attitude change. In G. Lindzey & E. Aronson (Eds.), *The handbook of social psychology* (Vol. 3). Reading, Mass.: Addison Wesley, pp. 136–314.

Miller, G. A., & Johnson-Laird, P. N. 1976. *Language and perception.* Cambridge, Mass.: Harvard University Press.

Piaget, J., & Inhelder, B. 1962. *Le developpement des quantities physiques chez l'enfant.* Neuchatel: Delschaux et Niestlé.

Ross, R. P., Cambell, T., Heislon-Stein, A., & Wright, J. C. 1981. Nutritional misinformation of children: A developmental and experimental analysis of the effects of televised food commercials. *Journal of Applied Developmental Psychology, 1,* 329-347.

Searle, J. R. 1969. *Speech acts.* Cambridge, England: Cambridge University Press.

Searle, J. R. 1975. Indirect speech acts. In P. Cole & J. L. Morgan (Eds.), *Syntax and semantics III: Speech acts.* New York: Academic Press, pp. 59-81.

Siegel, L. S. 1978. The relationship of language and thought in the preoperational child: A reconsideration of non-verbal alternatives to Piagetian tasks. In L. S. Seigel & C. J. Brainerd (Eds.), *Alternatives to Piaget.* New York: Academic Press, pp. 43-68.

Stern, C., & Bryson, J. 1970. Competence vs. performance in young children's use of adjectival comparatives. *Child Development, 41,* 1197-1201.

Turner, E., & Rommetviet, R. 1967. The acquisition of sentence voice and reversibility. *Child Development, 38,* 649-660.

Ward, S., Wachman, D., & Wartella, E. 1977. *How children learn to buy: The development of consumer information processing skills.* Beverley Hills: Sage.

Ward, S., Wachman, D., & Wartella, E. 1979. Oral testimony submitted to the Federal Trade Commission concerning children's television advertising. (Reference number: LL-157)

Wason, P. C., & Johnson-Laird, P. N. 1972. *Psychology of reasoning: Form and content.* Cambridge, Mass.: Harvard University Press.

Zwicky, A. M., & Zwicky, A. D. In press. Register as a dimension of linguistic variation. In R. Kittredge & J. Lehrberger (Eds.), *Sublanguage: Studies of language in restricted semantic domains.* The Hague: Walter de Gruyter.

Index of Commercials

Author Index

Subject Index

(Continued from p. ii)

PERSPECTIVES IN
NEUROLINGUISTICS, NEUROPSYCHOLOGY, AND
PSYCHOLINGUISTICS: A Series of Monographs and Treatises

FRANCIS J. PIROZZOLO and MERLIN C. WITTROCK (Eds.). Neuropsychological and Cognitive Processes in Reading

JASON W. BROWN (Ed.). Jargonaphasia

DONALD G. DOEHRING, RONALD L. TRITES, P. G. PATEL, and CHRISTINA A. M. FIEDOROWICZ. Reading Disabilities: The Interaction of Reading, Language, and Neuropsychological Deficits

MICHAEL A. ARBIB, DAVID CAPLAN, and JOHN C. MARSHALL (Eds.). Neural Models of Language Processes

R. N. MALATESHA and P. G. AARON (Eds.). Reading Disorders: Varieties and Treatments

MICHAEL L. GEIS. The Language of Television Advertising

LORAINE OBLER and LISE MENN (Eds.). Exceptional Language and Linguistics

In Preparation:

M. P. BRYDEN. Laterality: Functional Asymmetry in the Intact Brain

KEITH RAYNER (Ed.). Eye Movements in Reading: Perceptual and Language Processes

S. J. SEGALOWITZ (Ed.). Language Functions and Brain Organization